LINUX Start-up Guide

Springer
Berlin
Heidelberg
New York
Barcelona
Budapest
Hong Kong
London
Milan
Paris
Santa Clara
Singapore
Tokyo

Fred Hantelmann, born 1959, studied mathematics and computer science at the University of Hamburg (graduated 1988, Ph.D. 1993). Since 1994 he has been an assistant professor in the Department of Economic Science and Management, Institute for Computer Science, University of the Federal Armed Forces, Hamburg. With more than 80 technical publications on hardware and software topics, Fred Hantelmann is well known as a qualified technical author, especially in the Unix community.

Fred Hantelmann

LINUX
Start-up Guide
A self-contained introduction

With 57 Figures

 Springer

Fred Hantelmann
Felder Schlagbaum 6
D-21217 Seevetal, Germany

ISBN-13: 978-3-540-62676-3

Cataloging-in-Publication Data applied for
Die Deutsche Bibliothek - CIP-Einheitsaufnahme
Hantelmann, Fred:
LINUX start-up guide: a self-contained introduction/Fred Hantelmann. -
Berlin; Heidelberg; New York; Barcelona; Budapest; Hong Kong; London;
Milan; Paris; Santa Clara; Singapore; Tokyo: Springer, 1997
 Dt. Ausg. u.d.T.: Hantelmann, Fred: LINUX für Durchstarter
 ISBN-13: 978-3-540-62676-3   e-ISBN-13:978-3-642-60749-3
 DOI: 10.1007/978-3-642-60749-3

Typesetting: Camera-ready by author
Cover Design: Künkel+Lopka, Heidelberg
Printed on acid-free paper   SPIN 10569145 33/3142 – 5 4 3 2 1 0

Preface

The *Linux Start-Up Guide* has been written for both private and professional Linux users. Its purpose is to give a solid understanding of the Unix-like operating system kernel and its system commands.

This book is intended for beginners, system administrators, and people who have worked with other systems. Experienced Unix and Linux users will still find it useful, as all main Linux features have been treated extensive, reducing the need to study other documentation.

Without a doubt, it is not possible to give a comprehensive description of every typical Linux tool in just 300 pages. Therefore, I have concentrated on providing detailed and well structured explanations of the fundamental Unix commands, the most important editors, network applications, and the X Window System. I also thought it important to give a general idea of the concepts underlying each topic and to mention the historic milestones that influenced the current state of development.

Linux distributions are the result of various academic projects and private developments. The majority of the products that typify the performance of Linux distributions available today are subject to the General Public License (GPL), which defines the term "free software" according to the Free Software Foundation: Everybody has the right to make any number of copies of software following the GPL and pass it on, together with the respective program sources. The further development of Linux depends on people providing free software, so just do it! In conjunction with this, each and every user is urged to support the continued development of Linux by contributing free software.

V

Contents

Programs and Processes 39

Files and File Systems 55

File Oriented Commands 83

Editors   145

Shell Programs   187

Networked Systems   219

X Window Manager   299

Bibliography   319

Index   321

Figures

Introduction

Not so very long ago Unix was known to just a small group of computer experts. This was due to the fact, amongst others, that at that time Unix could only be used on special mini or supercomputers to which the average user had no access. Today microcomputers and especially PCs are so powerful that almost every home PC has all that is required for using Unix.

Until recently Unix could only be run on mini or supercomputers

Indeed there are plenty of other operating systems on the market, competing for new customers. With appealing user interfaces they promise optimized software ergonomics. Recent Unix variants and clones also have graphic interfaces, so they can easily keep up with their competitors in this respect.

Modern Unix variants include a graphical interface

However, the question of "security" has only been solved partly, if at all, for the majority of the established operating systems. Here lies the strength of Unix, as it integrates a tried and tested, and already mature, concept of data security, which bears close examination even beyond the bounds of the system.

Unix integrates a well thought-out security concept

Since the Unix clone Linux is available as freeware it seems that finally it is the customers' turn to speak: Why spend a lot of money on an operating system and several applications, when they can solve all their problems with an almost zero-cost Linux distribution.

Linux is a freely available clone of the Unix operating system

Linux was not developed by just one person. Development of the Linux operating system kernel was originated by Linus Benedict Torvalds, from whose name the word Linux is derived. By using the Unix teaching operating system Minix as a basis and by adding components developed by the Free Software Foundation (FSF), Linus Benedict Torwalds created an executable first Linux version, which he sent to interested Minix users for

The inspiration for the development of Linux was Minix

1

free. This had the effect that numerous amateurs and experts contributed their specialist knowledge, and the original operating system kernel was developed into a stable product.

The popularity of the kernel is due to the spread of Linux distributions

Linux distributions have been largely responsible for the rapid worldwide spread and growth in popularity of the kernel. These Linux distributions bundle the Linux operating system kernel together with numerous applications, basic Unix programs, and complete application packages.

Many basic applications have been developed by the FSF

Given the fact that a large number of Linux distributions are available, which are in no way uniform, the user gets with each Linux distribution a Unix-like operating system with mature C and C++ development environments, editors, command line interpreters, X Window System, network applications, TEX/LATEX, documentation system, and other assorted products, which cover a great number of application types.

1.1 Linux Versus Unix

Linux is a multiuser, multitasking, operating system kernel, allowing several users to work on one computer simultaneously and several programs to run at practically the same time. Linux cannot be equated to Unix, but it combines the most important features of System V, BSD and POSIX, so it shows a great similarity to Unix.

Linux combines features of System V, BSD, and POSIX

In contrast to Unix, all the source files of the Linux system are freely available, including the operating system kernel, device drivers, runtime libraries, development tools, and application programs. Linux can be run on hardware architectures that use CPUs from Intel (80[3–6]86), Digital Equipment Corporation (Alpha), Motorola (MC680x0, PowerPC), Silicon Graphics (MIPS) or Sun Microsystems (SPARC).

All components of Linux are freely available as source code

The most striking features of Linux are process management conforming to POSIX, support of pseudo terminals (`pty` devices) as well as national keyboards via dynamically loadable keyboard drivers, shared libraries, virtual memory management, and dynamically loadable device drivers (modules). Virtual terminals allow switching from one console login session to another. An integrated FPU emulator even allows Linux to run on hardware platforms lacking a floating point math coprocessor.

The Linux developers thought it important to make their product compatible with as many file system formats as possible. For example, Linux provides transparent access to MS-DOS partitions via common Unix commands. A special format "UMSDOS" serves to install Linux within a MS-DOS partition. Furthermore, Linux can operate file systems that have been formatted for Minix, Xenix, or System V.

Linux allows a transparent access to MS-DOS partitions

HPFS-2 format partitions created under OS/2 2.1 can be read by Linux, but so far not written to. Compressed partitions created by MS-DOS 6 are not supported at present and will probably not be supported in future. Compatibility with the VFAT format common to Windows NT and Windows 95 and the Amiga Fast File System Format (AFFS) has been achieved. Linux also supports the ISO 9660 format, which means that Linux can read all common CD-ROMs.

ISO 9660 compatibility allows access to common CD-ROMs

Linux includes a complete implementation of the Transmission Control Protocol/Internet Protocol (TCP/IP) specifications. Numerous device drivers for diverse Ethernet cards allow Linux PCs to be integrated into local networks. Additionally, Linux supports Serial Line Internet Protocol (SLIP), Point to Point Protocol (PPP), and Parallel Line Internet Protocol (PLIP) access to TCP/IP networks via serial or parallel connection, respectively. The compatibility with the Network File System (NFS) allows access to remote hard disk resources.

Support for TCP/IP, SLIP, and PLIP allow the integration of Linux PCs into a network

1.2   Kernel Architecture

The operating system kernel has amongst others the task of realizing the performance features listed in the previous section. It also manages processes as well as the system memory and it provides functions that offer access to the file system and the communication facilities. The latter are known as system calls; they form the interface between the applications and the operating system kernel.

The kernel is the interface between the applications and the hardware

3

To be precise, the operating system kernel is a program that consists of the following logical components:

process manager,

memory manager,

file system, and

I/O services.

Each of these "kernel modules" provides services that may be accessed on the user side via the system calls just mentioned. Operating the computer hardware is the task of a deeper underlying layer, which normally cannot be accessed by the user. The components of this layer include

scheduler,

I/O buffer, and

device drivers.

These components carry out the process scheduling. They are responsible for the administration and provision of main memory and they carry out the input/output functions, which are necessary on the lowest level. Figure 1.1 shows graphically the components of the operating system kernel.

Fig. 1.1
Components
of the operating
system kernel

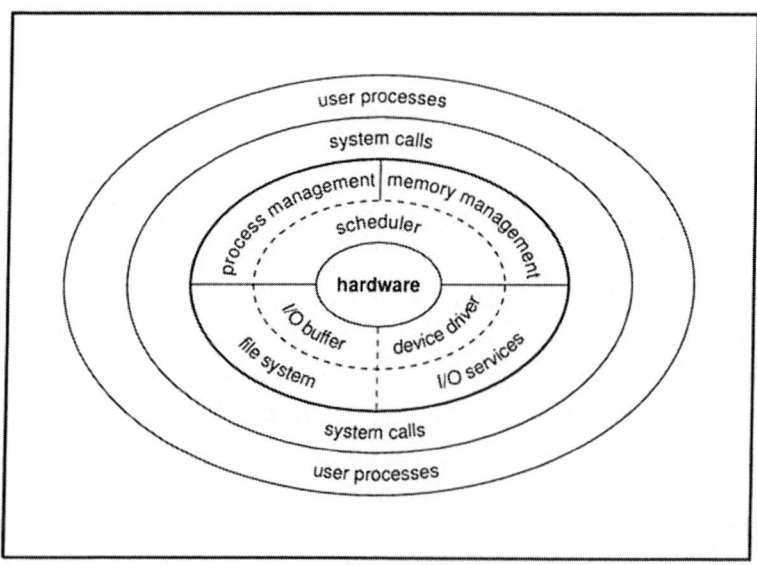

1.3 Guide

Linux Start-Up Guide is a practical textbook. It is mainly about the following topics: programs and processes, files and file systems, file oriented commands, editors, shell programming, networked systems, network applications, the X Window System, and the operation and configuration of the X Window Managers twm, olwm, and fvwm.

An important feature of the book is that it gives a comprehensive explanation of the conceptual background of the individual topics in order to enable the reader to see the features specific to Linux in their theoretical context.

Chapter 2 contains an overview of the historical development of Unix in general and of PC Unix variants in particular. The aim of this section is to list the different targets set by the several teams at the very beginning of Unix development, and to identify the concepts of the individual Unix derivatives that can now be found in almost every Unix version.

Historical development

Chapter 3 has been written especially for Linux beginners. First of all, the necessary steps for switching on and off the computer and for logging on and off are explained. A reproducible example of a session illustrates how to do so with a few frequently required Unix commands. Discussion of the Linux command line interpreter explain the command syntax, environment variables, the command line editor, redirecting input and output streams, command sequences, background processes, and pipelines. Section 3.4 shows the mechanism Unix uses for the identification of users. To complete the chapter, use of the online help and its internal construction are explained in detail.

Introductory seminar: usage and user profile

Chapter 4 handles the process management and control side of the operating system kernel along with program execution. The main topics here are process monitoring, creation of processes, process signals, independent processes, process priority, and daemons. Additionally, the reader is offered an explanation of interval and signal controlled daemons, which take on user and system management tasks within the framework of multiuser multitasking operation.

Process subsystem

Files, directories, file systems

Files and file systems are the focus of Chapter 5. The physical and logical structures of hard disks are explained in detail. The structure of the Linux directory tree and the roles of individual directories are presented, and different file types and the attributes associated with each file type are treated. An extra section is dedicated to the device files, and includes a table of the files that refer to the peripheral components. The final section lists Linux programs that configure or test hardware components.

Basic commands

Chapter 6 contains a structured explanation of the basic commands, found in each Linux distribution, which operate on files and directories. The presentation serves the purpose of augmenting the online manual pages with annotations on the usage of the respective commands, and illustrates their usage with examples. At the end of the chapter, a compact guide is given to the syntax of regular expressions.

Editors: sed, vi, and GNU Emacs

Chapter 7 deals with the use of the stream editor `sed`, which is now a indispensable aid, especially for the adaption and installation of freely available software packages, as well as the use of the Unix standard editor `vi` and the universal development tool GNU Emacs. The aim of this chapter is to make all frequently required standard commands and also the majority of the occasionally used editing commands familiar to the reader step by step.

Shell programming

Chapter 8 deals with the internal syntax of the command shell interpreters `bash`, `ksh`, and `tcsh`, which make the construction of simple and complex shell programs possible. Some of the topics already briefly mentioned in Sect. 3.3, but especially the concepts of variables in the various command interpreters, are worked through in detail here. Additionally, the system programmer is given an explanation of the input and output functions of the shell, the program flow control structures (switches, loops, functions), of internal and external utility programs, and the handling of signals.

Networking

Chapter 9 gives an explanation of the basic concepts of networked architectures, thematically structured into the areas of network topology, protocol families such as ISO/OSI in general and TCP/IP in particular and the different addressing schemes that secure a unique identification in local and global networks. Beyond that, the system administrator is given a treatment of the steps required to create serial login connections such as SLIP and PPP under Linux.

Chapter 10 explains the different Linux applications and Linux daemons that access TCP/IP based network services or enable remote systems to access local services. Following a comprehensive explanation of the tools for making network analysis, sections are dedicated to the program `telnet`, the Berkeley r-commands, data transfer, email, news, dialog programs, and information systems.

Network applications and daemons

Chapter 11 discusses the concepts and components of the X Window System. Following a historical account of the development of window systems, the architecture of X11 and the meaning of the widgets are explained. Section 11.4 is oriented to practice: it shows the methods for accessing X11, explains the concept of the X server addresses and access permissions, and classifies the basic applications, called MIT X clients. Further sections are dedicated to application-specific attributes, where the structure of X resources as well as the available methods for choosing character sets and colors are shown in detail.

X Window System

Finally, Chapter 12 explains in order the X Window Managers `twm`, `olwm`, and `fvwm`, which on the one hand influence the appearance of X11 based desktops, and on the other hand provide the main functions for its operation. For each of the three X Window Managers mentioned, the product-specific components of the window design and the window operations connected with them are explained. In this chapter, the reader is given an organized explanation of the configuration of each X Window Manager.

X Window Manager

1.4 Typographical Conventions

This book uses the following typographic conventions:

1. Command names, variable names, and parameters (options, arguments) are set in `Terminal font`.

2. Square brackets `[]` in syntax diagrams frame optional information which can be ignored. Square brackets in examples are syntactic elements and are absolutely necessary.

3. Items in syntax diagrams that are framed by braces `{}` are exclusive options; from the list given only one option is to be used. Braces in examples are syntactic elements and are absolutely necessary.

4. Angled brackets `<>` in syntax diagrams frame non-exclusive options: each letter in the list can occur exactly once in the command line options.

5. Three dots `...` following an item in a syntax diagrams say that the item may appear repeatedly.

6. When it occurs in examples at the end of a line, the backslash `\` indicates a continuation of the line. Within a command line the backslash is a syntactic element.

7. The prefixes `Alt-`, `C-`, and `M-` before a key name indicate the control keys Alt, Control, and Meta; the keyboard code following them should be entered together with the given control key.

8. Marginal notes either highlight the important information in a section or provide additional information.

Development of Unix

2.1 Academic Versions

The forefathers of all current variants of the multiuser multi-tasking operating system Unix are Kenneth Thompson and Dennis Ritchie. In 1969, in the laboratories of the North American telephone company AT&T, they developed the first Unix prototype, then still written in Assembler, on a PDP-7 system manufactured by Digital Equipment Corporation (DEC). The name "Unix" first derived from a pun on MULTICS, which was one of the first interactive operating systems. Based on the idea of creating a system, that would support the cooperation of several programmers in the team and communication between them, Thompson and Ritchie conceived the "UNiplexed Information and Computing System" Unics.

Kenneth Thompson and Dennis Ritchie programmed Unics in Assembler

A disadvantage of this doubtlessly revolutionary operating system was that it had been completely written in the assembly language of the PDP-7. Within two years a team managed to transfer the program code to the assembly language of the PDP-11. Additionally, the first functional extensions were integrated in the operating system kernel. The Unix Version 1 so created was in the following years mainly used as a word processing system by using the tools **ed** and **roff** which are still used today.

Porting to a DEC PDP-11 took two years

Motivated by the porting effort required to port Unix to a new architecture, Thompson invented the programming language B, from which Ritchie and Brian Kernighan then developed the language C. The aim was to combine the features of traditional high-level languages with the functionality of assembly languages in a portable programming language.

Dennis Ritchie and Brian Kernighan developed the language C

9

*Version 4 was
to a great extent
programmed in C*

A large part of the original Unix operating system was then rewritten in C. Version 4, introduced in 1973, included just a small part of an architecture-dependent assembler code. Version 6, presented two years later, was for the first time used outside the Bell Laboratories, mainly at universities.

*Version 6
was available
as source code*

A significant difference from other operating systems at this time was that Unix was written in a higher-level programming language, could be bought as source code, and already contained diverse and powerful base applications. Before it had matured into a marketable commodity (an initial commercial Unix version was offered by the Interactive Systems Corporation in 1977), the original prototype had undergone various changes, with the surprising result that two different operating systems with the name Unix were to become popular.

*BSD Unix and
AT&T Version 7
derived from
Version 6*

A team in the University of California at Berkeley modified the original specifications and presented the Berkeley Software Distribution to the public in 1977. The main feature of this variant, named BSD Unix, was the use of the C shell as the command interpreter. Shortly afterwards, AT&T introduced the Unix Time Sharing System V7, in which inputs from the user were interpreted by the Bourne shell, named after its developer Steve Bourne. V7 was the first portable version of Unix, as the system could run not only on the PDP-11 but also on an Interdata 8/32.

*C shell versus
Bourne shell*

BSD Unix gained a high degree of acceptance, especially at universities, as the C shell in comparison to the Bourne shell realized various concepts that made quick command input possible. The possibility of storing commands in a list (history), mechanisms for recalling previously used commands, modification of those commands, alias lists, and convenient process management convinced application developers, especially, that BSD Unix, compared to AT&T V7, was the "better" Unix.

*commercial:
System V*

The AT&T variant, however, was aimed instead at commercial usage. In 1983 the System V version was developed, and gained much popularity. Roughly at the same time Sun Microsystems introduced its first Unix workstation. This was supplied with the operating system SunOS, which included features of AT&T Unix as well as features of BSD Unix. Users of SunOS could use either the Bourne shell or the C shell as their command interpreter.

2.2 Commercial Breakthrough

Within a short time Unix advanced to being the standard operating system for workstations, which had meanwhile become part of the product spectrum of many hardware producers. On the other hand, the different Unix variants no longer had much in common; each system was been supplied with a Unix derivative customized by the manufacturer, which sometimes differed greatly from competitors' derivative. Committees representing all the producers tried to prevent the looming chaos.

Unix becomes standard operating system for workstations

System V style Unix implementations were coordinated by "Unix International" (UI), whose aim was to encourage the use of of Unix in commercial fields. BSD Unix, on the other hand, was primarily shaped by the requirements of scientific applications. Its further development was guided by the "Computer System Research Group" (CSRG) in the University of California at Berkeley. SunOS played an independent role and meanwhile acquired a few additional characteristics.

Three main streams: System V, BSD Unix and SunOS

Then, in 1988, representatives of these agreed to establish the System V Release 4 specification. SVR4 was intended to stop the existing three-way division that existed in the market and create the basis for a unique Unix by combining the distinctive advantages of the main development streams. The following features were taken over:

New standard: System V Release 4

system administration, terminal interface, Unix to Unix Copy uucp, printer control, STREAMS, Remote File System (RFS) from SVR3,

uucp, STREAMS

Sockets, `select()` (synchronous I/O multiplexing), Fast File System FFS, TCP/IP, C shell from BSD,

TCP/IP, C shell

virtual memory management, shared libraries, Network File System (NFS), OpenLook GUI, X11/NeWS from SunOS.

NFS. X11

Additionally, they took over internationalization (8-bit character set), the Korn shell `ksh`, ANSI C, and an "Application Binary Interface" (ABI) for the SVR4 specification. Furthermore, they demanded conformity with the standards of the "Portable Operating System Interface Specification" POSIX. The objectives

SVR4 conforms to POSIX and X/Open

of the X/Open committee, founded in 1984 by Bull, ICL, Nixdorf, Olivetti, and Siemens, which had the aim of establishing standards for software portability as well as the System V Interface Definition SVID. The results of their work were also defined as part of the System V Release 4.

Unix for
multiprocessor
systems: OSF/1

At the beginning of 1991 the Open Software Foundation OSF established a producer organization. Its first members were, among others, Apollo, DEC, HP, and IBM. They wrote a further Unix specification called OSF/1. Features of this operating system, which had been conceived especially for use on multiprocessor systems, included support of symmetric multiprocessor architectures, parallelized operating system kernel, threads, redundant disks, logical file systems, Unix File System (UFS), STREAMS, NFS, sockets, shared libraries, and extended safety rules according to level B1 or B2 of the safety categories listed by the American Department of Defense (DoD) in the "Orange Book".

Mach kernel:
tasks, threads,
messages, ports

OSF/1 uses the Mach micro kernel, which was developed especially for multiprocessor systems. The Unix process context is replaced by task structures containing a performance environment and threads, which run as sub-processes (lightweight processes) in a task environment. Several threads can use identical memory areas simultaneously. Communication with the operating system kernel is not via system calls, but via messages, addressed to communication channels.

Most popular:
BSD and System V

Today, Unix derivatives in use are mainly based on BSD and System V. Despite the current availability of multiprocessor architectures, OSF/1 is of secondary importance. Furthermore, it turns out in practice that after some modifications to the operating system kernel, the traditional Unix concept also harmonizes with multiprocessor systems.

From the user's point of view all Unix derivatives contain essentially similar tools. And yet a small number of utility programs with the same name in the Unix variants produce different results when using special program parameters (switches).

ps f does not
work uniformly

For example, when **ps -f** is called for single programs under System V, as well as getting the process number, running time (CPU time used), and the assigned input and output channel, the user also gets the user identification, the number of the parent process, and the time when the command was started. Under BSD Unix, however, the switch −f for ps has no meaning.

To end this section, Figure 2.1 summarizes the history of the Unix versions mentioned so far.

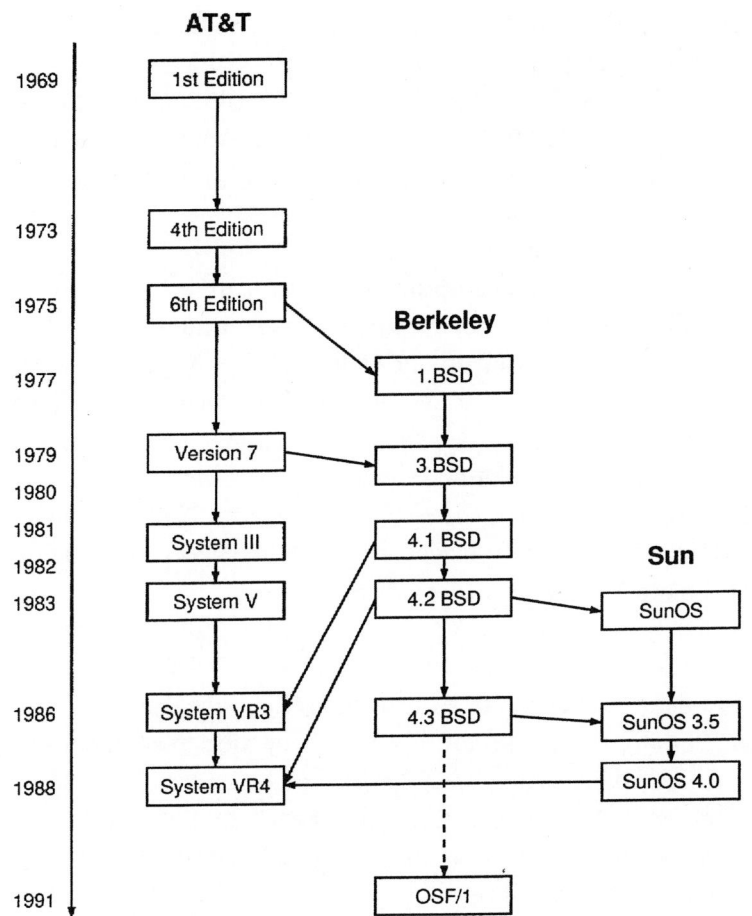

Fig. 2.1
Development
of Unix

2.3 PC Unix Variants

Using Unix on PCs first became possible in the 1980s, since, relative to the hardware common at that time, it put great demands on processor performance, main memory, and hard disk capacity. The first Unix-like operating systems for microcomputers were QNX presented in 1982 and PC/ix in 1983. Shortly afterwards Microsoft put the product Xenix on the market, which it developed in a strategic partnership with Santa Cruz Operation (SCO). This product, derived from AT&T Version 7, was conceived for 8088/8086 PCs. They chose the name Xenix because some years earlier AT&T had registered the name Unix as a protected trademark, so that no other enterprise was allowed to use the name Unix for any of its products.

Microsoft and SCO: Xenix for 8088/8086 PCs

Porting Unix to microprocessors was carried out early for Motorola's 68000 CPUs, which had been available as 16-bit processors before Intel produced the 80286. Apple developed Lisa 68K UNIX its Lisa systems but the product gained less popularity than it may have deserved. Higher acceptance was achieved by Tandy XENIX, which could be used for Z80 based Tandy Model II systems if they had a 68k extension board. Around 1985, with 250 000 copies, this product was more popular than an other Unix version at that time.

Lisa 68K UNIX and Tandy XENIX

Shortly after the broad availability of Intel 80286 processors in 1985, SCO presented Xenix 286 System V Release 2.0. As the processor was busy enough just controlling the operating system, initially it was hard for this implementation to compete with MS-DOS, which became established on the same processor type.

16 bit version SCO Xenix 286

Around 1986, shortly after the "birth" of the Intel 80386 processors, Interactive Systems,, then developer of AIX for IBM, pushed Interactive Unix onto the market. AT&T then added Xenix compatibility to Interactive Unix and publicly released this extended version, called SysV R3, in July 1987. Thereafter, more and more PC Unix variants were announced: X86 Sys V R3 (Microport), Esix (Everex), and Xenix System V/386 version 3.2 were released in quick succession. At the same time, Sun released its SunOS 4.x, together with a specially developed PC called "Roadrunner", onto the market.

Interactive Unix, AT&T SysV R3, X86 Sys V R 3, Esix, Xenix V/386

2.4 Free Unix Distributions

Another starting point to provide Unix for microcomputers was made by Andrew Tanenbaum, who published the PC based tutorial operating system Minix in 1987 while working as a professor at the Free University of Amsterdam. Minix was developed completely independently of the sources of AT&T Unix, but nevertheless it managed to attain the functionality of Version 7. The main feature of Minix was the availability of the system as source code, which could be acquired by everyone at an insignificant cost. Minix managed to spread worldwide and was ported by several programmers to Atari ST, Amiga, and Apple Macintosh. The author intended that Minix remain a teaching system; changing the system kernel for the benefit of applications, for example integrating the X Window System, was out of the question.

Minix as PC based tutorial operating system available in source code

Linus Benedict Torvalds from Helsinki, Finland, was one of those who had their first experience with Unix through using Minix. On the basis of Minix and with the C development system from the Free Software Foundation (FSF), which is freely available as source code, he had been working on a small operating system since March 1991, which he named Linux 0.01 and which he sent for free to interested Minix users in September 1991. Four months later he presented Version 0.12, consisting of a stable running operating system kernel with Bourne Again shell as command interpreter, GNU C compiler, Micro Emacs as text editor, and various service programs that had been developed by the Free Software Foundation (FSF), commonly called GNU utilities.

Linux 0.12 with bash, C compiler, and Micro Emacs freely available

At the beginning of 1992 the American William F. Jolitz presented Version 0.0 of 386BSD, which he also conceived as a freely available product, derived from the Networking Software Release 2. The latter had been developed in the EECS Department of the University of California at Berkeley, and to a great extent bears Bill Jolitz's mark. One of the first stable versions, based on an operating system kernel conforming to BSD, was Net BSD 0.8, released in November 1984. Shortly thereafter in December 1994, 386BSD was finally renamed "FreeBSD". None

BSD PC Unix 386BSD 0.0

of the freely available BSD PC Unix versions, however, attained the worldwide distribution that had been achieved by Linux at that time.

The basis for the success of Linux was doubtlessly its worldwide support from programmers and testers, who, linked just by communication via Internet, helped to develop the original operating system kernel. Between them they took care to structure the operating system kernel according to the POSIX standards so that it was compatible with a wide range of software that was freely available or had been developed at universities. Furthermore, integration of features of System V and of the BSD distributions support the porting of nearly all significant applications to Linux, so long they are freely available as source code. As a consequence, several well known software producers have now ported their commercial products to Linux.

Linux includes features of POSIX, System V, and BSD

Linux was originally conceived especially for PCs with Intel processors. Broad interest in the performance features of the operating system kernel finally led to the foundation of teams, whose aim was to adapt Linux for other hardware architectures. First trials were conducted on the Motorola 680x0 based Atari and Amiga systems. Shortly afterwards, Linux could be run on various 680x0 based systems. Later projects were launched that enabled further porting to DEC Alpha, MIPS, PowerPC, and SPARC architectures.

Linux runs on DEC Alpha, MIPS, PowerPC, and SPARC architectures

Since the release of Linux Version 2.0, the sources of the operating system kernel include all components necessary to adapt it to the processor types mentioned. Intel based multiprocessor systems have been officially supported since Version 1.3.71.

Operating Linux

Switching on a Linux computer for the first time, one is confronted with a large number of system messages that include information on the hardware devices. These messages are issued by the operating system kernel while booting the system. The system is only operational after this is completed. Then the user is invited to log in by a login prompt. The concept of virtual consoles realized under Linux offers the opportunity to log in more than once on the consoles of the system (see Sect. 3.1.1).

Logging in via a virtual console

The real task while working with Linux is to run commands by giving their command names and optional command line arguments. The latter control the way the command operates. Normally, the user interacts not directly with the operating system kernel but with a command interpreter. Its task is to accept command lines and, after analyzing them, either to execute the chosen command itself or to forward the command line arguments to another program.

The command interpreter analyzes the command line

Each Linux distribution has a variety of fundamental Unix commands, tools for system administration, and complex applications from a variety of areas. The user is provided with suitable information on the concept and purpose of each command, its calling conventions, and mode of operation in an online manual, which is part of the system's basic equipment and provides in effect a help function.

Basic commands and applications are explained in the online manual

The aim of this chapter is to show the necessary and the optional steps for logging in and out, to examine basic techniques for handling the command line interpreter, and to explain how to operate the online manual and understand the information it contains. Conceptual elements of Linux used here for illustration,

17

namely processes and files, will be discussed in detail in the following chapters.

3.1 Login, Logout, Shutdown

The login procedure (signing into the system) serves the purpose of assigning private data unambiguously to their owners and preventing undesired access by others to the data. The login procedure is as follows:

The login serves to protect data

- After the login

      login:

  one enters ones user name (for example, **marion**) and presses the return key.

1st step: Entering the user name

- Then Linux normally asks for the password, which was either chosen previously by the user or given to her by the system administrator. If, after the user name is entered, the system displays the message

      Password:

  this safety check has to be answered accordingly. One must ensure that the password is entered completely and without mistakes and is terminated with the return key. Linux will not display the password on the screen.

2nd step: Security check

In both cases one has to check capitalization, because Linux and every other Unix differentiates between upper and lowercase letters. If the system then displays the message

Check upper and lowercase letters

    Login incorrect

there can be two reasons for it: either the password has not been entered correctly or the user has made a mistake when entering the user name. In both cases the login prompt is repeated.

If the inputs have been entered correctly, the system starts an interactive session. To be more precise, Linux activates a command interpreter that then prompts for keyboard controlled command input.

A session starts in the home directory

Immediately after the login, the current working directory for the user will be his or her home directory. The system shows its readiness to communicate with the user with a ready sign, the shell prompt. The appearance of the prompt can easily be changed; the required command sequences are shown in Sect. 8.2.1 (p. 194). The default shell prompt of the LST distribution appears as follows:

The shell prompt awaits the input of commands

```
marion@jeannie:~$
```

A session is finished with the command `logout`. After this command is entered, the familiar login prompt is redisplayed on the screen. If one plans to switch off the computer completely, it is absolutely necessary to shut down the system before touching the power switch.

Shut down, then switch off

The reason for this is that to maintain for operational readiness the operating system starts a variety of control programs, which then continue to run with open files. Simply switching off the computer – which has the same effect as pressing the reset key – normally leads to a corrupt file system. In most cases Linux can repair corrupt file systems while re-booting. However, it is not advisable to use the reset key unless absolutely necessary, as repairing the file system involves time-consuming integrity tests.

Switching off the computer suddenly leads to corrupt file systems

Linux offers three commands for shutting down the system: `shutdown`, `halt`, and `reboot`. These commands are "privileged" and therefore can only be carried out by the system administrator. Since in many cases the Linux user is also the Linux system administrator, an explanation of how to get the right to execute these commands is appropriate here. One can either log in as superuser by entering `root` at the login prompt, or one can enter the command `su` during a normal session. In both cases, one then has to enter the password of the system administrator. Afterwards the user (more precisely, the system administrator) can shut down the system with one of the commands mentioned above.

shutdown, halt and reboot are privileged commands

The command `shutdown`, called without any additional parameters, shuts the system down after a waiting period of 2 minutes. During that time, Linux informs each user who is logged into the system of the impending shutdown at regular intervals. If another waiting period is desired, this can be controlled with the

Shutdown informs all users

argument **now** (immediately), **+mins** (after a specified number of minutes), or **hh:ss** (at a certain time). Five minutes before the shutdown, the system creates a file **/etc/nologin** that says the system will be shut down and users may no longer log in. Only the system administrator may log in during this period.

Further command line parameters accepted by **shutdown** cause the system either to stop after the shutdown (option **-h**, halt) or to reload the operating system kernel (option **-r**, reboot). Calling **halt** is equivalent to **shutdown -h now**. Similarly, **reboot** causes a **shutdown -r now**.

Restarting with reboot, system halt with halt

3.1.1 Virtual Consoles

Virtual consoles Alt-F1... Alt-F6

Virtual consoles offer the ability to operate several command interpreters one after another. The LST distribution sets up six virtual consoles. The user can switch between them with the key combinations **Alt-F1 ... Alt-F6**.

Several independent workstations

The concept of virtual consoles provides a way to run several programs simultaneously under Linux, and thereby to utilize the multitasking capability of the system. Each console appears to provide a full and independent workstation.

After it is switched to another virtual console, Linux initially displays the login prompt just as it did for the first login console and asks for the user name and the password before loading another command interpreter. So, in principle, it is possible (and permissible) to log in on every virtual console with another user name.

Compiling without leaving the editor

Programs started by the user from one virtual console continue running when the user switches to another. A possible use of virtual consoles could be to work on program text and to translate the saved version with a compiler to find syntactic mistakes. One need not leave and reload the editor, as one only has to change to another virtual console.

3.2 Quick Lead-in

After a successful login the user will be inclined to make some initial experiments, in order to get acquainted with the system. The aim of this section is to introduce some basic Unix commands and to explain their action briefly with the help of an easy-to-follow example session.

The user name under which the user has logged in is displayed by entering

```
whoami
```

More comprehensive information, which, along with the user name, also includes the host name (system name) and the domain name (the address of the organization), as well as the terminal used and the current date and time, is given by

who am i shows user host and domain name

```
who am i
```

Detailed information about the user identity, and all groups to which the user belongs, can be obtained by entering

```
id
```

By calling `set`, one can examine the context variables used by the command interpreter:

```
set
```

supplies values of set environment variables such as `USER` (user name), `UID` (user number), `SHELL` (current command interpreter), `PWD` (present working directory), and the search path `PATH`. The latter is important, as it causes the shell to search for executable programs in the directories listed by `PATH`, which have been called without stating the complete path.

PATH contains search paths to programs

Information on currently loaded programs (more precisely, the processes currently run by the operating system kernel) can be displayed with the command

```
ps -al
```

21

Options control the working mode of the programs

In this call **ps** is the program name and **-al** is a command line option. Nearly every basic Unix command accepts a number of command line options, which control the way it works. The majority of programs recognize command line options by the initial hyphen. If a program has to process several options, one can state them either individually or one directly after another. For example, **ps -al** can also be entered as **ps -a -l**.

To display the content of one or more directories in the Unix file tree, which stores all programs and data accessible to the system in a hierarchical structure, one can use the command

```
ls
```

ls -a also lists "hidden" directories

If **ls**, when used in the user's home directory, claims that there are no directories, this is because **ls** only displays the directories and files that do not start with a period. This can be remedied by running **ls -a**, as this displays at least both of the hidden directory files . (current directory) and .. (parent directory). Here a handy tip: **ls -F** marks executable files by adding an asterisk *.

The command **ls** lists the files and directories located in the current working directory or in another directory. For example, **ls** shows the contents of the current working directory, whereas **ls /usr/bin** lists the names of all files located in the directory /usr/bin, excluding the ones starting with a period, of course. However, the latter call has the disadvantage that one sees just the last lines of the display, as the complete display needs more space than the screen provides.

Unfortunately, **ls** provides no option that displays the content of the directories page by page. Instead, one has to apply a technique that is one of the outstanding features of Unix. One calls up a second Unix command

```
more
```

Pipelines connect programs

that for the most part serves to display information page by page, and asks this program to process the output of **ls**. To transfer data one uses a pipeline:

```
ls /usr/bin | more
```

causes the **ls** command to write its display into a kind of temporary file, which is then used as the input file by **more**.

Next, one might wish to look at the file contents. Again, the command **more** is most often used for this purpose. For example,

```
more /var/log/debug
```

displays the system messages that were displayed on the console while the system booted. These can accumulate: for every boot the operating system kernel adds messages about its current configuration. To see the last lines only, it is better to use the command **tail**, perhaps with a number of lines as an argument. For example,

/var/log/debug: contains system messages

```
tail -50 /var/log/debug
```

shows the last 50 lines of the file. For output page by page the result of **tail** should be pipelined to **more**.

Now it might be interesting to create some new files. It would be simplest to copy existing files. For example,

```
cp /etc/passwd ~
```

copies the table of the local user passwords into the home directory of the user (~ indicates the home directory). Now there is a file named **passwd** in the home directory, which would have been better under another name. But it is easy to rename the file with

/etc/passwd contains the user passwords

```
mv ~/passwd ~/list
```

It would certainly have been easier to give the target file its final name right from the start by copying with **cp**, which means entering

```
cp /etc/passwd ~/list
```

It is worth noting that the commands **cp** and **mv** can also copy several source files, but the target then has to be a directory. However, the operating system forbids copying files when the user has no write permission in the target directory. Renaming requires that the user has write permission in both the source and the target directory.

Copying and renaming demands write permissions

User directories are created by the command `mkdir`, followed by one or more directory names. This succeeds only when the user has the permission to write. This condition is normally fulfilled for the case of the user's own home directory. So

mkdir creates
subdirectories

```
mkdir ~/bin ~/tmp
```

creates two subdirectories and afterwards

```
cp /bin/c* ~/tmp
```

copies all files from `/bin` to `~/tmp` whose names begin with the letter `c`.

Things are more complicated if all files are to be moved from `~/tmp` to `~/bin` with one command, and additionally are to be renamed there. Such tasks require a small program using commands from the shell programming language. After entering the command

```
cd ~/tmp
```

the current working directory will be `~/tmp`. The following command moves all the files located there to `~/bin` and gives each file the suffix `.org`:

```
for i in *; do mv $i ~/bin/$i.org; done
```

In practice it is common to input such shell programs in several lines, using the return key instead of the semicolon. Furthermore one can write such shell programs into a file and then execute that.

The Unix screen
editor is vi

The standard tool for creating and processing "readable" files is the editor `vi`, which is not so easy to use, but is included in each Unix distribution and can always be operated in the same way. To create the shell program as file `~/tmp/mymv.sh`, first of all one has to enter

```
vi ~/tmp/mymv.sh
```

vi modes:
command, input
and ex

To change the editor from the command mode to the input mode one presses the `i` key, then one can enter the program. Pressing the escape key returns `vi` to its command mode. Entering a colon `:` changes `vi` to the `ex` mode, in which the individual command lines have to be completed with return. The command **w** saves the file created, and finally **:q** closes the editor. To leave the editor without saving the file, one keys the sequence **:q!**, assuming the editor is not in the input mode.

The newly created file has the status of a normal text file, and so cannot be executed directly. There are two ways of executing the program. Either one can enter

```
sh ~/tmp/mymv.sh
```

which asks the command interpreter **sh** to execute the contents of the file ~/tmp/mymv.sh line by line, or one can mark the file as an executable file with

chmod sets access permissions

```
chmod +x ~/tmp/mymv.sh
```

In the latter case, **ls -F** will indicate this by adding an asterisk to the file name.

Detailed information on the file contents is provided by the command **file**. For example, the command

file identifies file types

```
file /usr/bin/* | more
```

lists the file types of each file located in **/usr/bin**. Possible file types are "Bourne shell script text", "ELF 32-bit LSB executable i386", "symbolic link to ...", and so on.

Users with a printer you will surely be interested to know how to print the new program ~/tmp/mymv.sh.

Printing with lpr

```
lpr ~/tmp/mymv.sh
```

is the appropriate command. To copy the file onto a DOS format diskette one uses **mcopy**. This command is a tool from the package called "mtools" for handling DOS format diskettes. The command

```
mcopy ~/tmp/mymv.sh a:
```

copies the file onto a DOS diskette in drive A. This can then be confirmed by the command **mdir a:** which lists the files located there. To transfer files from a DOS formatted diskette to the Linux file tree, one simply changes the order:

mcopy handles DOS diskettes

```
mcopy a:mymv.sh ~/tmp
```

copies the file from the diskette to the given target directory.

An explanation of how to delete files from the file tree is still

rm removes files   required. The only basic Unix command for removing files is `rm`. It also deletes directories and the files and directories in them (recursively) when the `-r` option is applied. With

```
rm -r ~/bin ~/tmp ~/list
```

the user can remove all the files and directories created in this example session. This is harmless, as the only productive result has been saved on diskette and can be used in a later session by calling the command `mcopy` with the appropriate parameters.

3.3 Command Interpreter

The task of the command interpreter (of the shell) is to analyze,

Linux command   or to interpret, command lines entered by the user and to start
interpreters: bash,   any programs cited. Linux distributions include various command
ksh, and tcsh   interpreters, for example the Bourne Again shell `bash`, the TENEX style C shell `tcsh`, and the public domain Korn shell `ksh`. These are easy to use and have their own programming languages.

In the following subsections the structure of a command or a command line is explained. Some important features of the standard Linux shell `bash` which promote rapid work under

The Linux standard   Linux are listed: command line editing, using wildcards, and
shell is the bash   redirecting input and output. Furthermore, it is shown how to structure command sequences and how to start background processes, and the meaning of pipelines for work with Unix/Linux is briefly mentioned. Details of the language building blocks and the syntax of the shell's internal programming language are summarized in Chap. 8.

3.3.1 Command Syntax

Commands can consist of one or more words or symbol sequences, which must be separated by spaces or tab stops so that they form a command line. The first word in a command line corresponds to the command name, i.e., the name of a program. Subsequent words or symbols form command arguments. After a command line is completed by pressing the return key, the shell analyzes the command line and starts the cited program with the arguments supplied.

Command name
+ arguments
= command line

One must distinguish between two types of command arguments:

- normal parameters, which represent character strings or file names, and

- additional information (options), which control the way the program works.

There are two different kinds of command arguments

The command line

```
ls -l /usr /bin
```

for example, consists of the command name **ls**, the normal parameters **/usr** and **/bin** (strictly speaking, these are directory names), and the option **-l**, which asks the command **ls** to make a detailed list of the named directories.

File names can contain special characters, which have a special meaning for the command interpreter. Some letters, such as #, ?, and \, need to be masked by a preceding backslash \. So

*Special characters are masked by the backslash *

```
ls \#*
```

lists all temporary backup copies created by the program **emacs**. Otherwise, especially for character strings, it may be necessary, to set the parameter in single (´) or double (") quotation marks. This is a must especially for character strings containing a space character:

Quotation marks bracket character strings

```
grep "more characters" testfile
```

27

displays lines of the file `testfile` that contain the word sequence `more characters`. Without the quotation marks, `grep` would have understood `more` to be the character string sought, and `characters` would have been interpreted as a file name.

Many Unix programs expect a preceding hyphen – before an option. Often they accept groups of letters as lists of options, concatenated behind a single hyphen. Additionally, programs developed by the Free Software Foundation usually also process options formed from single or combined words.

These word options require two preceding hyphens and must be separated by a space or tab stop. It is a kind of trademark of many programs developed by the Free Software Foundation that they process both

GNU programs
process
--help and
--version

```
--help  and
--version
```

options and give brief help or display their version number when the respective option is used.

Unfortunately, not all "GNU programs" hold to this style. For example, calling up `bash --help` causes an error message, while `bash -help`, besides displaying its version number, starts an additional shell, but gives no hints on how to use it.

3.3.2 Environment Variables

Environment
variables
characterize
the process
environment

Unix command interpreters can define a context characterized by environment variables that influences the behavior of commands. Information on existing environment variables is obtained by the command `set`, and

```
export variable=value
```

sets a new variable or changes a variable's value. Important environment variables are `PATH`, where the command interpreter searches for executable files, `PS1`, which determines the appearance of the shell prompt, and `TERM`.

Incorrect or incomplete entries in **TERM** can cause the screen editor **vi** to unexpectedly present an unusable screen output, as the control sequences generated by **vi** do not match the terminal. In many cases the definition

TERM controls the screen structure

```
export TERM=linux  or
export TERM=xterm
```

will help. The first assignment ensures that the **vi** can be used on the Linux console without any problems. In the second case a subsequently called-up **vi** generates control sequences that are understood by the **xterm** application.

It is often necessary to examine the values of environment variables. To do so, the name of an environment variable is simply preceded by a dollar sign, so that the shell will replace the variable by its value. For example, the command

$PATH supplies the value of PATH.

```
echo $PATH
```

displays the directories that the command interpreter searches for executable programs.

3.3.3 Editing the Command Line

Within a command line the cursor can be moved back and forth with the left and right arrow keys (←, →). Convenient editing functions are provided for erasing characters as well as inserting missing ones. The built-in command line history allows command lines that have been executed previously to be recalled with the up and down arrow keys (↑, ↓). Users of the Bourne Again shell **bash** may search for a particular command line with the key combination **C-r** (Hold the control key and press **r**). Instead of the prompt the **bash** shows the text

Inserting, deleting, repeating, changing, and searching

```
(reverse-i-search)`´:
```

As soon as some characters are entered and **return** pressed, the **bash** searches through the command line history for the matching expression. It always displays the last matching command line in the sequence. Pressing the escape key and then < (**M-<**)

displays the last command saved, while **M->** displays the next command to be processed.

The number of commands stored by the command line (the history list) is controlled by the environment variable **HISTSIZE**. Its default value is 500. If the user ends a shell (with **exit** or **C-d**), then it saves its current history list in the file specified by **$HISTFILE** (usually this is **~/.bash_history**). The maximum number of lines occupied by this file is determined by the environment variable **HISTFILESIZE**.

~/.bash_history While initializing, a new shell fills its history list with the
saves "old" entries from **~/.bash_history**. Thus in the current session, the
command lines user can still recall command lines entered during the previous session.

3.3.4 Wildcards

The Linux command interpreters allow usage of wildcards, which
Wildcards represent any character, any character sequence, or a character
represent several within a given scope. Spaces separate words, so a wildcard can
characters never stand for a space. There are three different ways to use wildcards:

> **?** for any ASCII character,
>
> ***** for any (also empty) sequence of ASCII characters with the exception of the dot ".",
>
> **[range]** for any character within a range.

The following examples explain the usage of wildcards:

aaa, aba, a1a, ... **a?a** describes the set of all 3-character strings beginning with **a** and ending with **a**.

a1abc, alabaster, ... **a?a*** is interpreted by the shell as the set of all character strings with 3 or more characters that begin with **a** and contain an **a** as the third character.

UNIX, tEx, ... **?[A-Z]*** matches all character strings with at least 2 characters, where the second character is uppercase.

.[a-z]?* matches all character strings that begin with a dot, followed by a lowercase letter, and consist of at least three characters.

.exrc, .xinitrc, ...

3.3.5 Redirecting the Input and Output

Most Unix programs consume or produce data by reading the information to be processed from the standard input **stdin**, forwarding the results to the standard output **stdout**, and diverting any errors to the error stream **stderr**. These three standard streams are provided by the runtime system which is part of every program.

Programs read from stdin and write on stdout

Usually the runtime system assigns all three channels to the terminal; inputs are taken by the application from the keyboard, outputs are displayed on the screen. Internally, Unix (and Linux, too) uses stream numbers 0 for standard input, 1 for standard output, and 2 for standard errors.

To redirect these three streams to files, one has to ask the command interpreter to replace, via redirections, the standard streams with file streams. The **bash** allows these three channels to be redirected by using the redirection operators <, >, and 2>:

[n]< file opens the file **file**; when the program requires input from the standard input it reads **file**. With the optional numeric parameter n one can tell the shell to use **file** for the input on channel number n.

Redirections open files for data input and output

[n]> file specifies **file** as the output file. If the n is missing, the shell redirects stream number 1 (standard output) to **file**. To redirect the error stream, one has to use n=2.

If no output file exist, one is automatically created by the command interpreter. If there is already an output file, it will usually be overwritten. If the environment variable **noclobber** is defined in the user environment, the command interpreter refuses to overwrite the output file in question. If an output file should be overwritten nevertheless, the redirection >| or 2>| must be used.

noclobber prevents you from accidentally overwriting

31

Another redirection operator [n]>> allows program output to be appended to a file. If one wants to simultaneously redirect the standard output and error messages to a single file, one has *>& file combines* to use the syntax &> file or >& file. The third method of *stdout and stderr* redirecting the standard output and error messages to a single file is to use > file 2>&1. The following examples illustrate the usage of redirections.

>   ls > output
>   writes the result of ls into the file output,

>   more < output
>   displays the content of output page by page,

>   pr < output > formatted-output
>   formats output for printing and writes the result to formatted-output.

An important tool that simultaneously redirects the standard *tee multiplies* input to one or more files and copies the information read to the *stdout* standard output is the program tee. It is often used for saving interim results of command sequences, where a command forwards its results via a pipeline to a subsequent program. For example,

>   sort file | tee sorted | more

generates a backup copy sorted from the result of the sort program. Also, tee forwards its input data to more.

3.3.6 Command Sequences and Background Processes

Command Unix command interpreters allow several commands to be given *sequences* in a single command line. These can be separated by one of the *contain* following characters: ;, &, &&, or ||. The end of a command line *;, &, &&, or ||* is indicated either by ;, by &, or by the linefeed.

The semicolon ; and the logical operators && or || in a command line delimit several program calls from each other. A command sequence is processed sequentially, which means in the order entered. A command at the end of the command sequence will be started only after the command directly before it has been processed. In an execution sequence `command1 operator command2`

the operator controls the process as follows:

   `;` starts `command2` right after `command1`,

   `&&` starts `command2` only when `command1` has finished
      with status `0`,

   `||` starts `command2` only when `command1` finishes with a
      status other than `0`.

The `&` operator causes one or more programs to run in a sub-shell as background processes, and causes the command interpreter not to wait until the command has been processed, but instead to indicate its readiness for the next command directly after the program starts. The only messages given by the command interpreter after it starts the background processes are the job number and the process identification (PID) number allocated by the operating system kernel. *Background processes run in a sub-shell*

If a command sequence is to run completely in the background, the sequence must be grouped by brackets. The sequence

   `ls /etc/passwd && cat /etc/passwd > output &`

leads to the execution of the command `ls /etc/passwd` in the foreground; then, if no error occurred, `cat /etc/passwd > output` will be executed in the background. *Brackets combine processes in groups*

   `(ls /etc/passwd && cat /etc/passwd > output)&`

processes the complete sequence as a background process. The last example,

   `( ls -1R > list ; echo "Finished" ) &`

generates in the background a comprehensive list `list` of all files and directories, starting in the current working directory. After finishing, `echo` writes the text `Finished` to the terminal.

3.3.7 Pipelines

The pipeline operator links stdout with stdin

In the examples of Sect. 3.3.5 the command `ls` generated a file `output` by redirecting the standard output, and the command `more` finally uses `output` as standard input. Unix allows the standard output of a program to be pipelined to the standard input of a second program using the pipeline operator `|`:

```
ls | more
```

in general leads to the same result as calling `ls` and `more` separately using redirections. Linking programs via pipelines has the benefit that no additional intermediate file has to be created, that may need to be removed at the end.

Filter chains consist of linked sequences

Pipelines can connect a sequence of commands in series to form a chain of filters with every command altering the data generated by its predecessor and passing on the result it creates to yet another command. A command that prints the number of files located in the current working directory containing the character string `pas` in their file names can go as follows:

```
ls | grep pas | wc -1
```

The only result of this call is the output of the number of lines extracted by `grep` from the list generated by `ls`.

3.4 User Profiles

Unix user names are unambiguous within the system

Each Unix user has an unambiguous user name, with which to get permission to use the system. The system associates the user name with an unambiguous user identification number (UID). Additionally, each user is associated with at least one group name and a group identification number (GID). Users in the same group have the same GID, but different user UIDs. UIDs and GIDs are numbers from 0 to 32 767.

The file `/etc/passwd` collects these data in lines, along with the name of the user's home directory, his or her standard shell, a comment (for example his or her full name, and telephone number) and optionally his or her password, in encoded form.

The password is best stored in the file/etc/shadow, which can only be read by the system administrator. The meaning of the entries in /etc/passwd is shown in Fig. 3.1.

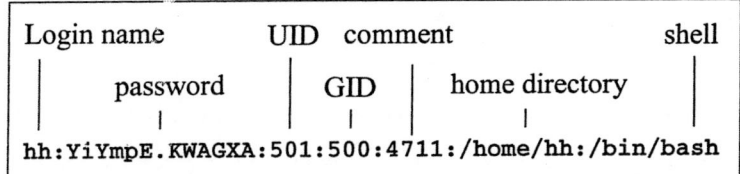

Fig. 3.1
Structure and
content of
/etc/passwd

Each user can belong to several groups. The assignment of user names to GIDs (and group names) is included in the file /etc/group. The list of groups to which a user belongs is given by the command groups.

The superuser root plays a special role amongst the users. Her or his UID and GID are 0, and she or he has unlimited access to system components. She or he is also responsible for entering new users.

New users are entered "by hand" in multiple stages. After the modification of /etc/passwd and /etc/group (probably also of /etc/shadow) a new home directory must be created with mkdir. Afterwards the superuser must transfer ownership of the new directory to the new user with the command chown. The command useradd, called up with the corresponding parameters, does the job in one step. lisa --useradm offers menu driven user administration to the LST system administrator.

User profiles
are located in
/etc/passwd,
/etc/shadow, and
/etc/group

3.5   Online Help

The basic equipment of a Linux distribution comprises various fundamental Unix commands that can be executed by every user. Additionally, the operating system includes privileged commands, which can only be used by the system administrator. Information on the operation of individual service programs is accessible online to each Linux user, via the command man. The syntax for calling the man command is

```
man [options] [section] topic
```

The online manual is structured in sections

where `options` may be one or more command parameters, `section` is a numeric value for choosing a chapter, and `topic` has to correspond to the name of a service program or a system file. For example, the call

```
man man
```

provides information on the usage of the `man` command itself.

All the documentation on fundamental Unix programs and system files that is available online is usually located in the directory `/usr/man`, compiled as an online manual. The online manual is divided into following sections:

1 user commands (application programs)
2. system calls
3 C library routines
4 descriptions of the device drivers
5 formats of special files
6 games
7 tables (for example: fonts, `*roff`-macros)
8 programs for system administration

Each entry includes subsections

Each page of the online manual follows a standard format that groups information by its content. The following are the commonly used headlines for subsections:

NAME command name and a short description of its function,

SYNOPSIS complete command syntax including the meaning of optional and required parameters,

DESCRIPTION comprehensive description of the command,

OPTIONS effects of optional parameters on the mode of operation of the program,

SEE ALSO commands with similar or supplementary function,

FILES files to which the command refers,

BUGS list of known errors, inconsistencies, or problems in connection with the execution of the program.

Linux distributions usually provide a number of online manuals, which include descriptions of program packages and can be found in different places within the file system. Documentation on locally installed applications, for example, is usually located in the directory `/usr/local/man`. Under `/usr/X11R6/man` information on the X Window System is summarized.

There are several online manuals

Before formatting and displaying a particular manual page, `man` usually searches through a number of directories. The configuration file `/etc/man.config` determines which directories are to be considered. Alternatively, the user can set an environment variable `MANPATH`. If `man` finds this variable in its process context, `man` uses the paths located there for its search for manual pages.

MANPATH determines where to search

Further support for locating commands that are linked to a special context is offered by the commands `apropos` and `whatis`. `apropos` searches in every path listed by `MANPATH` for a file `whatis`, and prints out all the lines in which the target keyword (more precisely the character string) occurs. `whatis` also searches through these files and displays all the lines in which the target command name occurs.

apropos and whatis search for keywords

The `whatis` files contain copies of the `NAME` subsections of individual pages of the respective online manuals, one line per manual page in fact. If a Linux distribution is extended with additional application packages, the result of `whatis` might no longer reflects the current state of the documentation. Therefore, it is recommended that the `whatis` files be recreated with `makewhatis` after additional software has been installed.

makewhatis updates the data basis

37

Programs and Processes

From the user's point of view, the operating system processes programs according to the program call entered. From the operating system kernel's view, however, the computer does not process a program, but a process derived from it. Programs are executable files, located anywhere in the file system, and a process is a context of the operating system kernel, which can run independently and which executes a program.

A program is an executable file

For each process the operating system kernel administers a number of data structures: program instructions in machine code, data representation in machine language, kernel stack memory, process table entry (the proc structure), user stack memory, and user structure. The operating system kernel stores the administrative data generated for all running processes in a process table. Furthermore, the operating system kernel administers a user process table, which contains a user structure for each process stored in main memory.

A process concentrates user and system structures

Entries in a proc structure include the following information:

- process status (task is sleeping, task is waiting, task is ready to calculate, task is idle, zombie, task is halted, loading or unloading taking place),

- swap status (process is in the main memory, cannot be swapped out, is swap blocked, a protocol is being created, it is a shared text segment, process is partly swapped),

- process priority,

- queued signals for the process,

*process groups
originate from a
common parent
process*

- name from the process with the highest level within the process group hierarchy as well as process identification from the generic process,

- address and size of the part that can be swapped.

- pointer to the corresponding user structure,

- time remaining until the process generates an alert.

For each program called up by the system or the user, the process manager of the operating system kernel creates this information.

Each Linux distribution is supplied with tools that give information on current running processes (**ps**), indicate system resources used (**top**), measure the total time for which a process *Processes use* uses system resources (**time**), send signals to running processes *system resources* (**kill**), or determine (**nice**) or modify (**renice**) the priority of individual processes. Section 4.1 deals with the first three commands mentioned. Following sections explain how the operating system kernel generates processes, the difference between foreground and background processes, which signal types are defined, and how to generate independent processes. Finally, Sect. 4.6 gives a brief explanation of daemons.

4.1 Process Monitoring

*ps and top show
the content of the
process table*

Like other Unix versions, Linux is equipped with the **ps** (process status) command. Depending on the options used, it gives information on one or all processes running. In contrast to most other Unix versions, the command **top** is a standard part of the Linux distributions. It reads the process table (to be more precise, the proc file system) at default intervals and shows among other things a list of the active processes sorted according to load on the CPU.

*time provides
information on the
system resources
used*

The command **time**, on the other hand, provides information on the system resources used by a program over its whole running time, for example the time used for the execution of the user program code, the time needed by the operating system

40

kernel for the execution of system calls, and the time that passed during the complete execution of the program.

4.1.1 ps

Comprehensive information on current running processes can be obtained with **ps -l**. The option **-l** (long) causes the output of a comprehensive list with roughly the following format:

Fig. 4.1

ps-output

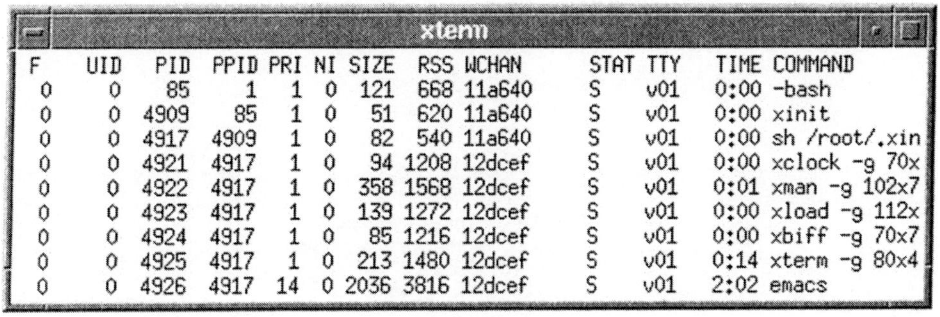

```
┌─────────────────────────────── xterm ──────────────────────────────┐
│ F   UID    PID  PPID PRI NI SIZE  RSS WCHAN     STAT TTY    TIME COMMAND      │
│ 0    0     85     1   1  0  121  668 11a640    S    v01   0:00 -bash         │
│ 0    0   4909    85   1  0   51  620 11a640    S    v01   0:00 xinit         │
│ 0    0   4917  4909   1  0   82  540 11a640    S    v01   0:00 sh /root/.xin │
│ 0    0   4921  4917   1  0   94 1208 12dcef    S    v01   0:00 xclock -g 70x │
│ 0    0   4922  4917   1  0  358 1568 12dcef    S    v01   0:01 xman -g 102x7 │
│ 0    0   4923  4917   1  0  139 1272 12dcef    S    v01   0:00 xload -g 112x │
│ 0    0   4924  4917   1  0   85 1216 12dcef    S    v01   0:00 xbiff -g 70x7 │
│ 0    0   4925  4917   1  0  213 1480 12dcef    S    v01   0:14 xterm -g 80x4 │
│ 0    0   4926  4917  14  0 2036 3816 12dcef    S    v01   2:02 emacs         │
└─────────────────────────────────────────────────────────────────────┘
```

A headline provides information on the content of the list, which is formatted in columns. Data created by calling up **ps -l** may be interpreted as follows: **F** shows process flags (usually **0**), **UID** the user identification of the process owner, **PID** the process number, **PPID** the process number of the parent process, **PRI** the current maximum computer time assigned to the process (in milliseconds) by the scheduler, **NI** the **nice** factor, **SIZE** the (virtual) memory used by the program, **RSS** the program size in the main memory, **WCHAN** the event that process is waiting for, **STAT** the process status (**R** running, **S** sleeping), **TTY** the terminal from which processes were started, **TIME** the computer time used (hours, minutes, and seconds) and **COMMAND** the name of the command.

UID shows who "owns" the process

An essential feature of the Linux version of **ps** is that the data are not obtained by a request to the operating system; kernel **ps** accesses the proc file system directly and formats the proc structures of each process stored there. In contrast to BSD and SysV versions, Linux **ps** does not run with the superuser's rights.

Linux ps is not a root process

The Linux **ps** options processed and output format sometimes differ greatly from those of the **ps** of other Unix derivatives. For a detailed description of the **ps** options and for further information on single processes given by **ps**, see the relevant manual pages.

4.1.2 top

The command **top** reads the proc file system at regular intervals and prepares a full screen table that contains detailed information on the current system data and the status of chosen processes, sorted by the load on the CPU. Figure 4.2 shows an example of the information displayed by **top**.

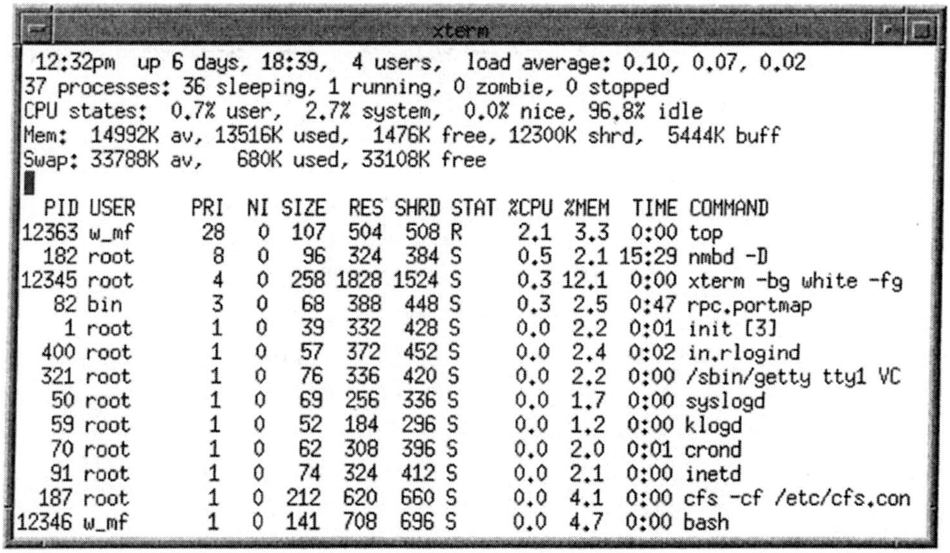

Fig. 4.2
Process
monitoring
with top

```
┌─                              xterm                         ┌─┐□
 12:32pm  up 6 days, 18:39,   4 users,  load average: 0.10, 0.07, 0.02
37 processes: 36 sleeping, 1 running, 0 zombie, 0 stopped
CPU states:  0.7% user,  2.7% system,  0.0% nice, 96.8% idle
Mem:  14992K av, 13516K used,  1476K free, 12300K shrd,  5444K buff
Swap: 33788K av,   680K used, 33108K free

  PID USER     PRI  NI SIZE  RES SHRD STAT %CPU %MEM  TIME COMMAND
12363 w_mf      28   0  107  504  508 R     2.1  3.3  0:00 top
  182 root       8   0   96  324  384 S     0.5  2.1 15:29 nmbd -D
12345 root       4   0  258 1828 1524 S     0.3 12.1  0:00 xterm -bg white -fg
   82 bin        3   0   68  388  448 S     0.3  2.5  0:47 rpc.portmap
    1 root       1   0   39  332  428 S     0.0  2.2  0:01 init [3]
  400 root       1   0   57  372  452 S     0.0  2.4  0:02 in.rlogind
  321 root       1   0   76  336  420 S     0.0  2.2  0:00 /sbin/getty tty1 VC
   50 root       1   0   69  256  336 S     0.0  1.7  0:00 syslogd
   59 root       1   0   52  184  296 S     0.0  1.2  0:00 klogd
   70 root       1   0   62  308  396 S     0.0  2.0  0:01 crond
   91 root       1   0   74  324  412 S     0.0  2.1  0:00 inetd
  187 root       1   0  212  620  660 S     0.0  4.1  0:00 cfs -cf /etc/cfs.con
12346 w_mf       1   0  141  708  696 S     0.0  4.7  0:00 bash
```

The five lines above the list show system-specific data:

uptime shows the
average CPU load

Uptime shows the current time, the time passed since the last system restart, the number of active users, and the average CPU load within the last 1, 5, and 15 minutes. This information is also provided by the Unix commands **uptime** and **w**; the latter additionally shows the activities of the users.

processes reflects all the processes of the system,
divided into idle, executable, scheduled, and halted
processes.

CPU states the current computer performance utilized
by the users and the system. The share demanded by
processes with altered **nice** factor (see Sect. 4.5)
counts twice for the user and system load. The sum
of user load, system load and idle computer capacity
therefore sometimes exceeds 100 percent.

*The field CPU
reflects the free
computer capacity*

memory states the current memory load. The line shows
the available main memory and its current usage
(used, free, shared memory, and memory used as a
buffer). Similar information is produced by the
command **free**.

*The command
free shows the
memory load*

Swap reveals the statistics for the swap area, if there is one
in the system. This information is also provided by
the command **free**.

In the list **top** displays the PID, user, priority, **nice** factor,
information on the memory required, status, percentage of the
CPU and memory load, computer time already used, and the
respective program call (truncated, if the screen is not wide
enough). Pressing the q key ends the program.

Moreover, **top** offers interactive process control in such a way
that the user can also send signals to single processes or change
their **nice** factor. Detailed information is given on the relevant
page in the online manual.

*top can also
send signals*

4.1.3 time

A useful tool for checking the system resources used by a
program or a command sequence during its whole running time
is **time**. Linux distributions include two versions of **time**: the
command interpreter **tcsh** contains an internal **time** function,
and in the directory **/usr/bin** there is a version of **time**
developed by the Free Software Foundation. Both variants
format their display according to a format definition. If the format

*The tcsh has an
internal time
command*

43

information is not given when `time` is called, then `time` analyses the environment variable `TIME`. If that too does not exist, then `time` uses a predetermined standard format.

The version of `time` integrated in `tcsh` called without options provides information on the computer time already used by the current shell. In contrast, `/usr/bin/time` always has to be used in connection with a further command:

```
time command
```

executes `command` and afterwards pipes the measured values of system resources used by `command` to the standard error stream. The output of `/usr/bin/time` usually has the form:

```
0.·01user 0.02system 0:00.12elapsed 25%CPU\
    (0avgtext+0avgdata 0maxresident)k
0inputs+0outputs (0major+0minor)pagefaults\
    0swaps
```

Form and content of the results of /usr/bin/time are controlled by a format string

according to the default format

```
%Uuser %Ssystem %Eelapsed %PCPU\
    (%Xavgtext+%Davgdata %Mmaxresident)k
%Iinputs+%Ooutputs (%Fmajor+%Rminor)pagefaults\
    %Wswaps
```

This information contains the time used (the actual time that passed, the time taken for processing the user program code and the system calls) and the percentage of the processor load allocated to the program. Information on the average size of the memory used (divided, undivided, resident) in kilobytes, the number of accesses to the file system (reads and writes), the number of accesses to swapped pages executed, and the number of swaps executed have the value 0, as Linux does not protocol these data. The manual page gives information on further data provided by `time` when the format is suitably specified.

4.2 Creating Processes

To create a new process, the operating system kernel uses the
system call `fork()`, which creates a child process as a copy of
a parent process, and then it uses `execve()` to overlay the code
segment of the child process with the program code of the new
program. The process context (current working directory, environment variables, etc.) is passed down complete to the child
process.

*The system call
fork() creates a
child process*

The child process is then executed, and the parent process is
usually idle until the child process tells the parent process of its
termination. In this case, the child process works as a foreground
process. If the parent process is to continue running in parallel
to the child process, then the child process has to be started as a
background process, say by to using the ampersand **&** as the last
character on the command line.

In practice the operating system kernel administers a process
hierarchy, starting with the process number 0 (**swapper**), which
first of all creates the **init** process. The latter starts, among other
things, a **getty** process for each defined terminal. This process
receives the user login and then, without creating a child process, is replaced by the **login** process, to check the login. After
successful user identification, the **login** process will finally
be replaced by the command interpreter. Then the user can start
user processes with a program call that, depending on the call
convention used, can have the status of either a foreground or a
background process.

*virtual terminals
are defined in
/etc/inittab*

4.3 Process Signals

The communication between a process and its environment is
controlled by signals, which are either sent or received by a
process. Sockets and shared memory areas are responsible for
the actual communication exchange. Linux defines 30 signals.
Figure 4.3 shows their names, internally used signal numbers, and
meanings. Linux signal numbers do not completely correspond to
the signal numbers used in other Unix operating system kernels.

*Processes send and
receive signals*

Fig. 4.3

Linux signals and

their meaning

Signal	Number	Meaning
SIGHUP	01	hang up
SIGINT	02	interrupt
SIGQUIT	03	quit
SIGILL	04	illegal instruction
SIGTRAP	05	trace trap ($\rightarrow$ debugger)
SIGIOT	06	IOT instruction ($\rightarrow$ debugger)
SIGABRT	06	abort
SIGBUS	07	bus error
SIGFPE	08	floating point calculation error
SIGKILL	09	kill
SIGUSR1	10	1st user defined signal
SIGSEGV	11	segmentation fault
SIGUSR2	12	2nd user defined signal
SIGPIPE	13	write to a pipeline without reader
SIGALRM	14	alarm clock
SIGTERM	15	software stop signal
SIGSTKFLT	16	stack error (coprocessor)
SIGCHLD	17	finishing the child process
SIGCONT	18	continue the halted process
SIGSTOP	19	stop signal
SIGTSTP	20	stop signal of TTSY
SIGTTSIN	21	read TTSY in the background
SIGTTSOU	22	write on TTSY in the background
SIGURG	23	important condition at the I/O stream
SIGXCPU	24	CPU time limit exceeded
SIGXFSZ	25	file size exceeded
SIGVTALRM	26	expiry of the virtual timers
SIGPROF	27	exceeding the profiling timer
SIGWINCH	28	changing the window size
SIGIO	29	I/O possible on a descriptor
SIGPWR	30	power supply interrupted
SIGUNUSED	31	not used

Upon receiving a signal a process either terminates itself, ignores the signal, or branches to another process. There are two methods of sending signals to a process from the command line:

C-c ends a running program, C-z halts it

foreground processes receive **SIGINT** when the user enters **C-c** at the terminal and **SIGTSTP** when **C-z** is entered.

background processes (and also foreground processes) can be sent any signal by using the internal shell command **kill**.

If a foreground process that has been started from the command line is finished with C-c or halted with C-z, the shell indicates its readiness with a shell prompt. Halted processes can afterwards be asked, with the internal shell command **bg**, to continue processing as a background process. If a halted process is to continue running as a foreground process, the internal shell command **fg** should be used, followed by a job number, if necessary. The command **jobs** provides a list of the background processes that have been started from a shell. Each shell administers its own list of jobs.

Halted processes can later continue to run as foreground or background processes

The internal shell commands **bg**, **fg**, and **jobs** are explained in the relevant manual pages of the command interpreters, albeit rather incidentally (note that **kill** also exists as **/bin/kill**). Due to the central significance of these commands for process control they are summarized here in a list:

bg %n causes job **n** to continue processing as a background process,

fg %n causes the continuing processing of job **n** as a foreground process,

jobs shows a list of the jobs that have been started from the current shell,

kill signal %n sends a signal **signal** to job n,

kill signal PID sends a signal **signal** to the process with the process identification **PID**.

4.4 Independent Processes

Usually, finishing a parent process leads to the termination of all child processes initiated by the parent process. If the user logs out from the system (**logout,**) all the jobs that have been started during the session are automatically deleted.

Independent processes ignore SIGHUP

The command **nohup** is useful here, as it causes the process started in this context to ignore the **SIGHUP** signal. In practice, one simply precedes the program call with the word **nohup** and to finishes the command line itself with **&**. For example,

```
nohup command [option]... [argument]... &
```

starts **command** together with the stated command line argument as a background process in such a way that it is "immune" to stopping the shell.

Results of nohup commands are placed in the file $HOME/nohup.out

Commands started with **nohup** do not write their results to the standard output, and any error messages do not appear in the standard error stream. Instead, **nohup** diverts both output streams to the file **$HOME/nohup.out**. If this file does not already exist, then it is created by **nohup** in such a way that only the owner has access permission to it (→ access permissions, see Sect. 5.4). Otherwise, any outputs are appended to the existing file.

nohup runs commands with lower priority

Command sequences can also be started as independent processes with **nohup**. To achieve this, the desired command sequence has to be written as shell script in a file.

A secondary effect of the usage of **nohup** is that the priority of the process thereby created increases by 5 points. The next section gives a detailed explanation.

4.5 Process Priority

Each of the processes to be processed gets a certain share of the available processor load from the scheduler. The percentage is determined by the priority assigned to a process by the system or the user.

nice factors are numbers between -20 and 19

If a process should be executed with a lower priority than others, the user can give it a **nice** factor at the program call. The values of the **nice** factor under Linux range from **-20** to **19**. The standard nice value for foreground processes is **0**; higher values imply lower priorities. By calling

```
nice [option]... [command]
```

the user gives the program **command** lower priority. The allocation of higher priorities is left up to the superuser. If **command** is missing then **nice** shows the **nice** factor that is in effect for the command interpreter.

If there is no option given, **nice** reduces the priority by **10** points, i.e., the **nice** factor is increased to **10**. The user can alter the `nice` factor with the option `-n`, where `n` can either be a positive or a negative number. If the `nice` factor, when changed this way, would exceed the maximum value **19** (lowest priority) or the minimum value, then `nice` sets the `nice` factor to the maximum or minimum value, respectively.

Lower priority implies longer running time

The `nice` factor of running processes is changed by

```
renice factor [[-p]PID] [[-g]PGRP] [[-u]user]
```

With `renice` the normal user can reduce the priority of one process by using the `-p` option followed by the desired process ID, of process groups by using the `-g` option, or of all his or her processes with the `-u` option. However, the user cannot increase the priority again. Only the superuser has unlimited permission to controlling the processes, which means he or she can increase or decrease the priorities of all processes. For example, if the superuser wants to set the `nice` factor of all the processes owned by the users `games` and `guest` and by another with the PID **217** to **8**, the following command does the job:

renice can increase or decrease the response time

```
renice 8 -u games guest -p 217
```

Usually, `nice` is only applied to background processes. Processes that work interactively should always run with high priority.

4.6 Daemons

In contrast to user-started processes, which are always bound to a user and a terminal and depend on the call convention used (either running in the foreground or in the background), daemon processes always run in the background. The operating system usually creates daemon processes when switching to the multiuser mode by executing the shell scripts located in `/etc/rc.d`.

Daemons run in the background

The main task of daemon processes is to process central services for all users. Examples are printer spooling by the line printer spooler daemon `lpd`, the control of network access by the Internet super-server `inetd`, or periodic repetition of commands by `crond`.

They provide user wide services

49

Daemons are
signal or interval
controlled

Normally, daemons carry out an activity on demand and suspend themselves afterwards for a certain time interval; then at a later point in time or alternatively because of a certain signal, they are called again for a new task. The life span of daemons lasts the whole running time of the operating system kernel, and only the shutdown of the operating system kernel leads to their termination. Only the superuser can start daemon processes.

4.6.1 Interval Controlled Daemons

sync compares
the disk cache
with the hard disk

Daemons that suspend themselves for a certain time interval include **bdflush** and **crond**. The task of **bdflush** is to make a **sync** system call every 30 seconds in order to synchronize the buffered data in the memory with the physical file system. **bdflush** is similar to **update**, which is common in Unix System V. The latter can be found in the file system as a link to **bdflush**.

Every 60 seconds, **crond** analyzes a number of files and searches through the directories **/var/spool/atjobs** and **/var/spool/cron/crontabs** for commands that are to be executed once or periodically, respectively. If so entitled by the system administrator, each user may draw up his or her own tables for commands that should be executing periodically or at particular times. The structure of such an entry is as follows:

```
minute hour day month weekday command
```

Minute: 0-59,
hour: 0-23,
day: 1-31,
month: 1-12,
weekday: 0-6,
$0 \cong Sunday$

Entries are separated by either space or tab characters. Times are either numbers, sequences of numbers separated by commas (**0,3,6**), or ranges of numbers (**4-8**). If a command has to be executed every day, at every full hour, and so on, one can also enter an asterisk ***** in the respective line position instead of the full list. For example, the line

```
0 9-18 * * * date > /dev/console
```

daily writes at every full hour between **8** and **18** hours the current date and time to the console.

Commands to be executed once at a certain time are initiated by the user with the **at** command. **at** builds a shell script in `/var/spool/atjobs` which is later analyzed by `crond`. The Linux version of `at` uses the syntax

at jobs are started later

> `at [option]... [-f file] time`

`time` can be given in the form `HHMM`, `HH:MM`, `MM/DD/YY` or as `now + n Units`, where `Units` stands for `minutes, hours, days,` or `weeks`. Further possibilities for specifying the execution time are explained in the online manual.

The command to be executed must either be entered at the terminal (after starting `at`, finish with `C-D`) or written in a file, whose name `at` must be given after the `-f` option. Any output from commands started in this way is sent to the user via electronic mail. Other commands associated with `at` are:

The user receives the results of at commands via electronic mail

`atq` lists the commands due for processing and later,

`atrm` removes commands from the `atjobs` list.

4.6.2 Signal Controlled Daemons

Linux offers almost every system service known from other Unix systems. The kernel log daemon `klogd`, for example captures messages from the operating system kernel and stores them in a central file. The line printer spooler daemon `lpd` receives printing orders from the user, puts them in a waiting queue, and passes them on if the appropriate printer is ready.

The Internet daemon `inetd` plays a central part in the network capability of Linux. Its main task is to receive any network requests and to call up a sub-daemon that suits the network service requested:

inetd starts sub-daemons

`bootpd:` transfers files to remote systems, thereby supporting the booting of remote systems without local hard disks (i.e., diskless clients).

also supports X terminals

`in.comsat:` informs the user of received mail.

`in.fingerd:` provides remote systems with a list of all active users or with detailed information on a certain user.

in.ftpd: opens remote access for file transfer and checks the access permission of the remote user.

in.rexecd: checks the access permission of a remote user and, when successfully validated, executes a task requested by the library function **rexec()** of a remote application.

Enables log in via a network connection

in.rlogind: controls the login of users who wish to access the local system from the network and, if successfully validated, opens a pseudo terminal. If there is a file **rhosts** on the local system in the home directory of the chosen user, and if the remote user is entered there, then no password is required.

in.rshd: checks the access permission of a remote user and, when successfully validated, locally executes a remotely started command.

in.talkd: tells the user that another user requests bidirectional information exchange (real-time dialog).

Similar to in.rlogind, no analysis of$HOME/.rhosts

in.telnetd: analogous to **in.rlogind**, controls the logins of users who wish to access the local system from the network. After successful validation, it opens a pseudo terminal.

Is often used by X terminals and diskless clients

in.tftpd: opens the remote access for file transfer without password inquiry; normally used for the transport of files that in any case can be accessed by everyone.

in.timed: compares the local computer time with the time of other systems on the network.

imapd: supports the interactive mail access protocol IMAP (specification for the manipulation of a remote mailbox).

IMAP is more "powerful", POP is more widespread

ipopd: supports TCP/IP based access (Post Office Protocol POP) on a mailbox server and the transfer of data located there. **ipopd** supports POP version, 2 and 3.

These sub-daemons that **inetd** starts on demand are active only while they run special services; afterwards they terminate.

A further class of network services is based on the Remote Procedure Call mechanism developed by Sun Microsystems. The central interface is the portmapper daemon `rpc.portmap`, which accepts requests from remote RPC applications and then provides them with a port number, saying where the respective services are offered. Sub-daemons called by the portmapper and RPC based services act as follows:

RPC services address the portmapper

`rpc.mountd`: enables remote systems to bind local file systems or their subdirectories into the remote file system.

`rpc.nfsd`: controls access to remote file systems connected via the Network File System (NFS) protocol. NFS file systems often contain data used by several systems, for example the online manual or X fonts.

rpc.mountd exports, rpc.nfsd imports

`rpc.rusersd`: provides remote systems with information on users logged in locally.

`rpc.rwalld`: controls the sending of messages to the users who are active in the network.

Additionally, Linux distributions include a number of other daemons that are usually started by the system while booting and are similar to the main daemons already mentioned. To complete the picture, we list these daemons:

`amd`: (the automounter) automatically binds remote file systems to a directory especially prepared for this purpose whenever someone accesses the directory.

`httpd`: controls the access to locally provided information that is formatted according to the Hypertext Transfer Protocol (HTTP).

Netscape uses the http service

`named`: converts system names, usually consisting of host name and domain name, to Internet addresses.

`sendmail`: represents the transport layer when sending electronic mail (e-mail) across the network.

Files and File Systems

Files collect data into groups, and directories structure files. Directories and file systems are logical components, on physical data storage media. At least that is the quick explanation of the difference between the specialist terms that this chapter deals with. For a deeper understanding of these conceptual elements, which play a central role in the way Unix and Linux work, such a brief definition of the terms is utterly inadequate.

Files and directories are logical components on physical data storage media

The aim of the following sections is therefore to deal with the difference between physical and logical data storage, and with the logical structure of file systems. They also give an explanation of file system elements such as the inode block and the data block area, among others. After this examination of the file system from the operating system side, the directory tree structure used under Linux is the topic of a separate section. There it is shown, among other things, which elements of the file system are used by the operating system, where users can find executable programs, where they can store private data, and how the operating system protects itself and the user against unauthorized access.

The Linux directory tree structures programs and user data

5.1 File Systems

The basis of each file system is a physical medium in the form of a floppy disk or a hard disk or a logical partition imposed upon a disk. Each partition can hold its own file system. Therefore it is possible for a hard disk to contain several file systems with different structures, or even several operating systems. In practice, each partition can be addressed as an independent

A hard disk can contain several operating systems

hard disk. Theoretically it would be possible to partition floppy disks, but due to the small storage capacity of currently available diskette media, this is not of practical value. Figure 5.1 shows the theoretical structure of a hard disk on which three partitions as well as the components of a Unix file system have been created.

Fig. 5.1
Physical
hard disk and
Unix file system

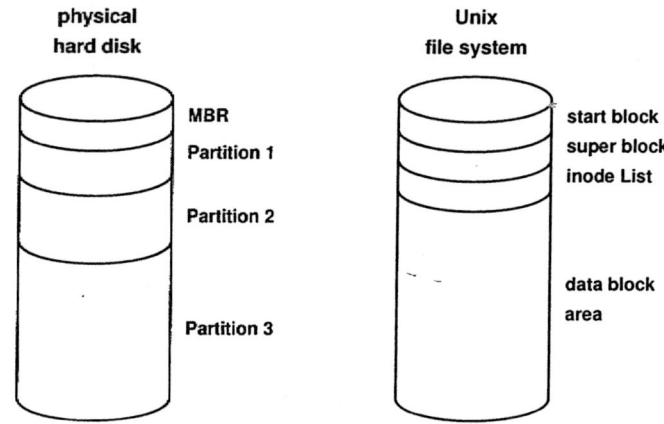

Information on the logical structure, i.e., the number and size of partitions, is stored in the first sector of a hard disk, the master boot record (MBR). When the computer is switched on (assuming there is no diskette in the disk drive), it first of all reads the MBR of the first hard disk, identifies the partition marked active, and then loads the first sector, i.e., the start block from that partition. Information located in the start block is an encoded program that loads the operating system kernel, which is located on the addressed partition, and then starts the kernel running.

The master boot
record holds
partition
information

The start block is one part of a logical file system. Unix file systems are further divided into a superblock, an inode list, and a multitude of data blocks.

Linux can bind in
DOS file systems
transparently

A Unix directory tree can consist of several Unix file systems. Linux allows transparent binding of file systems that adhere to the specifications of MS-DOS, OS/2, System V/386, Coherent, Xenix, or in the ISO 9660 CD-ROM format.

When a file system is created, information on the structure and status of the file system, such as the number of inodes and the number of existing and free data blocks, will be entered into the superblock. The inode list contains information regarding the position and size of every file located in the data block area, as well as other administrative data necessary for accessing the files. The file names are not in the inode list, but are listed in a directory in the data block area that linking each file name to an inode number.

The inode list stores the complete administration data

When creating a file system, the underlying block size is of practical importance, as large blocks increase the reading and writing speed. Although the data block is the smallest physical memory unit, a large part of the theoretical capacity remains unused when a file system prepared with a large block size houses mainly small files. Typical values of the block size of Linux file systems are 1024, 2048, or 4096 bytes.

The block size affects the reading and writing speed

Use of the `ext2fs` file system format is generally recommended for Linux. File names with up to 255 characters are permissible, and the maximum partition size is 2 GB. In principle it is possible to use one of the alternative file system formats, for example `Minix` or `xiafs`, which, in comparison to `ext2fs`, need less space for administrative structures. It is also possible for the directory tree to be composed of file systems with different formats. This has the effect that the operating system kernel must grow to support each additional file system type.

ext2fs supports partitions up to 2 GB

5.2 The Directory Tree

As under Unix, the basis for file administration under Linux is the directory tree stemming from a unique root / (`root`). Hierarchically structured elements beneath the root represent either a file, a directory, a link, or a device driver. Attributes assigned to each element of the file system mark the file type, include certain time stamps, and form the basis of data security. .

Directories are hierarchically structured, files are the "leaves"

The security concept of the Unix directory tree consists of an access permission scheme, classifying Unix users as user, group or other, and administer permissions for writing, reading, and executing within each class. This information is not part of the directory tree but among the file attributes.

User classes: user, group, other

All directory tree entries include the file name and a reference to an inode. The inode points to one or more data blocks where the actual file data is stored.

57

For administrative reasons, Linux has a directory tree structure that realizes a clear distinction between service programs, system files, and user files. This division has been repeatedly modified in the course of the development and today it corresponds to the following scheme, established under the title "Linux File System Standard" (FSSTND):

Fig. 5.2
Contents of the
root directory

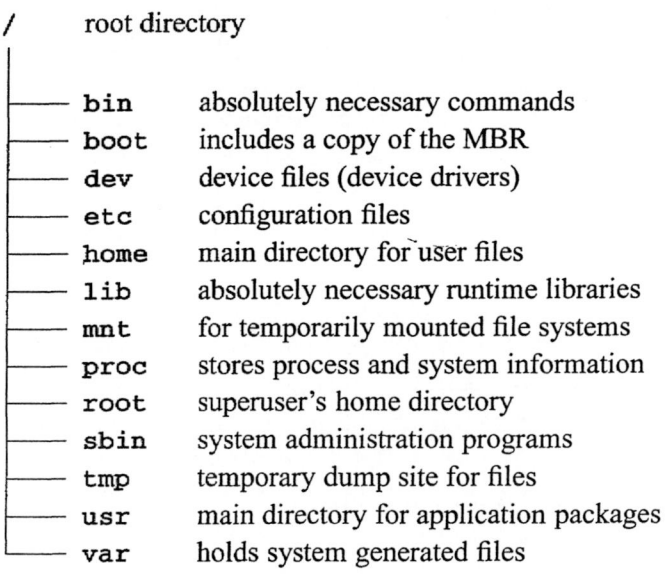

/	root directory
bin	absolutely necessary commands
boot	includes a copy of the MBR
dev	device files (device drivers)
etc	configuration files
home	main directory for user files
lib	absolutely necessary runtime libraries
mnt	for temporarily mounted file systems
proc	stores process and system information
root	superuser's home directory
sbin	system administration programs
tmp	temporary dump site for files
usr	main directory for application packages
var	holds system generated files

The system administrator can find all the files relevant for control of the operating system and user administration in *System files are located in /etc* /etc. Among these files are the user and group tables (**passwd**, **group**), the printer list (**printcap**), file systems to be mounted automatically (**fstab**), the host tables (**hosts***), and the configuration files for the Internet super-server daemon (**inetd.conf**, **rpc**, **protocols**, **services**). In the subdirectory **rc.d** there are various shell scripts that are executed by the **init** process while initializing the operating system. They are divided into scripts for single-user, multi-user, and **halt** mode.

In the **home** directory there are usually only sub-directories, each of which represents the home directory of a user. On systems *User data are located beneath /home* with relatively few users, these directories are usually located directly beneath **/home**, otherwise these home directories are often embedded in an additional directory hierarchy, for example sorted into user groups **staff**, **guests**, **students**, etc.

Significant for both the system administrator and the user is the hierarchy found under **/usr**. According to the FSSTND it is divided as follows:

/usr main directory for application packages

Fig. 5.3
Contents of the
/usr directory

├──	**X11R6**	X Window System, Version 11 Release 6
├──	**X386**	X Window System, Version 11 Release 5
├──	**bin**	additional user programs
├──	**dict**	dictionaries
├──	**doc**	additional documentation
├──	**etc**	configuration files
├──	**games**	games and teaching programs
├──	**include**	definition files for C development
├──	**info**	GNU Info system
├──	**lib**	libraries
├──	**local**	locally created additional applications
├──	**man**	online manual
├──	**sbin**	additional administration programs
├──	**share**	architecture-independent data
└──	**src**	program source code

The **/usr** directory is the main directory for user programs and data, which means it includes all system-wide accessible software components for application development and end-user applications. When several Linux systems are linked with each other in a network, it is usual to create the **/usr** directory on just one computer and to "export" it to the other computers. To this end, the system administrator creates an entry in the **/etc/exports** file of the system where the **/usr** directory has been created. On all other systems, he or she furnishes the file **/etc/fstab** with a line that mounts the remote **/usr** directory. Additionally, the NFS daemon **rpc.nfsd** and the mount daemon **rpc.mountd** have to be activated on the systems involved.

/usr includes
user applications

Networked systems
need only one /usr

The **/var** directory has great significance for the operation of the system services, as it is, in effect, the working directory for the operating system kernel and all active daemons. This is not the place to give a complete explanation of the subdirectories located

/var is the working
directory for the
Linux operating
system kernel   **59**

there, but it is worth pointing out that the line printer daemon lpd
stores the print commands in the directory **spool** located there
and that all incoming mail is placed there, among other things.

If the /var directory is in the **root** file system, one runs
the risk that the system will become inoperable when a large
number of incoming e-mail messages or a long printing queue
exhausts capacity of the **root** file system. This can have the effect
that some applications stop running (for example the C compiler),
because they want to put temporary files in the /tmp directory. If
the capacity of the **root** file system is exhausted, the operating
system kernel puts out the message "file system full".

*On server systems
an independent
/var file system
should be created*

In this case, the remedy is to distribute some main directories to different file systems. One possible division scheme is to
install the information necessary for the configuration of the local system on a small **root** file system, and place the application
packages on a much larger **usr** file system. Furthermore, it may
be desirable to separate user files from system files by placing the
/home directory, too, in an independent file system. If it is not
possible to create a file system for the /var directory as well, it
is recommended that /var/spool is established as a soft link
pointing to a directory located in another file system.

*/ needs about
10-15 MB, /usr
at least 70 MB*

Finally, files are usually only placed in /tmp for test purposes
or when they include interim results. Under no circumstances
should critical data be put there, as this directory is deleted at
every system restart, or in some configurations at periodical intervals. Sometimes /tmp is created as a RAM disk to achieve
maximum access speed.

In the conception of a directory tree architecture that is to
consist of several file systems it is necessary that the directories
/bin, /dev, /etc, /lib, and /sbin be part of the **root** file
system. The programs and configuration files located there are
absolutely necessary for basic administration tasks. /root and
/boot are optional directories, which are usually also located
in the **root** file system. /mnt is an optional entry, that helps
the system administrator to temporarily mount other file systems.
/proc is necessary if the proc structures are to be accessible as
files.

*/bin, /dev, /etc, /lib,
/sbin, /boot, /mnt,
/proc, and /root
belong in the root
file system*

5.3 File Types

Each of the elements in the directory tree represents one of the following file types:

Normal files consist of byte sequences and either include readable text information or unreadable binary information. Normal files are documents, data files, programs, shell scripts, and so on.

Directory files are, in a way catalogs of the file system. Each directory file (/ included) includes at least two files that are also directory files. The first is called .. and is a reference to the parent directory. The second is called . and refers to the directory itself. The entry .. in the root directory refers to /.

Access rights decide whether or not the content of directories is readable

Special files (references, devices) differ from the two preceding file types as follows: references (soft or hard links) are neither normal files nor directory files, but they can point to either a file or a directory. Device files on the other hand provide for the access to devices. They are the input and output interface to the keyboard, the mouse, serial and parallel and Ethernet interface, floppy drive, tape cartridge, the hard disks, and so on.

/dev/mouse is often a soft link to /dev/ttyS0

FIFO files (pipes) mainly serve for information transfer between processes, to be more precise for data transfer from parent to child process. The command interpreter can only create unidirectional pipes, thus a child process cannot transfer data to its parent process. But in principle pipes allow bidirectional communication.

X applications communicate with the X server via sockets

Directory files can include directory files as well as files. References "point" to any file element type desired and, in the case of soft links, can also refer to themselves. If a file referred to by a soft link is removed or deleted, then the soft link points nowhere, so to speak.

The difference between the two link types mentioned is the following: A hard link to a file is a directory entry pointing to the same inode as the referenced element. Hard links can only refer to file elements located on the same file system as the

61

original file. Additionally, normal users can only create hard links to normal files. Only the superuser has permission to create hard links to directories. Soft links, on the other hand, are directory entries that refer to an inode other than that of the original file. The only content of the assigned data block is the path of the file referenced. Soft links can refer to any directory tree element including directory entries on other file systems.

Hard links refer to an inode, soft links include pathnames

To be able to recognize the content of a common file by the file name, it is customary to use file name extensions. The file name extension .c, for example, indicates that the file is C source code. Analogously, Fortran sources have the suffix .f, Pascal sources are identified by the suffix .p, and so on. Using several name extensions is also allowed, for example to identify files with similar content but different version numbers. Executable files normally have a name extension only when they combine programs calls in batches. These files called shell scripts can be recognized by the ending .sh, .csh, or .ksh. Compressed files have the ending .z, .Z, .gz, .taz, or .tgz.

The ending identifies the file type

5.4   File Attributes

All file elements of a Unix directory tree, for short called files, are associated with a block of information. These file attributes, administered in the corresponding inode to each file, include the access permission scheme mentioned already as well as information on file type, number of hard links to the file, file size, owner and group identification of the owner (who created the file), date of creation, date of last access, and date of last modification. When creating a file the operating system kernel enters this information in the corresponding inode and updates it whenever a user accesses the file.

The inode stores file type, file size, owner, group, and access permissions

The basis for access control is a division of all system users into the owner (user), user groups (group), and everyone else (other) who has access to the system. A special role is assigned to the system administrator root who always has access to all files. Based on this division into three classes, Unix differentiates between the permission to write, read, and execute files as well as to search or change in directories.

Access criteria: read, write, execute

Additional attributes control the access rights from an application program to files. The set user ID bit, also called the magic bit, and the set group ID bit transfer to a program the file access permission of the owner of the program file or of the group to which he or she belongs. This mechanism is especially necessary when a user calls up a program that operates on protected files. For example, a user who wishes to change his or her password uses the program **passwd**, which belongs to the system administrator.

S bit programs run with the access permissions of their owner

The program **passwd** always belongs to the superuser. It modifies a password entry located in the file **/etc/passwd**. The file **/etc/passwd** belongs to the system administrator, who is the only one with write permission for it. But because the set user ID bit (and also the set group ID bit) is set in the access permissions of the program **passwd**, every user may modify the file **/etc/passwd** to the extent that the program **passwd** allows.

passwd is S bit root and is therefore allowed to modify /etc/passwd

Another attribute is the sticky bit. If two or more processes simultaneously execute the same program, they can both use the physical memory. Programs with the sticky bit set remain in the (virtual) main memory even when the program is no longer used by anyone. If a user calls up the program again later it will be available instantly.

If the sticky bit is set for a directory, the files located there can only be deleted or renamed by their respective owners. This is also the case if a file has write permissions for group or other set. The superuser, on the other hand, has permission to access such files freely in every case. The command **ls -l** provides information on the attributes of a file. Figure 5.4 shows the structure of the output from **ls** and explains the information included.

The initial letter provides information on the file type. A minus sign indicates that it is a normal file, while **d** indicates directories and **l** soft links. Device files are marked by either a **c** (character oriented) or a **b** (block oriented). Finally, FIFO files are indicated by a **p** (pipe) or an **s** (socket).

The subsequent nine letters include the access permissions. Starting from the left, they identify the read, write, and execute permissions, for owner, user, and other, using 3 letters for each. Refused access permissions are indicated by a minus sign. For

Denied permissions are displayed by ls -l as minus signs

soft links, all access permissions are always set. When using a soft link, the file it refers to determines the access permission.

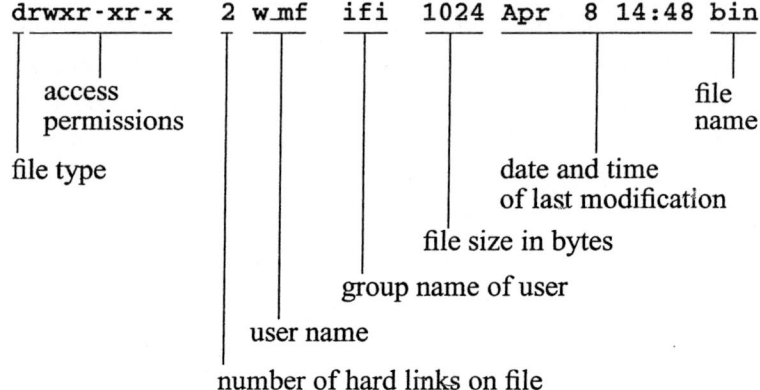

Fig. 5.4
File attributes

If the set user ID bit or the set group ID bit is set for a file, then instead of **x** the letter **s** is placed in the owner or group permissions. Files and directories for which the sticky bit is set have **t** instead of **x** in the "other" position. If one of these bits is set without the corresponding execution and search bit being set, a capital letter (**S** or **T**) appears in the **ls -1** output.

Internally, the access permissions are encoded in a 4-digit octal number or four 3-digit bit fields. The digits identify (starting from the left) system-specific attributes as well as access permissions for owner, group, and other (Fig. 5.5).

755 corresponds to rwxr-xr-x

Fig. 5.5

Octal values

of the access

permissions

Octal value	Meaning
4000	set user ID bit
2000	set group ID bit
1000	sticky bit
400	read access owner
200	write access owner
100	execution/search access owner
40	read access group
20	write access group
10	execution/search access group
4	read access other
2	write access other
1	execution/search access other

5.5 Device Files

All devices accessible via the operating system kernel are entered in the directory /dev as device special files. The command ls -l uses the type identifications c for buffered character oriented, u for unbuffered character oriented, or b for block oriented for these files to indicate the operation mode.

Character oriented devices always work sequentially, whereas block oriented devices can randomly access any data in a record. To read a particular record, one need only position the file pointer suitably before reading, so it is not necessary to search through the file from the beginning. Terminals and serial and parallel interfaces are examples of the first group. Diskette drives, hard disks, and CD-ROM drives belong to the second group.

Block oriented devices support random data access

The output of ls -l does not display a file size for device files, as is usual for other file types, but rather two numbers separated by a comma. The first number, indicating the type of device, is the major device number. If there are several devices of the same type in a system, their second value, the minor device number, will be different. For each type of device, the operating system kernel has a special hardware driver.

The kernel needs a driver for each type of device

There are about 500 predefined device names in the /dev directory. Additional device names may be created using the command MAKEDEV, which implicitly calls mknod:

```
mknod [option]... file {bcu} major minor
```

creates a block (b), character (c), or unbuffered character oriented (u) device file file. Calling mknod or MAKEDEV to create additional device files is a job for the system administrator.

Since kernel version 1.3.25 the sources of the operating system kernel come with a documentation directory. There, in the file devices.txt, is a summary of device names and the respective major and minor device numbers. Note that only those device files are accessible, for which the operating system kernel contains corresponding hardware drivers. Figure 5.6 summarizes the most important device files that access peripherals.

devices.txt includes a list of the Linux file types

Fig. 5.6

Some Linux

device files

Device name	Type	Device
atibm	c	ATI XL bus-mouse
audio	c	sound card, Sun compatible I/O
aztcd	b	Aztech CD-ROM
cdu535	b	Sony CDU-535 CD-ROM
cdrom	l	soft link on CD-ROM
console	c	system console
cuaN	c	callout devices (COM1...)
dsp	c	general sound card I/O
fd0	b	1st diskette drive
hda	b	1st IDE hard disk
ht0	c	1st IDE tape drive
lp0	c	1st parallel interface
js0	c	1st joystick
mcd	b	Mitsumi CD-ROM
midi00	c	1st MIDI interface
mixer	c	audio mixer
modem	l	soft link on modem interface
mouse	l	soft link on mouse interface
psaux	c	PS/2 compatible mouse
ptyN	c	pseudo terminals
sbpcd0	b	SoundBlaster CD-ROM interface
sda	b	1st SCSI hard disk
sequencer	c	audio sequencer
sonycd	b	Sony CDU-31A/33A CD-ROM
sr0	b	1st SCSI CD-ROM drive
st0	c	1st SCSI cartridge tape drive
tape	l	soft link to tape drive
ttyN	c	virtual consoles
ttySN	c	serial interfaces
xda	b	1st XT hard disk

*cdrom, modem,
mouse, and tape
are soft links*

The four soft links **cdrom**, **modem**, **mouse**, and **tape** are optional and are usually generated when setting up the system. For example, **mouse** and **modem** refer to serial interfaces like **ttyS0** and **cua1**.

*4 IDE and
16 SCSI
hard disks
at the most*

Hard disks are accessible either whole (**hda**, **sda**, **xda**) or by partition. The first partition of the first SCSI hard disk, for example, is called **sda1**, the second partition **sda2**, and so on. At first, after the installation of a Linux distribution, there will usually be device files for four IDE and four SCSI hard disks (**hda...hdd**, **sda...sdd**) along with 15 partitions (hda1...hda15, etc.) for each. SCSI drives can have 15 partitions at the most, and the maximum number for IDE drives is 63. Due to the IDE/EIDE specification, a maximum of 4 hard disks of this type (including IDE CD-ROM drives) may be connected. The limit on the number of usable SCSI hard disks is 16.

For cartridge tape drives (ht0, st0) there are additional "non-rewind" device files, which prevent rewinding when using the tape drive. These device files must be addressed whenever a cartridge tape medium is to save or contain several archive files one after the other.

Tapes can store several archive files

Diskette drives are normally addressed in "autodetect" mode. In this case the operating system kernel checks their type (3.5 or 5.25 inch) and their capacity. If a diskette has to have a particular format, characterized by the number of tracks and number of sectors per tracks, the device is addressed via an alternative device file. For example, with fd0D720 the operating system kernel is asked to address the drive as a 3.5 inch diskette with 80 tracks and 9 sectors per track (total capacity 720 KB), while fd0E2880 addresses a 3.5 inch diskette with 80 tracks, each with 36 sectors (2880 KB).

fd0 is an autodetect device driver

fd0H1440 corresponds to 3.5 inches HD format

The letter N, added to virtual consoles or serial interfaces, stands for a device number (0, 1, up to 63). The number of virtual consoles to be supported can be configured in /etc/inittab by the system administrator.

Serial interfaces correspond to the COM ports of the computer hardware. COM1 corresponds to ttyS0/cua0, COM2 is ttyS1/cua1, and so on. cua0 is a callout device that operates the same physical interface as ttyS0.

modem is a soft link to cua*, mouse points to ttyS*

Pseudo terminals are numbered from p0 to sf. The operating system kernel supports up to 64 pseudo terminal masters and 64 pseudo terminal slaves (ttyp0 ... ttysf). They serve to control terminal connections via network interfaces, for example SLIP or Ethernet.

67

5.6 Device Administration

Each Linux device driver takes its operating parameters from special configuration files. This section names the files and explains the tools that allow the system administrator to change existing configurations.

5.6.1 Keyboard Adaption

Linux includes about 40 national keyboard tables

It is relatively easy to configure the keyboard. For the users of the LST distribution, the installation tool `lisa` enters a sequence in the configuration file `/etc/sysconfig/keyboard`. This data is stored as environment variables and read by the initialization script `/etc/rc.d/init.d/keytable`, which loads an adapted keyboard table. For other distributions it may be necessary to add an instruction sequence like

```
if [ -f /usr/lib/kbd/keytables/us.map ]; then
        loadkeys /usr/lib/kbd/keytables/de.map
fi
```

Key bindings under X11 are controlled by /etc/XF86Config and xmodmap

to the start up file `/etc/rc.d/rc.local`. Naturally, in place of `us.map` a keyboard table from `/usr/lib/kbd/keytables` that corresponds to the keyboard currently connected has to be stated. However, this method just defines the keyboard setting for one session at the console. Users of the X Window System have to set the key bindings in the file `/etc/XF86Config` and load a special configuration with `xmodmap` when necessary.

Aside from `loadkeys`, Linux includes other tools for configuring individual keyboard parameters. For example,

Delay is a value in milliseconds, ranging from 250 to 1000 ms

```
kbdrate [-r Rate] [-d Delay]
```

sets the number of characters generated by the keyboard per second (`-r Rate`) when holding down a key, and the time a key has to be pressed until the "autorepeat function" is activated. The command

```
setleds [{+-}num] [{+-}caps] [{+-}scroll]
```

shows, sets, or removes the status of LED flags. For example, setting the `Caps` LED inverts the effect of the `Shift` key, and the `Num` LED influences the interpretation of the keys from the number block.

The program `setmetamode` alters the effect of the `Alt` key. If the meta mode is set to one of the values `esc`, `prefix`, or `escprefix`, the keyboard driver generates 2 characters when the `Alt` key is pressed together with a second key (pressed key with preceding escape character). Otherwise (`meta`, `bit`, `metabit`), a sign is generated for which the 8th bit is set. `dumpkeys` copies the keyboard table currently located in the keyboard driver to the standard output formatted according to the input requirements of the program `loadkeys`.

In meta mode Alt-a produces ß and Alt-A produces ü

5.6.2 Graphics Mode

During the boot sequence the operating system kernel initializes the graphics card for depiction of 80 characters and 25 lines. Other screen resolutions can be freely chosen by the system administrator by using the boot option `VGA=ASK` or requesting with

Standard resolutions are 80×25 and 80×50

```
rdev -v -3
```

that the kernel ask which resolution to use during system start. When the system is already running, the user can configure the screen to `R` rows and `C` columns with

```
resizecons CxR
```

The program `restorecons` then searches in the directory `/usr/lib/kbd/videomodes` for the file `CxR`. Initially there are no screen files. The system administrator creates the necessary configuration files by sequentially initializing the kernel with the desired resolutions and by saving the status with

Video files are built by the system administrator

```
restoretextmode -w /usr/lib/kbd/videomodes/CxR
```

Resolutions for use in the X Window System must be entered in `/etc/XF86Config` by the system administrator.

69

The text output on a Linux console is generated by an internal character generator that makes fonts with sizes of **8x8**, **8x14**, and **8x16** pixels. The latter are loaded from a file located in `/usr/lib/kbd/consolefonts`. The default setting is `default8x16`. The command

*The fonts are
generated by
a character
generator*

```
setfont [Option]... file
```

offers the user a selection of about 100 different screen fonts.

5.6.3 Hard Disk Administration

During initial setup, the creation of file systems is, to a large extent, executed automatically. Adding further hard disk capacity to the system, however, requires some effort to prepare the medium, create the file systems, and integrate the generated file systems into the Linux directory tree. These actions can only be executed by the superuser.

The first step to be taken is setting the partition structure with `fdisk`. The call syntax is

*fdisk divides a hard
disk into partitions*

```
fdisk [Option]... [device]
```

Entering the command m after `fdisk` leads to the output of a command summary. The partition table is displayed by the command p.

The system administrator can allocate new partitions with the n command. Then `fdisk` asks whether a primary or an extended partition is to be made. A hard disk can administer 4 primary partitions at the most. If a larger number of partitions is desired, an extended partition should be created, within it is possible to create further logical partitions. On additional hard disks often only one partition is set up.

*An extended
partition includes
logical partitions*

After successfully partitioning the hard disk, the final structure should always be viewed again (with p) and verified (with v). Furthermore, the partition identification **Id** should be checked. Linux uses the type **83** (Linux native). Finally, the partition information must be written on the hard disk by `fdisk` with the command w, and the system rebooted.

The second step is to create a file system. For this purpose, Linux provides the program

    `mkfs [-V]] [-t type] [Option]... partition`

mkfs generates Minix or ext2 file systems

If the type `ext2fs` is to be created, it also provides the more convenient program

    `mke2fs [Option]... partition`

For a more comprehensive explanation of the `mke2fs` options, see the online manual.

The third and final step is to make a mount point, modify `/etc/fstab`, and integrate the now prepared file system into the directory tree. The mount point is a simple directory entry made with `mkdir`.

fstab entries are automatically mounted by the kernel

The required modification of `/etc/fstab` is the entry of an additional line. For example,

    `/dev/sdb1 /usr/local ext2 defaults 0 3`

mounts the first partition of the second SCSI hard disk to the directory `/usr/local`. The fourth parameter (in the example `defaults`) can be a list, separated by commas, of `mount` options that among other things control the operation mode (read only, etc.). The fifth parameter is significant for the `dump` command. If there is any value other than 0 in this position, `dump` takes the partition into consideration when saving data. The last field indicates the order in which the file systems are checked by `fsck` (file system check) during the boot process. If the entry is missing or its value is 0, the respective file system will not be checked.

rw mounted file systems should always be checked by the kernel while booting

When integrating a new file system the first time, the super-user is recommended to make a file system check, for example by calling up

    `fsck /dev/sdb1`

Afterwards the file system can be integrated into the directory tree with, for example, the command

    `mount -t ext2 /dev/sdb1 /usr/local`

or simply with `mount -a` (which integrates all partitions entered in `/etc/fstab`).

5.6.4 CD-ROM Operation

CD-ROMs are removable data media that can be addressed by
Linux as data or audio CDs. Most data CDs on the market are
constructed according to the ISO 9660 standard and can easily be
mounted in the directory tree as read-only file systems, whereas
audio CDs have no file system structure and cannot be integrated
by `mount`.

Integrating data CDs in the directory tree is achieved with the
command

```
mount -r -t iso9660 /dev/cdrom /cdrom
```

If the superuser wants to change the CD-ROM, the first step is to
remove the file system from the directory tree, for example with

```
umount /dev/cdrom
```

The new CD-ROM
can only be
accessed after it
has been mounted
again

But this action will fail if the file system is still being used by
an application, for example if a command interpreter is using a
directory on the CD as the current working directory. After the
data CD-ROM is changed, the command `mount` must be called
once again, so that the data and files are accessible in the directory
tree.

5.6.5 Diskette (Floppy) Operation

Diskettes are like CD-ROMs removable, but that they provide
read/write file systems. Pre-formatted diskettes can be used practically immediately. Otherwise the medium has to be formatted
first, and depending on the intended use, a file system must be
made on it.

Brand new diskettes may be formatted by the program
`fdformat`. As argument, `fdformat` needs the name of a fixed

fdformat only
operates on device
files with fixed
format

format device file ("autodetect" is not possible for unformatted
diskettes). For example,

```
fdformat /dev/fd0H1440
```

creates 80 tracks, each with 18 sectors, on a 3.5-inch diskette. **fd-format** also checks the medium. Thus prepared diskettes can be used directly for data storage, and can be read from and written to with **dd**, **cpio**, or **tar**. Integrating diskettes in the directory tree also means creating a logical structure on the medium. As it does with hard disks, **mkfs** creates a standard Linux file system. Alternatively the command **mformat** makes a DOS-like structure, consisting of boot sector, file allocation table (FAT), and root directory. DOS diskettes can be mounted in the directory tree with, for example,

mformat creates a logical DOS structure

```
mount -t msdos /dev/fd0 /floppy0
```

To support work with DOS diskettes, Linux distributions include an **mtools** packet that provides various commands for access to DOS diskettes. In **mtools** syntax the device name **a:** addresses the first diskette drive and **b:** the second one. Subdirectories are separated with the usual Unix path separator **/**. Figure 5.7 lists the **mtools** commands.

Program	Task
mattrib	changes DOS file attributes
mcd	changes to another DOS directory
mcopy	copies DOS files to the Linux directory tree and vice versa
mdel	removes DOS files
mdir	shows the contents of a DOS diskette
mformat	generates a DOS format structure
mlabel	sets a DOS volume label
mmd	makes a DOS subdirectory
mrd	removes a DOS subdirectory
mread	copies DOS files to Unix
mren	changes the name of a DOS file
mtype	shows the content of a DOS file
mwrite	copies Unix files to DOS

Fig. 5.7 mtools programs

73

5.6.6 Magnetic Tape Drives

Magnetic tape drives are the preferred medium used for saving
and swapping data. Their memory capacity usually matches the
capacity of a hard disk. Linux can operate various common SCSI
DAT and streamer drives as well as some cheap systems that can
be connected to the floppy disk controller.

Cartridge tapes
do not contain
any file system,
they store files

In comparison to hard disks, diskettes, and CD-ROMs, cartridge tape drives operate sequentially. They are not intended for
use as a file system. Recording of files or of general data streams
is as a sequence of bytes on removable tape cartridges. Some of
the Unix tools available for this purpose are: `cpio`, `dd`, `dump`, and
`tar`. For example,

```
tar cvf /dev/rmt0 /usr
```

makes a backup copy of all files located beneath `/usr` onto the
first cartridge tape drive. Working in the other direction,

```
tar xvf /dev/rmt0
```

extracts a backup located on the first cartridge tape drive and
copies the extracted directory hierarchy into the current working
directory. For restoring data, it is recommended to use the same
command with which the backup was created.

In the non-rewind
mode a cartridge
tape can record
several files

If a cartridge tape is to record several backups, the user must
address the device in the "non-rewind" mode. Instead of `rmt0`,
one simply addresses the corresponding non-rewinding device
`nrmt0`. Then the addressed drive is stopped but not rewound after
each file is recorded.

For the operation of cartridge tape drives, Linux distributions
also include the control program `mt`, which provides basic
functions, such as positioning, rewinding, or erasing a tape. For

mt sets parameters
and offers basic
operations

processing tapes that have been written on another system,

```
mt -f /dev/tape setblk 0
```

is the recommended way to set the block size used by the hardware to "variable".

Basic operations of `mt` include positioning and rewinding of
the medium block by block or file by file. For example, with

```
mt -f /dev/nrst0 fsr 1
```

the user can move the tape forward one block. The latter is often
helpful if the medium is faulty. If an error occurs during a read the   *Faulty,*
user can move the tape forward slightly and try to extract further   *non-compressed*
data with **dd**. When the records are not compressed, some of the   *records are partly*
data may be "recovered" using this technique.   *recoverable*

5.6.7 Serial Connections

The serial connections, called COM ports in the DOS world, are
provided with two device drivers per physical interface under   *Linux differentiates*
Linux. The Linux operating system kernel differentiates between   *between outgoing*
outgoing (**cua***) and incoming (**ttyS***) connections. In practice,   *and incoming*
a serial mouse is often addressed via **/dev/ttyS0** and an exter-   *connections*
nal modem via **/dev/cua1**.

For technical reasons, in PCs two hardware parameters are
responsible for the successful operation of serially connected
peripheral devices. Values for interrupt and I/O address are set
from the hardware side and have to correspond with the data used
by the drivers. However, operational problems can also be due to
different signal parameters, for example the transfer rate or the
number of stop bits.

With the program **setserial** the system administrator
can inform the kernel about configuration of interrupt and I/O   *setserial*
addresses if they differ from the default values. One should   *configures*
remember that **setserial** does not program the hardware, but   *hardware*
just modifies some kernel parameters. For further information see   *parameters*
the manual page about the program **setserial**.

If hardware addresses and kernel parameters correspond with
each other, the system administrator can then test with

```
cat < /dev/mouse
```

whether or not the operating system kernel receives data from the   *Mouse type*
mouse. If this is the case and the mouse nevertheless refuses to   *and baud rate*
operate properly, then most likely either the wrong mouse type   *have to suit*
has been selected or the baud rate is set incorrectly. Standard
transfer rates for serial mice are 1200 and 9600 baud.   75

*Other parameters
have a special
significance for
printers and
terminals*

The baud rate is also a key parameter for the problem-free operation of serial printers or terminals, but it is not the only one. Other configuration parameters affect the character length (7 or 8-bit), the number of stop bits, the type of synchronization (RTS/CTS or XON/XOFF), and so on.

Information on preset attributes for a terminal interface is provided by the command `stty`:

```
stty < /dev/ttyS0
```

*stty displays and
sets configuration
parameters*

displays baud rate, various signal parameters, and some other configuration parameters for the first serial interface that control the interpretation of control characters, among other things.

The program `stty` also serves for setting terminal attributes. For example, if the backspace key **DEL** creates a special key `^?` instead of deleting the preceding character, the user can tell the operating system with

```
stty erase ^?
```

to use DEL as the "erase character". `/etc/termcap` defines terminal attributes that are used by special screen-oriented applications but cannot be set with `stty` (see Sect. 7.2).

*getty controls the
login access*

Sessions via terminal connections under Linux are started or ended with a `getty` program, which is configured in the file `/etc/inittab`. Entries located there follow the structure:

```
id:run level:action:program
```

*Actions are
respawn, wait,
once, or boot*

The first entry consists of an identification with two letters. That is followed by a list of kernel run levels in which the **action** can be executed. **action** is a signal for the **init** process as to whether and how the following **program** is to be executed (once only, repeatedly, after a signal). The necessary signal parameters are finally to be given as command line arguments to the `getty` program, located in the fourth field.

5.6.8 Printer Administration

The Linux printing system consists of the line printer daemon lpd and the four application programs lpr, lprm, lpq, and lpc. lpr accepts print jobs from the user and forwards them to the lpd. The latter puts the printing job in a waiting queue that has been assigned to the printer addressed. The command lpq displays the contents of a printer queue, lprm removes printing jobs, and lpc mainly offers interactive access to print queues, including opening, closing, and resetting.

The Linux printing system creates and processes waiting queues

All the important information for controlling printing is read from the file /etc/printcap by lpd. The structure roughly corresponds to the structure of /etc/termcap. Each printer is described by a line, which defines various options, following the printer name. A simple entry for example is

The control file of the print system is /etc/printcap

```
lp|laser:lp=/dev/lp1:sd=/var/spool/lp:sh:mx#0:
```

The so-defined queue lp with the alias name laser addresses the device driver /dev/lp1. Print jobs addressed to the printer lp are copied into the spool directory /var/spool/lp by lpd. After the complete print job has been sent to the printer the spool file is removed.

lpd creates spool files

The two remaining entries tell lpd not to put out a header page (suppress header sh) and to take on files with unlimited size (maximum file size mx). printcap entries can define up to 40 different attributes. If a printcap entry is distributed over several lines, then each line break has to be masked with a backslash \. Figure 5.8 explains some frequently used options.

lp=	name of the device file
sd=	name of the spool directory
lf=	file for error messages
if=	name of a filter program
rm=	name of a remote printing host
rp=	name of the printer on the remote host
sh	suppresses the output of a banner page
sf	suppresses the output of a form-feed character at the end of a print job
mx#	maximum size of the print file

Fig. 5.8

printcap options

A filter program, labeled by `if=`, has the task of converting the data to be printed to a protocol that can be understood by the printer. A favored printing filter for Linux is the program `apsfilter`, which converts ASCII files as well as various document and graphics formats to protocols that can processed by dot matrix, ink-jet, and laser printers.

apsfilter converts printing protocols

`lpd` recognizes printers connected to a remote host by the entry `rm=`, but there also has to be a colon immediately after the `lp=` label. An entry to address a matrix printer on the host **ares** can go as follows

The printing service operates across the network

```
dotpr:lp=:rm=ares:sd=/usr/spool/dotpr:
```

If the printer has a different name on the target system, `printcap` will also need the option `rp=`. Furthermore, the local system has to be entered as registered host on the remote system, either in the file `/etc/hosts.lpd` or in `/etc/hosts.equiv`.

The superuser creates empty files .seq, status, and lock with touch

Users of the LST distribution can install additional printers with `lisa` via menus. A printer installation "by hand" requires modifying `etc/printcap` and creating the directory entry for spool files, the empty files `.seq`, `status`, `lock` located there, and if necessary a file for error messages. The spool directory and all included files must belong to the **root** user and the group **lp**. Furthermore, the access permissions have to be set to **775**.

5.6.9 Ethernet Configuration

Files located in /etc/rc.d/rc.inet*, configure the Ethernet interface

During installation, the configuration of a network interface usually causes very few problems. Firstly, the operating system kernel in most cases automatically recognizes the Ethernet card and sets the hardware parameters. Secondly, the installation script obtains all the necessary logical addresses and then makes the required entries in `/etc/rc.d/rc.inet*`. Virtually every Linux distribution includes a suitable tool (`netconfig`, `lisa` etc) for adjusting the configuration.

Nevertheless, Ethernet configuration is a relatively difficult task, as it requires comprehensive knowledge of network addressing. The basics will be explained in Sect. 9.5. In this section we discuss the Linux commands for Ethernet configuration.

During the boot process, the operating system kernel configures the network interface by executing the commands `ifconfig` and `route` from `/etc/rc.d/rc.inet1`. Firstly,

ifconfig sets
IP addresses

```
ifconfig lo 127.0.0.1
```

sets up the loopback interface `lo` and assigns the identification (IP address) `127.0.0.1` to it. Furthermore, this interface implicitly gets a netmask, consisting of four 2-digit hexadecimal numbers. If the netmask is linked to the local host address, the result will most probably be the network address.

The netmask
can also be set
explicitly

In the second step, the command

```
route add 127.0.0.1
```

tells the network subsystem that the local system is its own "gateway", which means it forms the router to be addressed in order to establish a connection to the local host. This configuration is not necessary for communicating via point-to-point connections (SLIP, PPP) or for local network services, as the target automatically constitutes the router.

a gateway provides
a connection to the
target address

A second `ifconfig` call to the device `eth0`, along with some further parameters, initializes the Ethernet interface:

```
ifconfig eth0 192.47.11.129\
          netmask 255.255.255.128\
          broadcast 192.47.11.255
```

When called up
without argument,
ifconfig returns
the current
configuration

assigns the IP address `192.47.11.129` within the network and `192.47.11.128` to the local computer. Optionally, `ifconfig mtu num` can set the maximum allowed packet size for the device to `num` (default value: 1500) or activate or deactivate the interface.

Afterwards, the script `/etc/rc.d/rc.inet1` calls the command `route` a second time:

The route command
identifies gateways

```
route add -net netmask 255.255.255.128
```

extends the routing table with another network route and

```
route add default gw 192.47.11.254 metric 1
```

specifies the system `192.47.11.254` as junction point to the world outside. `route del host` removes the route `host`.

Without additional arguments, the commands `ifconfig` and `route` return information about the currently applied configuration. Appropriately parametrized, they can also modify driver characteristics during running operation.

For testing the network interface, Linux provides the programs `ping` and `traceroute`.

For testing the network interface, Linux provides ping and traceroute

```
ping 127.0.0.1
```

checks whether the loopback interface is working, and

```
traceroute jeannie
```

shows a list of every gateway a data package passes on its way to the target system `jeannie`. The resolver, a collection of library functions in the runtime system, translates the host name into the respective IP address required for this kind of command.

/etc/hosts connects the host name with the IP addresses, /etc/resolv.conf refers to the name server

The way the resolver should resolve the host name is controlled by the file `/etc/host.conf`. Normally, this says that the resolver should first examine the entries in the local host table `/etc/hosts` and then ask the name server for the corresponding IP address.

A second configuration file `/etc/resolv.conf` contains the domain name of the local system, and the IP address of a name server. The name service is usually only operated in large networks or when some systems within the net cannot resolve host names locally. The name service configuration is described in great detail in the book *Linux Network Administrator's Guide*, written by Olaf Kirch (Germany) in 1992.

5.6.10 Audio Configuration

While configuring the kernel, all the configuration data for sound
cards should be stated. For this purpose, the system administrator
needs to know the details of the sound card: the sound processor *Hardware data of*
type, the interrupt and DMA channel set by the hardware, and *sound cards are*
the I/O address used. If the Linux sound driver is included in the *kernel parameters*
kernel, then it can also be configured via boot parameters. The
file **Readme.linux**, located in **drivers/sound** relative to the
main kernel sources directory, includes a list of the relevant boot
parameters.

The configuration used on the operating system side is written
to the file **/var/log/debug**, for example. Instead of searching
through it for the last boot messages, however, it is easier to start
the program *dmesg displays all*

boot messages

```
dmesg
```

and to locate the character string **Sound** there. If the data
displayed matches the hardware identifications, then the call

```
cat /dev/sndstat
```

should provide a comprehensive list of the configuration data.

81

File Oriented Commands

Creating, removing, listing, renaming, copying, and reloading are the main actions performed on files and directories. Typical Unix distributions also include a variety of commands for extracting special information from binary and text files. A further group of Unix programs serve for management of file systems. However, the commands available for these purposes are accessible not all to the average user, or are available only with limited features.

File systems can only be created by the superuser

6.1 Changing the Working Directory: cd

The Unix command **cd** may be second only to **ls** with respect to its frequency of use by Unix users. Although it is for altering an environment variable, it only operates on directory names, and has the syntax

`cd [directory]`

cd

cd sets the current working directory to **directory** in the environment context of the command interpreter. If **cd** is called without an argument, then it sets the current working directory to the user's home directory, or more precisely, to the value of the environment variable **HOME**. If **cd** is passed the minus sign – instead of a directory name as the argument, then the current working directory becomes the value of the environment variable **OLDPWD** (**bash**) or **owd** (**tcsh**).

cd sets the current working directory

If the specified directory name cannot be accessed in the form stated, then **cd** analyzes the environment variable **CDPATH** and searches for the target directory under one of the "search paths" it lists. The current working directory will not be changed if the path given does not exist or the user does not have permission to search the directory.

Examples

Programs located in the current working directory are always found by the shell if . is included in PATH

cd sets the current working directory to the user's home directory.

cd /usr/local sets the current working directory to the directory **/usr/local**.

cd /./usr/local also sets the current working directory to the directory **/usr/local**. Starting from the root, the path describes the root, then the directory **usr** located below it and finally **local** below **/usr**.

Changing the current working directory has above all practical advantages. Since the shell starts each command as child process, and the child always inherits the context from its parent process (in this case, the shell), the files and directories located in the current working directory can be directly accessed by the command. Hence, the complete path beginning with the root does not need to be stated. **cd** is a internal shell command.

6.1.1 Displaying the Working Directory: pwd

Information on the current working directory is provided by the command

pwd

pwd

Linux distributions include two different **pwd** commands. Firstly, the command interpreter **bash** has an internal **pwd**, and secondly, the path **/bin** houses the GNU **pwd**. The latter always displays the absolute path of the current working directory and replaces directory links with the real path. **bash**'s internal **pwd** command displays links only when the user has set the **physical** attribute for **bash** by applying **set -P** or when **bash** has been told with **enable -n pwd** not to use the internal **pwd**.

For example, if the user has set the current working directory to /usr/X386 with cd (X386 is a link to X11R6), the internal bash pwd supplies /usr/X386. The result of the call /bin/pwd, however, will be /usr/X11R6.

*After set -P is
called, bash's
internal pwd
displays the
physical path*

If the environment variable PS1 or prompt (see Sects. 8.2.1 and 8.3.1) is suitably configured, the current working directory will be indicated in the shell prompt. Though this has practical advantages it sometimes results in very long shell prompts. Therefore, the shell prompt is often configured in such a way that it does not display the complete path, but instead only the directory name.

6.2 Creating and Removing

Usually, each user can do as he or she wants with his or her home directory, and it is up to them to create or remove any files and directories there. While mkdir is the only command for creating directories, Unix offers several ways for producing files. In practice, every command can create a file if its output is copied to a file via redirection operators.

Removal of files and directories is done by rm. With rmdir the user can remove "empty" directories. Of course, creating as well as removing files and directories requires the appropriate access permissions. Creating files is possible whenever the user has write permission. Only those files and directories that belong to the user or those for which the user has write permission may be deleted (also see Sect. 5.4).

*Creating and
removing files
requires write
permission*

Directories with the sticky bit set play a special role, as they can only be deleted by their owner. For this reason, the directory /tmp is always has the sticky bit set. Anyone can create or delete files and directories there, but the directory itself can only be removed by its owner root (the superuser).

Unix and Linux distributions also include commands for creating device files (mknod) and file systems (mkfs) as well as for integrating file systems into the directory tree (mount); umount removes file systems from the directory tree. The command mount can also be called by the average user, but without any arguments. In this case, the result is a list of the mounted

*mount also informs
the user of the
access permissions
of mounted file
systems*

file systems. In normal operation, the four commands mentioned manipulate system files and therefore may only be executed by the system administrator.

6.2.1 Creating Directories: `mkdir`

The command

mkdir

```
mkdir [-p] [-m mode] directory...
```

creates the directory entry **directory**, or several entries if a list of directories has been given. If a chosen **directory** does not contain any special characters describing a path, then `mkdir` creates the entry in the current working directory. If the entry already exists as file or directory, then `mkdir` emits an error message.

The option **-p** (parent) has the effect that `mkdir` automatically creates subdirectories if necessary. The option **-m mode** sets the access permissions for each directory created according to **mode**. Further information on the make up of **mode** is given in connection with the command **chmod** in Sect. 6.5.1. By default, `mkdir` sets the access permissions according to the environment variable **umask**. **022** is the default value and has the effect that group and others do not get write permission.

Symbolic mode:
u=rwx,go=x
Octal mode: 711

Examples

mkdir src bin tmp creates the subdirectories **src**, **bin**, and **tmp** in the current working directory.

mkdir ../local creates the subdirectory **local** in the parent directory.

6.2.2 Removing Directories: `rmdir`

The command

rmdir

```
rmdir [-p] directory...
```

removes empty directories that contain the entries . and .. only. If the option **-p** is given in the command line, `rmdir` also removes the parent directory provided it is empty after **directory** is removed.

Examples

rmdir /tmp/newtmp removes the directory **/tmp/newtmp** if only the directories **.** and **..** are left. The directory **/tmp** will not be removed.

rmdir -p local/tmp removes the directory **local/tmp** relative to the current working directory, and also removes **local** if only the entries **.** and **..** remain after removal of **tmp**.

6.2.3 Creating Files

As already stated in practice one can use any Unix command to create files by applying redirection operators.

Examples

echo text > file creates a file **file** with the content **text**, followed by a line-feed character.

ls -l /bin > /tmp/list creates a file named **/tmp/list**, containing the result of the command **ls -l /bin**, in the directory **tmp**.

cat > file reads from the standard input, i.e., the keyboard, until the user enters the end of file character **c-d**. It then copies all characters entered, including line-feeds, into **file**.

It is common practice to use either the line editor **ed**, the Unix standard editor **vi**, or the multi-purpose tool **emacs** to create files, since these programs can be used not only for creating but also for editing the files. Note that **emacs**, unlike the other two editors, can also process binary files.

From time to time, the user probably wants to create a file containing just a single line. For this sort of application,

echo [option]... [text]...

is preferred. The command interpreters **bash** and **tcsh** have internal **echo** commands. In addition, the directory **/bin** contains the **echo** command from the Free Software Foundation which offers some additional abilities over and above those of the internal shell **echo** commands.

/bin/echo *can create any* *character desired*

/bin/echo allows any file desired to be created, even binary ones. Usually, **text** must be written within double quotation marks **"** to prevent the shell misinterpreting the meta character \ which is processed by /bin/echo. Then any character can be created with \nnn, where **nnn** is the octal value of the desired character and must be a value between **000** and **377**. Additionally, /bin/echo understands the special characters \t (tabulator), \n (line-feed), and \f (form-feed). A file containing just three lines is created by

```
/bin/echo "\t1\n\t2\n\t3" > file
```

In each line a tab character is followed by the line number.

This method is certainly rather inconvenient. Also, the command /bin/echo can only create files of relatively small size. By calling /bin/echo repeatedly and using the redirection operator >> from the second call on, one can also create larger files. For example, with

```
echo "alias ls=´ls -F´" >> ~/.bashrc
```

the user can extend **bash**'s start-up file with an alias definition.

umask determines *the access permis-* *sion of new set files*

Like **mkdir**, each new file is created with access permissions inherited from the environment variable **umask**. New files created with the methods mentioned are given no search/execute permissions. The default value **022** for **umask** gives read and write permission to the user. The group and others only get read permission.

touch creates *"empty" files*

Normally permission to execute is not set by editors or the command interpreter when creating a file. For example, if the user has created a shell script by using an editor, then he or she needs to set the execution attribute with the command **chmod** in order to ensure that the file is executable. On the other hand, application programs created with a compiler automatically receive this attribute. Furthermore, the command **touch** can create empty files (with file size **0**).

6.2.4 Removing Files: `rm`

The command

`rm [option]... file...`

deletes all files stated, provided that the user has the necessary write permission. As Unix normally does not include a mechanism for recreating deleted files, it is advisable to handle the `rm` command carefully.

Usage of the option `-i` (interactive) provides a certain degree of protection, as in this case the user is asked to confirm the deletion of each and every file with `y` or `Y`. It is recommended in every case to enter an alias definition

Deleted files cannot be restored

> `alias rm=´rm -i´`

in the start-up file (`~/.bashrc`, `~/.kshrc`, `~/.tcshrc`) consulted by the shell is used. After the alias is set, `rm` only deletes without the user's confirmation if it has been called as `\rm` with no options.

Even if called without `-i`, `rm` may still ask for confirmation before deleting a file. This is case when either the file belongs to the user or it is located in a directory belonging to the user but for which he or she does not have write permission. The `-f` option will force the deletion.

If `rm` is to remove directories and the files and subdirectories located there, the user must call the command with the option `-r` or `-R` (recursive).

rm removes files and directories

Examples

`rm -i ./.[A-Z]*` removes all files in the current working directory beginning with a dot followed by an uppercase letter. Before a file is deleted, the user will be asked for confirmation.

`\rm -rf /tmp/newtmp` removes `/tmp/newtmp` as well as all files and subdirectories located there recursively. Use of this call method will not replace `rm` by any alias definition that may exist.

Command names preceded with the backslash \ are not replaced by their alias

6.3   Displaying Contents

Information on currently mounted file systems is provided by
mount, and the free space on all mounted file systems by df.
The contents of a directory are shown by ls which with with the
option −1 also displays the size and attributes of the files. The
command du displays the space taken up by the directories, their
subdirectories and the files they include.

To access the contents of a file, Unix offers the commands
cat, more, pg, pr, and, if one is only interested in the first or last
lines of a file, head and tail. Commands cat, head, and tail
can display text as well as binary files, whereas more, pg, and pr
can usually only be used for text files. Information on the file type
is provided by file, which tries to identify the contents of one
or more files and then classify them.

file analyzes files
and displays the
file type

Other Unix tools for displaying the contents of binary files are
od for converting octal values or integer or floating point numbers
to readable ASCII characters, strings for displaying character
strings that are embedded in a binary file, and nm for extracting
the names of the symbols from a library or an object file. od
and strings can also be applied to text files, whereas this is
not possible with nm.

6.3.1   Information on File Systems: mount and df

The command

mount

mount

provides a list of all currently mounted file systems. The listing
gives the device name, mount point path in the directory tree containing the file system, file system type, and general attributes.
The latter determine the type of access (read only, read and write,
etc.) to files located there. mount is only available in this operation mode for the average user.

The command

df

df [option]... [file system]...

displays the free space in mounted file systems. The parameter
file system can also be a directory name. In this case, df

supplies the free space of the file system which contains the chosen directory name. If `file system` is not stated, then `df` displays the free space of every file system mounted.

Called up with the option `-T`, `df` additionally displays the file system type. `df -t type` limits the display to file systems of the type `type`, whereas `df -x type` only displays file systems of type other than `type`.

df indicates whether or not the current working directory can take a "large" file

`df` provides information on the number of free data blocks, based on a block size of 1024 bytes, or, if the environment variable `POSIXLY_CORRECT` is set in the shell environment, of 512 bytes. To obtain information on the number of used and free inodes, the user should call the command `df` with the `-i` option.

6.3.2 Directory Information: `ls` and `du`

The command

```
ls [option]... [file]...
```

ls

prints the contents of directories or indicates whether or not the given files exist. If the parameter `file` includes wildcards, then `ls` displays all files that match the pattern. If `ls` is called without any `file` arguments, then it displays the contents of the current working directory.

The `ls` command, along with the already mentioned `cd`, is one of the Unix commands used most often. There are more than 30 options controlling what information is displayed and how it is formatted.

When called without any options, `ls` prints all file and directory names with the exception of those beginning with a dot. With the option `-a`, it also displays such "hidden" files. With the option `-i`, not only the file name but also the number of the corresponding inode is displayed. The option `-l` adds the file type, access permission, number of hard links, name of the user and group to which the file belongs, file size, and the last modification time for the file name. The option `-R` (recursive) displays all hierarchically lower directories and their files.

Files, beginning with a dot are usually not displayed by ls

91

Normally the output format to the screen is sorted in columns and the file names are sorted alphabetically from top to bottom. But if the output is transferred to a file or forwarded to another command by a pipe, the output will contain only one column and *ls options control* each line just one file name. If the output needs to be formatted *the output format* in columns in any case, then the option −c must be used. The option −m has the result that file names are separated by a comma and a space, and that each line contains as many file names as the number of character columns on the terminal permits.

Alternative sorting criteria are set by −t (sorted by the modification time), −s (file size), −x (horizontally), −X (alphabetically), and −f (according to the order of the directory entries).

Examples

ls −alt displays comprehensive information on all files of the current working directory, sorted by their modification time. Files and directory names beginning with a dot are displayed as well.

ls −RFC /usr outputs in lines all the files from /usr, and all the subdirectories located there and appended with a type identification character. Files and directory names beginning with a dot are not displayed.

The command

du

du [option]... [file]...

displays the space taken up by the given element file. If file *du -c displays* is a directory, du displays the space taken by this directory and *the total sum of* all subdirectories below it. If the argument file is missing, then *all arguments* du gives information on the current working directory.

Like df, du provides information on the basis of a block size of 1024 bytes. A block size of 512 bytes will be used if the environment variable POSIXLY_CORRECT has been set. To obtain values directly in bytes instead, the option −b should be set.

6.3.3   File Type Identification: `file`

The command

`file [Option]... file...`

tries to identify the content of one or more files and classify them.

`file` carries out three tests. A file test on the basis of the system call `stat()` checks whether or not the `file` is empty and whether or not it corresponds to a special file type (directory file, link, socket, etc.). If `file` includes a magic code which can be a binary code or a character string, then `file` classifies the file according to the entry from a "magic file" `/etc/magic`. If `file` includes ASCII data, then `file` tries to guess whether or not the content matches a certain programming language.

*/etc/magic
links magic code
to file types*

If the list of files to be analyzed is very long, the option `-f list` can be used to instruct the program to take the names of the files to be classified from the file `list`. If `file` is to use an alternative magic file, the option `-m magic-file` should be set. This magic file which usually has to be created by the user, can also be checked syntactically by `file` (option `-c`).

Soft links are recognized by `file` as link files, but when `file -L` is called it displays the type of the file referenced. `file` also analyzes compressed files when the `-z` option is applied.

*file -z analyzes
compressed files*

Examples

`file /etc/*` shows the file type of each file located in the directory `/etc`.

`file -z /usr/man/cat1/a*` analyzes all files of the directory `/usr/man/cat1` whose names begin with a lower-case a, including compressed files.

`file -f filelist` determines the file type of every file name listed in the file `filelist`. The latter file is normally created using the command `ls` or `find`.

93

6.3.4 Displaying Files: `cat`, `head` and `tail`

The command

cat

```
cat [option]... [file]...
```

cat does not create
paged output

copies the given files to the standard output, in the order stated in the command line. If the argument `file` is missing, then `cat` reads from the standard input. If `file` is replaced with a minus sign `-`, then again `cat` reads from the standard input. If the user wishes to furnish the file with an introduction to be input via the keyboard and furthermore add something to the end, then

```
cat - file -
```

is the command line for the job. First, `cat` reads from the keyboard until the user enters the end of file character `c-d`. Next, it copies `file`. Afterwards, it reads from the keyboard again.

cat can
concatenate
binary and
text files

`cat` is mainly used for concatenating several files together into a new one created by using the redirection operator `>`. The input files to be processed are not just limited to readable files. `cat` can also concatenate binary files. However, if `cat` has to display binary files on the terminal, there could be certain difficulties, as the terminal may have to process non-printable characters, such as control characters, which cause it to switch to an unreadable character set. The `-v` option is the remedy here. It causes the ASCII control characters (i.e., characters between octal `000` and

cat -v displays
encoded non-
printable
characters

`037`) with the exception of tab, line, and form-feed characters, to be encoded with a `^` followed by a printable character from the range `100` to `137` (octal). Additionally, `cat -v` encodes the characters whose 8th bit is set (octal `200` to `377`) with a preceding `M-` (Meta). The DEL character (octal `177`) appears as `^?`.

cat -s reduces all
successive blank
lines to a single
blank line

`cat` is also able to number sequentially all text lines processed (option `-n`) or all text lines with the exception of blank lines (option `-b`). If `cat` is to replace several successive blank lines by one single blank line, the option `-s` must be used, but note that this has a different meaning under other Unix versions. Also, `cat -E` adds a dollar sign `$` to the end of each text line.

Examples

`cat *.out >outfile` creates a new file `outfile`, consisting of the contents of all files of the current working directory that have the suffix `.out`.

cat only creates new files when redirection operators are used

`cat ~/src/*.c | wc` connects all C program sources from `~/src` in alphabetical order. The following command `wc` outputs the number of characters, words, and lines of all C program source code.

`cat -sn ~/src/*.c | lpr` copies the cited files to the standard output. Here `cat` replaces successive blank lines by a single blank line and numbers all output lines. The result is forwarded to the printer.

Linux also includes the command `zcat` which unpacks and copies compressed files to the standard output. `zcat` is a soft link to `gzip` (see Sect. 6.9.2). `zcat` does not process the options `-b`, `-n`, `-s`, or `-v`.

The command

`head [option]... [file]...`

head

sends the first ten lines of the given file or files to the standard output. If `file` has not been stated or a minus sign – has been used in place of `file`, then **head** takes the information to be processed from the standard input.

head outputs a greater or lesser number of lines if the user uses the option `-num` where `num` is the number of lines to be output. If **head** has to process several files, each file gets a preceding headline in the output. The headline contains the name of the file that the following text has been taken from. The `-q` option causes the output of the file name to be suppressed.

head does not create page formatted output

Linux distributions include the **head** variant developed by the Free Software Foundation which can also process binary files. The option `-c num` determines how many bytes **head** has to copy to the standard output. A letter suffix to `num` indicates whether `num` is to specify number of 512-byte (`b`), kilobyte (`k`), or megabyte (`m`) blocks.

Binary files are always displayed unencoded by head

95

Example

`head -20 /var/log/messages` displays the first 20 system messages on the terminal.

The command

`tail [Option]... [file]...`

copies the last ten lines to the standard output. If no input file has been stated, `tail` takes the information to be processed from the standard input. It also does so if `file` has been specified with the minus sign -.

When the option -num is used, `tail` outputs the last num lines. `tail +num` copies the contents of `file` from the line num to the end of the file to the standard output. For example, if one wishes to display lines 17 to 25 of `file`, one uses `tail` in combination with `head`:

If not followed by a head, tail displays each line until the end of the file

`tail +17 file | head -9`

does the job.

If `tail` is to process several files, then each information block is preceded with a headline giving the respective file name. The option -q suppresses the output of the headline.

`tail -f` (follow) allows a special mode of operation. This option tells `tail` not to terminate after the last line of the stated file has been displayed. Instead, the command continues to copy, to the standard output, any data added to the end of the file by another process. `tail -f` is often used for watching protocol files, for example, which are created by commands that have been started as background processes with output redirected into a file.

tail -f does not work on pipelines

The "Linux `tail`" was developed by the Free Software Foundation and, like `head`, it allows the processing of binary files with the option -c num. A letter added after num indicates whether num is to specify the number of 512-byte (**b**), kilobyte (**k**), or megabyte (**m**) blocks.

6.3.5 Displaying Text Files: `more`

The command

`more [option]... [file]...`

displays text files on the standard output page by page. After one page is displayed, `more` prompts the user for input. Entering space or `f` displays the next page, `n` followed by space displays the next `n` lines, `c-d` displays 11 more lines, and a line-feed (RETURN) leads to the output of one more line. `more` takes the page length from the `termcap` description of the terminal used. The display is scrolled back page by page by entering `b` or `c-b`. The command = displays the current line number.

The page length is determined by TERM

If `more` is to start the output at a line containing a certain character string `text`, the option `+/text` should be used. While `more` is running, the user can scroll to a line containing the chosen text pattern by using the command `/text`. In both cases `text` can be a regular expression (see Sect.6.10). The command `n` scrolls to the next occurrence of the last pattern sought. `N` searches for the pattern in the reverse direction.

more offers commands for interactively scrolling back and forth, and for searching

From the `more` command the user can also start Unix commands. This is done by entering an exclamation mark `!` followed by a command line. The command is then executed in a subshell. In connection with this, a special role is assigned to the Unix standard editor `vi` when it is called up from `more` upon entering the `v` command. `vi` uses the currently displayed line as its starting point.

The command v starts the editor vi

If several file names were listed in the command line, `more` displays the first file in the command line first. With the `:n` command the user can switch to the next file; `:p` switches back to the previous file. After `:f` is entered, the name of the currently processed file is displayed. With `q` or `Q` the user can finally terminate the `more` command.

:n and :p move back and forth between files

The interactive commands `b`, `f`, `/pattern`, `n`, `:n`, and `:p` can be preceded by a number. This causes the particular command to be executed as often as demanded. For example, when `3b` is entered, `more` scrolls back three pages.

It is not possible to scroll back page by page or file by file if **more** is used as a "filter", i.e., when it receives its input from another program. This holds in particular for the command chains

```
ls -R | more   and   cat * | more
```

less is an
extension
of more

Linux distributions are therefore additionally supplied with the command **less** which completely buffers the standard input and allows backward scrolling even in this operation mode. In some Linux distributions **more** is a soft link to **less**.

Like for **cat**, the option **-s** for **more** leads to the output of a single blank line where there are several successive blank lines in the input file. If **more** is to consider certain options, the user can combine them all in the environment variable **MORE**.

6.3.6 Displaying Binary Files: od, nm and strings

After the sequence
ESC-[7m has been
sent to the console
letters appear in
inverse video

Displaying binary files on the standard output can lead to unintended side-effects if one of the commands **cat**, **more**, **head**, or **tail** is used for this purpose. This is because the terminal used may interpret any control sequences included.

To display the contents of binary files in a readable format the call **cat -v** can be used, although this will only provide results of a limited utility. Better commands for this task are **od**, **nm**, and **strings**.

The main task of **strings** is to extract character strings, while nm displays symbols of an object module, e.g., names of subprograms. On the other hand, **od** converts binary files and displays binary encoded integer and floating point numbers as sequences of readable figures.

The command

od

```
od [option]... [file]...
```

converts input data into various formats. **od** is used for converting binary data to octal, decimal, or hexadecimal numbers or to integer or floating point numbers or ASCII characters. When no input file is specified, **od** takes information from the standard input.

The output format is selected with the option -t type.
Supported values for type are a (ASCII characters), c (ASCII
characters or octal numbers), d (signed decimal numbers), f
(floating point numbers), o (octal numbers), u (unsigned decimal
numbers), and x (hexadecimal numbers).

With the exception of the a and c options, a number can be
added to the type specifier. This number specifies how many bytes
the conversion process should consider at a time. Permitted values *Format options*
are 1, 2, 4, and 8. In place of one of these numbers, od also under- *are similar to*
stands a letter analogous to the syntax within the C programming *the conversion*
language. The letters c (char), s (short), I (int) and L (long) may *specifiers of the C*
be used with whole number types (d, o, u, x) and the letters F *function printf()*
(float), D (double), and L (long double) may be used with floating
point numbers.

od understands following short forms for the specification of
the output format:

Option	corresponds to	Option	corresponds to
-a	-t a	-h	-t x2
-b	-t oC	-i	-t d2
-c	-t c	-l	-t d4
-d	-t u2	-o	-t o2
-f	-t fF	-x	-t x2

With the option -j num the user can specify the byte in the
file where the conversion starts. The number of successive bytes
od processes is determined with the option -N num, where num
is interpreted as a decimal number, or if it begins with 0x, as a
hexadecimal number. An optional letter suffix to num indicates a
multiplier: b corresponds to 512, k to 1024, and m to 1 048 576
bytes.

The output of od is displayed line by line. Each line is pre- *The file offset is*
ceded with the file offset. By default the offset is displayed in *displayed in octal,*
octal. With the -A base option the user can tell od to display the *decimal, or*
offset in decimal (base=d), hexadecimal (base=x), or not at all *hexadecimal*
(base=n).

By default, od displays 16 bytes per line. A different number
of bytes per line can be specified with -w bytes.

When successive lines have the same content, od normally only displays the first line with that content. If all lines should be displayed in the output, then the −v option must be used.

The further option −s [num] results in displaying only the byte sequences that represent a character string consisting of at least num bytes (default setting 3). This is similar to the handling of binary files by strings.

Examples

od −j 47b −N 8 −f /bin/bash converts 8 bytes from the file /bin/bash to 2 floating point numbers, beginning in the 47th block.

od −A n −s4 /usr/bin/od extracts all the character strings consisting of at least 4 letters from the stated file. The file offset is not displayed at the beginning of each line. The result of this call is similar, but not identical, to the result of strings −a /usr/bin/od.

The command

nm

nm [option]... [file]...

nm displays the names of the subprograms

extracts symbols representing the names of subprograms from file (to be precise, from a runtime library or an object module). If nm is called up without file, then nm searches in the current working directory for the file a.out and displays the symbols included in it.

By default the displayed output is a combination of symbol name, symbol type, and a "value" that indicates the relative address of the symbol within the object module as a hexadecimal number. With the −t basis option, the value is displayed either as a decimal (basis=d) or as an octal number (basis=o). The output format is controlled by the −f format option. Values allowed for format are bsd (default), posix, and sysv. When stated in the short form, nm additionally recognizes the options −B (bsd) and −P (posix).

For each symbol name, nm encodes the symbol type with A (absolute), B (uninitialized data area), C (common), D (initialized data area), I (indirect reference), U (undefined), or T (program code). If the symbol type is indicated by an uppercase letter, it is a global (externally accessible) reference, otherwise it is a local one. Undefined symbols have no value.

Externally accessible subprograms are identified by a capital letter

In addition to the the local and global symbols that are normally displayed, nm -a also provides those symbols that include the object module for making analyses with a debugger. The user also has to differentiate between normal and dynamic symbols. The latter occur in dynamic objects only (e.g., shared libraries) and nm only displays them when using the option -D. If nm is to limit its output to external symbols, the option -g must be used. nm -u provides undefined symbols only. When processing several files the option -A has the result that each symbol is identified with the name of the file the symbol has been taken from.

Finally, we mention the possibility of creating sorted outputs. By default, nm displays the symbols in alphabetical order. The option -v leads to output sorted by values. When called up with -r, nm displays the symbols (according to the context chosen) in reverse order. Sorting can be suppressed with -p.

nm -r displays the symbols in reverse order

Examples

nm -g /lib/libc.so.5 displays the list of external symbols included in the C runtime library.

nm -u /usr/X11R6/lib/libXpm.so displays all the symbols needed by /usr/X11R6/lib/libXpm.so.

The command

strings [option] ... file...

strings

searches through each stated file for ASCII sequences consisting of at least 4 letters and copies the result to the standard output. It copies the relatively readable text from binary files. strings can be used, for example, to analyze programs with regard to the names of environment variables they use or the names of the files to which the program refers.

strings extracts readable character strings

The minimum length of character strings to be output is controlled by the options **-n len** and **-len**. If **strings** is to prefix each character string found within the file with its relative position, then the **-t base** option must be used. As with the **od** and **nm** commands already mentioned, **o** (octal), **d** (decimal), and **x** (hexadecimal) are permitted values for **base**. The option **-o** is the short form of **-t o**.

strings -a
displays all
character strings

When working with **strings**, note that this command normally considers the initialized data area of a file only. If **strings** is to process the complete file, the option **-a** must be used. If the option **-f** is used when calling up **strings**, each extracted character string is prefixed by the name of the file.

examples:

strings -a /bin/bash displays all character strings of the command interpreter **/bin/bash** that consist of at least 4 ASCII characters.

strings -f -n 10 /lib/* extracts from files in **/lib/*** the strings that consist of at least 10 ASCII characters. In addition, each character string is prefixed by the name of the file it has been taken from.

6.4   Renaming Entries

The command

mv

```
mv [Option]... source... target
```

removes the directory entry **source** and creates a new directory entry **target**. The file itself remains in the same data block of the file system if the renaming takes place within one file system (i.e., the inode remains unchanged). If **target** is a directory,

mv can
rename files
and directories

then all files **source** will be entered in the directory **target**. If **target** is a file name, then **mv** creates the directory entry stated (provided the target directory exists). In this operation mode only one **source** argument is allowed. If several source files are stated, the target must be a directory name.

Already existing target directories are overwritten by **mv** when renaming. There are two options that can protect the user from this: **mv -i** prompts the user for confirmation, while **mv -b** makes a backup of the file to be overwritten. By default, it will appear under the original name with a tilde character ~ appended. If the user has set the environment variable **SIMPLE_BACKUP_SUFFIX**, then the backup copy gets the suffix that it specifies. If **mv** finds the environment variable **VERSION_CONTROL** in the user's environment context, then **mv** will apply the backup method determined there.

When using the option **-S ending, mv -b** creates the backup with the suffix **ending**. Alternatively, the option **-V method** gives the user the opportunity to choose between three methods. **-V numbered** creates numbered backups. The first gets the ending ~1~, the second ~2~, and so on. **-V existing** creates numbered backups only if backups already exist. Finally, **-V never** always creates copies with "simple" endings.

mv -b creates
backup copies

Example

mv *.c ~/src moves all C source programs located in the current working directory to the directory **src**, relative to the user's home directory.

The command

```
ln [option]... source [target] and
ln [option]... source... target
```

ln

create links. If exactly one source **source** has been stated but no **target**, **ln** creates a link to **source**, using the same name, in the current working directory. If **ln** is to create several link files in one call, then **target** must be a directory.

Normally, **ln** creates hard links. As stated in Sect. 5.3, these have to be created in the same file system as the referenced file, and only the superuser has the right to create hard links to directories. Soft links created with **ln -s** are also allowed to refer to directory entries, especially to those located on another file system.

hard links to
directories can
only be created by
the superuser

103

Analogous to **mv**, **ln -f** overwrites any existing target directories. When used together with **-b**, **ln** makes a backup of the target directory to be overwritten. The user can control the ending of this directory with **-S ending**, **-V method**, or the environment variables **SIMPLE_BACKUP_SUFFIX** or **VERSION_CONTROL**.

Examples

ln /bin/less /bin/more creates the entry **more** in the directory **/bin**. It refers to the same inode as **less**. When calling up **more** afterwards, the command **less** will be executed.

/usr already includes the soft link X11 that refers to X11R6
ln -s /usr/X11R6 /usr/X386 creates a soft link **X386** in **/usr** that points to **X11R6**. Thus all the files and directories located beneath **/usr/X11R6** can also be accessed via pathnames beginning with the string **/usr/X386**.

ln -s source creates a link to itself. Though such links are senseless, they are not prevented by the operating system kernel.

6.5 Changing Attributes

As explained in Sect.5.4, file attributes summarize characteristic file features such as the access permission scheme information on the file type, number of hard links to the file, owner and group identification, creation time, modification time, and last access time.

ls -il displays almost all file attributes
The file type (normal file, directory, socket) is an attribute that the operating system kernel assigns to each file element when it is created. This is valid for the entire "lifetime" of the file, so it will never be changed. Whereas the number of hard links is changed by the operating system whenever an additional hard link is made or an element whose inode is referred to repeatedly in the directory tree is deleted.

All the other attributes are variable information that can be accessed by the user. This means, on the one hand, that the operating system kernel automatically changes the modification time and the access time. On the other hand, there are Unix commands that modify date entries (`touch`), owner and group identification (`chown`, `chgrp`), and access permission (`chmod`), according to options given by the user.

6.5.1 Changing Access Permissions: `chmod`

The command

`chmod [option]... mode file...`

changes the access permissions for files, directories, etc. `chmod` accepts the argument `mode` as an octal number or as a symbolic expression in the format

`<ugoa>{+-=}<rwxXstugo>`

The letters from the first block determine the user classes for which the access permissions are to be modified (owner **u**, group **g**, others **o**, all **a**). Next, an operator has to be given to determine whether access permissions are to be added (**+**), removed (**-**), or given exclusively (**=**, removes all other access permissions for the classes of users). Letters following the operator determine which access permissions are to be modified by `chmod`.

u=rwx gives read, write, and execute permission to the owner

In detail, `chmod` sets or removes the permission to read (**r**), write (**w**), and execute a file or access a directory (**x**). Furthermore, `chmod` can change the values of the sticky bit (**t**), the set user ID bit, and the set group ID bit (**s**). If one of the letters **u**, **g**, or **o** is used in the third block, then `chmod` sets the access permissions that are currently valid for owner, group, or others. On the other hand, **X** causes `chmod` to set the search/execution permission only when it already exists for the owner, group, or others in the respective file.

g=u gives "group" the access permissions of the owner

If `chmod` is to execute several symbolicly formulated changes of the access permissions in one call, the expressions need to be separated by commas. `chmod` executes the chosen operations in the order stated.

Alternatively, `chmod` exclusively sets the access permissions according to a 4-digit octal number or four 3-digit bit fields. The desired access permission must be formed by adding single permissions, using the list of octal values in Fig. 5.5 (Sect. 5.4).

Passing an octally encoded mode to chmod sets the access permissions for owner, group, and other

The value **640**, for example, indicates, that the owner has read and write permission, group has read permission, and others have no access permission at all.

Average users are only allowed to change the access permissions of files they own. When an unauthorized attempt is made to modify the access permission, **chmod** gives out an error message and the modifications are not carried out. Note that the **-f** option suppresses the error message. If **chmod** is called with **-R** (recursive), the program also changes the access permissions of all the files included in any subdirectories that may exist. **chmod -v** also provides the access permissions of all the files mentioned as octal numbers and as encoded character strings. The option **-c** limits this output to files whose access permissions have been changed.

Access permissions of a file can only be modified by the owner or by the superuser

Examples

chmod u+x $HOME/.xsession gives the user the execution right for his or her XDM start-up file **~/.xsession**.

chmod a-rwxst,u+rw,g+r file sets the access permissions on **file** in such a way that the owner has read and write permission, group has read permission, and others have no access permission at all.

After this the access permissions on files will have no meaning for group and others

chmod 700 . modifies the access permission of the current working directory in such a way that only the owner and the superuser will be able to look at its content. The group and others will not be not look at file contents located there either.

6.5.2 Changing File Owners: **chown**

The command

chown

chown [option]... [user][:.][group] file....

transfers ownership of the file(s) stated to **user**; the latter parameter can either be a user name accepted by the command **login** or the corresponding user identification number (user ID) stored in the file **/etc/passwd**.

If **user** is directly followed by a period or a colon and that in turn is followed a group name or a group identification number (group ID), then **chown** additionally modifies the group attribute of the files addressed. If **user** is followed by a period or a colon, but no group name thereafter, then **chown** will assign the chosen files to the group to which the user, specified by **user**, belongs. If a period or a colon followed by a group name has been stated, but no user name has been given, then **chown** does the same job as **chgrp** (see Sect. 6.5.3).

The owner attribute can only be modified by the superuser

Modifications of the owner attribute are left up to the superuser. The average user can only transfer files to groups to which he or she belongs.

Possible options for **chown** as well as the resulting operation mode are mainly identical to the options for **chmod**. **-f** suppresses the error messages created by **chown** in response to an unauthorized access. When modifying user or group ownership, **-R** also considers possible subdirectories and files included there. For each file addressed, **-v** shows whether and how the owner and group identification have been modified. **-c** only displays the files whose owner and group identification have been modified by **chown**.

chown -R transfers a directory hierarchy

Examples

chown adm /var/adm transfers ownership of the directory /var/adm to the administrator (**adm**).

chown -R 25101:25000 /home/mf transfers the directory /home/mf and all included files and subdirectories to the user with UID **25101**. Also, when this command is used, all file elements will get the group identification **25100**.

chown accepts the user name and identification

6.5.3 Changing the Group Identification: chgrp

The command

chgrp [option] ... group file ...

chgrp

modifies the group identification of **file**. Like **chown**, **chgrp** accepts the parameter **group** in the form of a group name or the corresponding numeric identification (group ID) according to the entry in /etc/group.

The average user can only transfer files to those groups to which he or she belongs. Permitted options for chgrp, as well as the resulting operation mode, are identical with chown (Sect. 6.5.2). A detailed list of the options is not given here.

6.5.4 Modifying Time Stamps: touch

The command

touch

touch [option]... file...

sets the time stamps for the last access or the last modification of file to the current date or the date given. If file does not exist, touch creates a new file file of length 0, i.e., with no content, provided that the user has write permission in the directory in question. Average users can modify the time stamps of all files that they own. This is also valid for all files that can be "written" by the user.

touch changes modification and access time

When called without any options, touch sets the time stamp for the last access and the last modification. touch -a only changes the time of the last access, touch -m the time of the last modification. If a date other than the current date should be set, the user can either apply the time stamp of a reference file, by using -r reference, or use

-t MMDDhhmm[[CC]YY][.ss]

touch -t needs values for month, day, hour, and minute

to set the specified date, consisting of month, day, hour, minute. Century, year, and second are optional. touch is often used for encoding version numbers of program packages as time in the modification time of appropriate files.

Examples

touch * sets the time stamps of all files located in the current working directory to the current date. Hidden files are not changed.

`touch $HOME/.emacs` creates a new file `.emacs` in the user's home directory, if one does not already exist. Otherwise, the time stamps of the stated file will be modified.

`touch -t 01010000 *.c` gives time stamps dated January 1st, 0 hours, to all `*.c` files in the current working directory.

6.6 Copying, Saving, Reloading

There are only a few Unix basic commands for copying, saving (archiving), and reloading files. This is rather advantageous for the user, however, since he or she only has to know a few commands for the task at hand.

For copying files within the directory tree, it is best to use the command `cp`. With a few restrictions, it can also be used for saving data on diskettes. But this area of application is unusual for Linux users, as a file system must be created on the diskette and this file system has to be mounted with `mount` in the directory tree. With reference to Sect. 3.2, `mcopy` is recommended for saving data onto diskettes.

cp copies within the directory tree, mcopy operates on DOS diskettes

`cpio` and `tar` are virtually unlimited with respect to copying and archiving files. These commands combine individual files or file groups into an archive file or, in the opposite direction, extract files that have been saved in such archives. The sources and targets for `cpio` and `tar` are normal files and device files. The two commands are universal Unix tools which support data transfer between different Unix systems. `cpio` supports various archive formats, for example the `tar` format. `tar` processes normal and compressed `tar` archives.

cpio and tar operate on archive files

`dump` is intended for saving all data on a system, as it archives the complete contents of a file system. Normally, a cartridge tape is used as archive medium. If one cartridge tape does not offer the capacity needed, `dump` can distribute the backup over several tapes. Its counterpart `restore` only serves for reloading all or certain of the files saved previously with `dump`.

dump saves file systems, restore reloads dump backups

Finally, with **dd** the user can copy a file from any source to any target medium and, if necessary, carry out conversions, e.g., translating the character set or swapping the byte order. Also, **dd** is the only Unix command that can generate bootable Linux diskettes.

6.6.1 Copying Files: cp

The command

cp

```
cp [option]... source... target
```

copies files **source** to **target**. If several sources are given, then *Normally cp* **target** must be a directory. Otherwise, **target** can be a file or *duplicates the* directory name. In this case, **source** either gets a new file name *data block area* or is copied to another directory under the same name. **cp** can also create a target file as a link to the original file, either as a hard link (**-l**) or as soft link (**-s**).

Any existing target directories are overwritten by **cp**. Like **mv**, **cp** allows the usage of two options, **-i** (interactive) which *cp -i produces* prompts the user to confirm the operation, and **-b** (backup), which *backups* automatically makes a backup. **cp** creates backups in the same way as **mv** (see Sect. 6.4) by evaluating the environment variables **SIMPLE_BACKUP_SUFFIX** and **VERSION_CONTROL**. **cp -f** (force) overwrites in every case but **cp -u** (update) does so only when the target directory is an "older" one.

If **cp** is also to copy subdirectories and any files they contain, *cp -r and cp -R* the program must be called with **-R** or **-r** options. **cp -R** copies *copy directory* normal files, directories, device files, and soft links in such a way *hierarchies* that the target directory is of the same type as the source file. Note that the normal user cannot copy device files. **cp -r** does not copy any soft links, but rather the files to which they refer. When the option **-x** is given in addition, **cp -R** and **cp -r** leave out all subdirectories located on other file systems.

cp -P path copies files in such a way that they are placed in the subdirectory **path** relative to **target**. Any subdirectories are needed for this purpose are made automatically by the command.

Files copied with **cp** always get the user and group identification of their user. With **cp** the superuser can retain user and group identifications when copying (option **-p**). The superuser can also use the full functionality of **cp -a** (archive), which combines the options **-d** (soft links remain), **-p**, and **-R**.

Copies made with cp belong to whoever used cp

Examples

cp $HOME/.bashrc /tmp copies the **bash** start-up file of the user to the directory **/tmp**.

cp -u *.c ~/src copies all C program sources into the directory **src** relative to the home directory of the user. Files of the same name located there are not overwritten by **cp** if the modification time of the target directory is more recent.

6.6.2 Archive Programs: **cpio** and **tar**

The commands

```
cpio -o [option]... [< list] [> archive]
cpio -i [option]... [pattern]... [< archive]
cpio -p [option]... target [< list]
```

cpio

copy files into or out of archive files. An archive file bundles several file elements, including file information about pathnames and attributes (owner, group, access permissions, time stamp). Archive files are normal files that can be on a hard disk or a cartridge tape or in a pipeline. Archive files generated with **cpio** have a standard format, so they serve for transferring data between different computer systems.

cpio archives serve for transferring data between Unix systems from different producers

The three operation modes of **cpio** have the tasks of generating archive files (**-o**, output), extracting all or just certain files (**-i**, input), and copying files to another directory (**-p**, copy-pass).

By default, **cpio** makes the backup in the binary format. **cpio** creates different archive formats if the user calls up **cpio -o -H format**. Available formats are:

111

Option	archive format
-H bin	binary format (standard)
-H odc	old portable POSIX-1 format
-H newc	portable SVR4 format
-H crc	portable SVR4 format with checksums
-H tar	tape archive format
-H ustar	POSIX-1 tar format
-H hpbin	HP-UX binary format
-H hpodc	portable HP-UX POSIX-1 format

When extracting files, cpio recognizes the archive format.

Files that are to be copied to an archive are directed to the program via the standard input, for example by redirecting a file containing the names of elements to be copied to the standard input, or by transferring file names generated by ls, find, etc., via a pipeline.

If cpio -o is to store the generated archive in a file, the user must use either a redirection operator or the option -O file. Optionally, file can be preceded by the name of another system or by the name of an authorized user, according to the syntax

This operation
mode requires a
suitable .rhosts
entry on
the target system

```
-O [[user@]host:]file
```

cpio -oA allows files to be added to an existing archive file.

To extract files, cpio reads either the standard input or a file. The program has to be told about the latter by means of -F file. Analogous to the -O option, one can put the name of another system and the name of an authorized user in front of file.

When "unpacking", cpio -o copies the archive files according to their complete pathnames. Any required subdirectories that do not already exist are only created by the program when the -d option is used. Existing files are normally overwritten by cpio -i only if the existing file is older than the one to be extracted. Called up with the -u option, the program overwrites already existing files in every case. Furthermore, cpio -ir allows the user to interactively rename files while they are being unpacked.

cpio -od creates the
subdirectories
necessary for
unpacking

If cpio -i is to extract certain files only, then the user must state one or several patterns pattern in the command line (as regular expressions, see Sect. 6.10), or the program must be told to take `patterns` to be analyzed from `file` using `-E file`. If the `-f` option is given as well, then `cpio -i` extracts all files that do not match `patterns`.

The contents of an archive file are displayed with `cpio -it` (the files are not copied). An additional option `-v` results in the output of a comprehensive summary. Called up with `-n`, the program outputs user and group identifications in numeric form.

cpio -ivt displays file names and /newline file attributes

In the copy-pass mode it is possible to generate soft links (`cpio -pdl`) or to replace soft links with the files they refer to (`cpio -pdL`) instead of making a backup of the data block area of single files. The second option can also be used for creating an archive file (`cpio -oL`).

`cpio -o` usually modifies the access time of the processed files. The option `-a` causes the program to reset the access time to the last one before the reading process. Similarly, `cpio -i` sets the modification time of files to be saved to the current date. The option `-m` causes entry of the original modification time.

cpio can modify or preserve the access times

The program transfers unpacked files to the user and his or her group. The superuser can additionally assign all the extracted files to a certain user (`-R [user] [:.] [group]`).

Further options that are especially useful for the transfer of archive files between systems with different architectures allow the order of half-words in data words (a data word consists of 4 bytes) and the order of bytes within the half-words to be swapped (`-b`), or alternatively just the bytes of half-words (`-s`) to leave the half-word order unchanged. These options are only available for `cpio -o`. The user can also specify the block size to be used, e.g., for optimizing access on cartridge tapes. Options available for this purpose are `-B` (block size of 5120 bytes), `--block--size=number` (block size of `number` * 512 bytes), and `-C size` (one block consists of `size` bytes).

cpio can swap the data byte by byte or word by word when unpacking

Examples

`ls | cpio -o > /dev/fd0` generates a `cpio` archive including all files located in the current working directory. `cpio` also archives any directory files that may exist, but not the files and subdirectories that they include.

`cpio -ivt < /dev/st0`   displays the content of a `cpio` archive recorded on cartridge tape.

cpio –pdl generates
hard or soft links

`find . -depth -print | cpio -pd /mnt`   copies the complete directory tree located beneath the current working directory to `/tmp`.

The command

tar

`tar option... file...`

is an all-purpose tool for creating and unpacking normal or compressed `tar` archives. The user can also specify most of the options for `tar` without a preceding minus sign. In some cases,

Many Linux however, a preceding minus sign is absolutely necessary.
distributions are   `tar` provides seven operation modes. The operation mode of
sold as collection the command is specified by the first option:
of compressed tar
archives
A adds the content of other `tar` files to an archive file,

c generates a new archive file,

d shows the differences between the files of a `tar` archive and files situated locally in the file system,

r adds files to an existing archive file,

t displays the contents of an archive file,

u adds only those files to the archive file that have a more recent modification time than existing ones,

x extracts files.

In contrast to `cpio`, `tar` can only process `tar` archives, which can also be compressed, however. The option **Z** generates or extracts files packed with `compress`. Called up with **z**, `tar` uses `gzip` or `gunzip`. An alternative compression program is used by `tar` if the user states the option `--use-compress-program prog`.

By default   In comparison to `cpio`, `tar` does not expect to obtain the
tar operates the information to be processed from the standard input and does
first cartridge not automatically transfer generated archives to the standard
tape drive output. Normally, `tar` operates the first cartridge tape device
(`/dev/rmt0`). Other devices, such as a floppy drive (`/dev/fd0`)

or normal files, can be chosen with **f archive**, and the standard input and output with **f -**. The argument following the **f** can also have the form **host:archive**.

Both when creating and when extracting, **tar** processes the subdirectories stated on the command line. The option **T file** causes **tar** to take the list of files to be considered from **file**. Conversely, the user can exclude a file (**--exclude file**) or a list of files (**X file**). **tar** displays a list of the processed files only when the program is called with the **v** option.

When using special options (beginning with two minus signs), it is also necessary to enter "simple" options one by one and to introduce each of them with **-**.

If the capacity of the medium used is smaller than the archive file (this will often be the case for diskettes) the user can create multiple volume archives using the **M** option. The need for a new medium can additionally be controlled via **L num**, where **num** describes the capacity as a multiple of 1024 bytes.

tar M processes multiple volume archives

Examples

tar ztvf /dev/st0 displays the content of a compressed **tar** archive recorded on a cartridge tape.

tar xvfC - /tmp takes a **tar** archive from the standard input and extracts the files in it to the directory **/tmp**. Note that options written directly one after another and requiring additional arguments take those arguments in the same order as the options themselves are stated.

tar -c --remove-files -f - . writes the directory tree, which starts in the current working directory, to the standard output using the **tar** format. **tar** simultaneously removes all processed files from the file system.

tar cf - . | rsh ares dd of=/dev/tape copies the file hierarchy beginning at the current working directory to the standard output, then the **rsh** command copies the data to the host **ares**, and **dd** writes it onto the magnetic tape **/dev/tape** of the host **ares**.

115

6.6.3 Copying and Converting: dd

The command

dd

```
dd [option]...
```

copies one or more files or parts of them and carries out conversions. When called without any options, dd reads from
dd operates the standard input and writes the result to the standard output.
on a normal The user has to inform the program about alternative input and
or device file output files by using if=input and of=output. Both input
and output can be the names of normal files or device files.

The count=n option limits the number of blocks to be processed, and sets the block size bs=size used for reading and
writing to size bytes. With the options ibs=size (input block
size) and obs=size (output block size) it is possible to separately
set the block sizes used for read and write operations. A letter
(optional) following size determines how tar should use the
factor size: c=1, w=2, b=512, k=1024 bytes, and xm=n sets the
multiplier to any number n.

Furthermore, the user can cause dd to begin reading only from
a certain block number onwards (skip=n) or to start copying
only n blocks after the head of the output file (skip=n).

Conversions can be made by dd, when stated immediately
dd changes after the option conv=, to change the character set from ASCII
character sets to EBCDIC (ebcdic), or to the EBCDIC format commonly
and carries out used for IBM systems (ibm), the other way round (ascii), or
an exchange byte changing small letters to capitals (ucase), or vice versa (lcase).
by byte dd can also swap successive bytes (conv=swab), but not successive half-words. If dd is to carry out several conversions, they
must be written one after the other, separated by commas.

The operations Files generated on older systems often have a block-oriented
conv=block and archive format, where single lines always have a certain num-
conv=unblock ber of characters. Instead of the end-of-line character, the end
change between a of a block indicates the end of a line. For converting between
fixed and a variable such formats and typical Unix formats, dd provides the conver-
record format sion methods block (replacing the end-of-line character by
as many spaces as are needed to fill the block) and unblock
(replacing trailing spaces by an end of line character). The size

of the conversion buffer that **dd** should use is specified with the **cbs=n** option.

Examples

dd if=/vmlinuz of=/dev/fd0 generates a Linux boot diskette.

dd if=/dev/hda1 of=/dev/hdb2 mirrors the complete content of the first partition of the first hard disk to the second partition of the second hard disk.

dd duplicates hard disks

dd if=/dev/fd0 of=/tmp/floppy1 copies the bit-by-bit contents of a diskette to a file.

dd if=/tmp/floppy1 of=/dev/fd0 makes a copy of a diskette that has been read in previously.

6.6.4 Saving Files and File Systems: dump

The command

dump [option]... source

dump

serves for backing up files and file systems, typically by copying all files, or just the ones that have been changed since the last **dump** was carried out, to an external storage medium (tape, hard disk) in the **dump** format. The basis for the "dump level" is a number between 0 and 9 which has to be stated as an option. The number determines whether all files are to be considered or just the files with the same or a lower dump level that have been changed since the last backup. Level 0 means that all files are to be saved. The standard value is 9. Only the superuser can make a data backup with **dump**.

dump is the standard Unix tool for periodically making data backups

   dump usually makes backups to the cartridge tape drive which is addressed as **/dev/rmt8**. If another device is to be used for the backup, the option **f file** must be used. In particular, this means that **dump** is a tool that makes it possible to mirror file systems. If the parameter stated after **f** has the format **host:file** or **user@host:file**, then **dump** writes to **file** on the remote system.

dump backs up to local or remote media

117

If the target device does not have sufficient capacity to take all data, as will always be the case when "large" partitions are to be saved on "small" tapes, then **dump** distributes the backup over several tapes. If the tape drive cannot generate end of media messages, then the **dump** command also has to be informed about the capacity of the medium.

The capacity of the target medium can be set with -d density and -s feet

The capacity can be estimated from the writing density (set with **-d density**, standard 1600 bpi) and the tape length in feet (option **-s feet**). The superuser can set the capacity with the number of records (**-B records**) that are to be written and the record size to be used (**-b block-size**, record size in KB).

Examples

dump duplicates hard disks

dump 0f /dev/sdb1 /dev/sda1 writes all the data located on the first partition of the first SCSI hard disk to the first partition of the second SCSI hard disk.

dump 0sf 600 /dev/rst0 /dev/hda3 makes a level 0 backup from the third partition of the first IDE hard disk to the first SCSI cartridge tape drive.

6.6.5 Restoring Files and File Systems: restore

The command

restore

restore option... [file]...

allows the superuser to reload files that have been saved with **dump** to the current working directory. The default device read by **restore** is **/dev/rmt8**, which is not included in the Linux directory tree by default but can be created by the superuser as a soft link to the existing tape drive (e.g., **/dev/st0**). The superuser can choose alternative backup media with the option **f file**. If **file** has the form **host:file** or **user@host:file**, *restore restores* **restore** uses remote backup media.

parts or all of the backup

restore can also be used, for example, to reload files after (unintended) loss of data, or convert file systems to another file system format (first, make a backup with **dump**, second, create a new file system, finally, reload with **restore**). The following four options control the operation mode of **restore**:

r fills newly created file systems,

x extracts only the files stated in the command line,

i allows the files for reloading to be chosen interactively,

t displays the contents of a backup medium.

Sometimes, **restore** can only restore part of a **dump** backup that is spread over several media, say when a backup medium is faulty. In this case, the option **R** makes it possible to interactively choose a particular backup volume.

multiple volume backups can be partly restored with restore

The **b blocksize** option enables the block size to be set, and **s num** causes **restore** to restore a certain file from a backup medium. This will always be necessary when several **dump** files have been created, one after the other, on a backup medium with high capacity, and when the read head should not be positioned as it is normally.

Examples

restore rf /dev/st0 loads all files of a **dump** backup from the first SCSI tape drive. Before using this call, it is advisable to recreate the appropriate file system (**mkfs**) and put it in place within the directory tree (with **mount**).

dump 0f - /usr | (cd /mnt; restore xf -) copies the contents of the **/usr** file system to a file system linked to **/mnt**. The data transfer is carried out via standard input and output.

6.7 Searching, Comparing, Sorting

A Unix directory tree usually houses some 1000 entries and it is almost impossible for the user to keep track of them. **find** purposefully searches for certain files or for files whose names follow a certain pattern. Furthermore, **find** can apply certain actions to the "hits", the is files that correspond to the given search criteria.

find locates files in the directory tree

grep searches
through file for
character strings

Often it is necessary to locate a file that includes a certain character string, e.g., the name of a variable in a program source. **grep** was made for exactly this task. It can also locate text patterns that can be written as regular expression.

cmp and diff
compare files
and show the
differences

Another task that occurs from time to time is checking whether or not files correspond with each other. Here, one has to differentiate between binary files, representing executable programs or including binary encoded data, and text files, e.g., configuration files or program sources. Unix programs that serve this purpose are **cmp** and **diff**. The latter is a relatively powerful tool as it can also generate scripts which can be used by the Unix editor **ed** or by the program **patch**, for updating an "older" file.

The command **sort**, which sorts single text files or merges several already sorted files, is explained in Sect. 6.7.4.

6.7.1 Searching for File Names: find

The command

find

```
find [path]... [expression]... [action]...
```

searches through the file system or through a part of it for files that correspond to a given pattern. **find** analyzes logical expressions for each file element located in the chosen directory hierarchy. The command carries out one or more actions **action** for each element identified as hit according to the stated criteria. Frequently used search criteria:

> **-empty** searches for files that do not include any data, and for directories that do not include any files.

Search criteria: file
name, time stamp,
access permission,
file type, owner

> **-name name** searches for files named **name**. If there are files to be found that match a mask, the wildcards of the shell can be used; **name** must be put in inverted commas in this case.

> **-newer file** searches for files that are newer than the reference file **file**.

> **-perm value** searches for files with the access permission **value**.

-type **type** searches for files of the type **type**. Permitted values for **type** are **b** (block-oriented device), **c** (character-oriented device), **d** (directory), **f** (normal file), **1** (link), **p** (pipe), and **s** (socket).

-user **user** searches for files that belong to the user **user.**

The file name of each file that matches the chosen criterion is piped to **action**. Some of the most important actions:

-exec **command** \; executes **command**. All the characters that follow after **command** are interpreted by **find** as command parameters. The end of the command line is indicated by a semicolon with preceding space and backslash (\). The command line should include a pair of braces {}. **find** replaces them by the current path name.

The action -exec has to be concluded by a masked semicolon \;

-fprint **file** writes all pathnames that match the chosen criteria to the file **file.**

-ls copies the pathname together with additional information (according to the call **ls -dils**) to the standard output.

-ok corresponds to -exec and additionally prompts the user to confirm the action.

-print copies the pathname to the standard output.

Examples

find ~ -name ".*rc" -print searches for files whose names start with a dot, end with the letters **rc**, and are located below the user's home directory.

Wild characters must be isolated with quotes

find / -name core -exec rm {} \; carries out the command **rm** for all files named **core** located in the directory tree.

find /tmp -user mf -print copies all names of the files of the directory hierarchy /tmp to the standard output belonging to the user **mf.**

121

6.7.2 Searching for File Contents: `grep`

The command

grep

`grep [option]... expression [file]...`

displays all lines of files (one or more) that include a particular expression, and copies them to the standard output. If the `file` argument is missing or a minus sign – has been used instead, then `grep` takes the information to be processed from the standard input. There are three options that determine the operation mode of `grep`:

grep, egrep, and
fgrep search for
character strings or
regular expressions

`-G` instructs `grep` to interpret **expression** as a regular expression (see Sect. 6.10),

`-E` results in **expression** being treated like an extended regular expression,

`-F` allows several listed expressions, which are usually located in a file (use the option `-f file`) and separated by line-feeds, to be sought.

If none of the options mentioned have been stated, the program works as if `grep -G` were used. For the other operation modes, either the command `egrep` (basically corresponds to `grep -E`) or `fgrep` (identical with `grep -F`) can be used. Linux distributions include the `grep` versions developed by the Free Software Foundation, which allow extended regular expressions for all operation modes.

By default, `grep` provides the line of each file that includes the stated expression. Additionally, the option `-num` results in the output of **num** lines before and after the line containing **expression**. If just the preceding or following lines are desired, the options `-B` (before) or `-A` (after) have to be used.

Normally, `grep` differentiates between capital and small letters; `grep -i` prevents this. Further important options are: `-n` for outputting the line numbers in which the **expression** has been found, `-h` for suppressing the file name output by `grep` when processing several files, `-c` for showing the number of

grep –i handles all
letters like small
letters

"hits", and −l for displaying only the names of the files that include **expression**. Inverted searching means displaying all lines that do not include **expression**, and that is done by **grep −v**.

Examples

grep −n −A 2 inetd /etc/rc.d/* displays all lines, with their line number, in all files located in the directory **/etc/rc.d/*** that include the character string **inetd**. In addition, **grep** displays the 2 following lines.

strings −a /bin/bash | grep −i version first extracts the readable text from **/bin/bash** and then filters out all the lines containing the character string **version**. No distinction is made between upper and lowercase letters.

grep is often used together with strings

grep −e ´\<F[A−Za−z]\{2\}\>´ *.tex searches in all files ***.tex** in the current working directory for words that match the stated regular expression, i.e., that start with a capital **F** and consist of exactly 3 letters (see Sect. 6.10).

6.7.3 Comparing File Contents: cmp and diff

The command

```
cmp [option]... file1 [file2]
```

cmp

compares two files with each other (or a file with the standard input) and, if there is any dissimilarity, displays the file position where the first difference occurs and the byte located there. **cmp** terminates with exit status 0 if the files match each other and with 1 if there are any differences. The −s option (silent) suppresses the output. In this case, the identity of of two files can be seen by the exit status of **cmp**.

Called with the −l option, **cmp**, displays all the differences with their file offset as a preceding decimal number, followed by the octal values of the bytes of both files at those lines. The option −c additionally outputs the octal value and the corresponding symbol of each such byte. Like **cat**, in this operation mode **cmp**

diff

-v indicates control characters with a preceding ^, and characters with the 8th bit set are indicated with a preceding `M-`.

The command

```
diff [option]... file1 file2
```

diff compares files and directories with each other

compares two files, `file1` and `file2`, with each other. The lines in `file1` that would have to be changed in order to be equivalent to `file2` are displayed on the standard output. If `file1` is a directory, `diff` compares `file2` with the file from the directory `file1` that is named `file2`. If `file1` and `file2` are both directories, `diff` compares files from `file1` with those of the same name from `file2`. In this case, with the right options, `diff` treats non existent primary (`-P`) or secondary (`-N`) files as if they were empty. Additionally, `-r` results in a recursive comparison, i.e., all subdirectories are considered.

`diff` is mainly intended for comparing text files. It can also handle binary files, but for comparing binary files `cmp` is recommended. When called up with `-s` or `-q`, `diff` outputs the names of identical or different files, respectively. Otherwise, the program generates a sequence of marked lines that indicate where the differences of the processed files are how they differ. The output looks roughly like:

a,c and d stand for append, change and delete

`n1an3,n4`	for lines to be added,
`n1,n2cn3,n4`	for lines to be changed and
`n1,n2dn3`	for lines to be deleted,

where `n1`, `n2`, `n3`, `n4` indicate line numbers. First `diff` writes the relevant lines from `file1`, then the ones from `file2`. The lines taken from `file1` are indicated with a preceding left angle bracket <, the lines added to `file2` with a right angle bracket >. Furthermore, `diff` adds a line with 3 minus signs after the lines from `file1`, if information from `file2` follows in the same block (this is only relevant in connection with the `-c` option).

diff can format the output for ed or patch

If `diff` is called up with the `-e` option, the output will appear in a format that can be used as a command sequence by the Unix line editor `ed` for modifying `file1` to look like `file2`. Alternatively, `diff -c` formats the output in the "context format" that meets the demands of the `patch` program.

When using the option **-y**, **diff** displays the contents of the files side by side and highlights the lines where **file2** differs from **file1**. Usually the line width is 130 characters; an alternative column number is set by **-W num**.

A further operation mode **diff -D name** allows two C program sources to be merged. Corresponding lines are copied unchanged to the standard output, and lines that differ are reframed with the preprocessor directives **#ifdef name** or **#ifndef name**, **#else**, and **#endif**.

diff –D merges C programs

The normal operation mode of **diff** is intended for comparison character by character. Called up together with the **-i** option, **diff** suppresses the distinction between capitals and small letters, with **-w** it removes any spaces before the comparison is made, with **-b** it reduces multiple blank lines to a single line, and with **-B** it ignores spaces. Furthermore, when **diff** is called up with **-I RegExp**, all the compared lines that match a regular expression **RegExp** are ignored.

diff -i treats capitals and small letters equally

Examples

diff rc.local rc.local~ outputs the differences between the current system start-up file **rc.local** and a backup **rc.local~**.

diff -crN old new > new.patch compares all the files from the directory hierarchy **new** with those from **old**. The patch file generated can then be used to modify the directory hierarchy **old** to bring it up to the state of **new** (**patch -p < new.patch**).

6.7.4 Sorting Text Files: sort

The command

```
sort [option]... [file]...
```

sort

sorts the lines of the stated files or of the data lines read in from the standard input and copies the result to the standard output or, when called with **-o file**, to a file. **sort -c** just checks whether

sort sorts a single
file or merges
several presorted
files

or not the data is already sorted. If the input file is not sorted, sort terminates with exit status 1. The contents of several files can be merged together to a a single output file, provided the input files involved are already presorted, by using sort -m. With -u the file will be filtered, so that identical lines occur once only in the output.

The lines in the input files are seen by sort as a sequence of fields, separated by a separator. Usually, the separator is a blank character (space or tab) between a non-blank character and either the next non-blank character or another blank character. The separator character used by sort may be specified with -t x. Note that a hyphen can never be part of a field.

+pos1 –pos2
specifies which
key-fields are to be
used for the sort

With +pos1 [-pos2] or -k pos1[,pos2] sort is told to use only the data in fields from pos1 to pos2 for the comparison. The field descriptors pos1 and pos2 can have the form f.c, where f is the field number and c the position of the character from which the comparison is to begin. The first field has the position number 0.

Normally, sort sorts according to the lexicographical order of the underlying machine character set, that is it uses the octal value of each character in the line and sorts the lines in ascending order or, with the -r option, in descending order. When two lines have equivalent first fields, the following fields determine the order. Spaces and tabs at the beginning of a field are ignored by sort if the program is called with the -b option.

Limitations on the character set to be considered by sort for the comparison can be set with the options -d (only letters and numbers) and -i (only characters from the octal numbers 040 to 176). On the other hand, sort -f changes the small letters in a line into capitals before making the comparison, so that for example d and D can be regarded as equal.

sort -M
sorts months

An alternative sorting criterion is used by sort -M, which regards the first three letters of a line as months. Lines of a file are then sorted in the following order JAN < FEB <...< DEC. Invalid month data are put before JAN.

When called together with the option -n, the program sorts character strings at the beginning of the line according to their arithmetic value. Numeric character strings consist of preceding spaces, followed by a prefixed sign and any number of digits, optionally extended by a decimal point and further digits.

Examples

`sort /etc/passwd` displays the contents of the password file, sorted on user names,

`ls -l | sort -M +5` sorts the complete list of files located in the current working directory on month data (6th field).

The first field has number 0

6.8 Formatting Files

From time to time it is necessary to prepare or format files suitably before making the output. The aim of this section is to explain some further Unix commands that serve in the broadest sense for the formatting of files.

One of these commands is `pr`. It prepares text files for printer output. With `pr` one can process several files in parallel and set out the contents of each file side by side in columns.

pr creates text outputs in printable format

Further programs intended for dealing with columns are `expand` and `unexpand`. The sole tasks of these commands are, respectively, to replace tabs by a suitable number of blank characters and, conversely, to replace blank characters by tabs.

Text files with long lines often cause problems, as the output device is "too narrow" for the output of all characters on a line. This problem can be solved with the program `fold`, which breaks long lines at a given position.

fold breaks lines and paste puts lines together

The opposite program, `paste`, removes line-feeds and combines all lines in a file into just one line. Furthermore, `paste` can put together text lines with the same line number from several files to form a single text line. The result will be several lines showing the content of the combined files in columns.

As well as the `head` and `tail` commands, already mentioned, which extract certain lines or parts of a document, all Unix distributions also include the command `cut`, which limits the output to certain columns or fields.

The application area of **awk** is much greater, as aside from outputting field elements from a line, it provides its own programming language (**awk** is, so to say, a programmable filter).

There is also the command **tr**. The main task of **tr** is to transform certain or all characters of a file to an alternative character set. Possible uses of **tr** are to transform all the small letters into capitals, to replace all the numbers with blank characters, etc.

tr converts the character set

6.8.1 Preparing Printer Output: `pr`

The command

pr

```
pr [option]... [file]...
```

outputs text files in print format. If the argument **file** is missing, **pr** takes the information to be processed from the standard input. The **+page** option causes **pr** to generate the output from **page** onwards only.

pr divides the output into several pages and provides each page with a headline including the name and modification time of the text file as well as a sequential page number. The option **-t** suppresses the headline. Furthermore, **pr -h text** replaces the file name in the headline by the character string **text**.

When using the option **-num**, **pr** lays the text out in **num** columns. When in addition the **-a** option is given, **pr** orders each line side by side (otherwise one below the other). If the program has to process several files in parallel, the **-m** option results in the output of each file in its own column. In this case, it is not permitted to use **-num** and **-a** as well.

pr -m prints multiple files next to each other in columns

The width to be used for each column is calculated by **pr** as the page width divided by the number of columns. A page width differing from the default value of 72 can be set with **-w num**. If a line of text is longer than the column width, the line will be shortened, which means the text will be truncated suitably.

When a multiple column output is chosen pr "length" shortens text lines

A page is normally 66 lines long: **pr** is thus optimized for the 11 inch printer paper common in the USA. An alternative number of lines for each page can be set with the option **-lnum**, where **pr** does not output a headline when a number smaller than 11 has been chosen for **num**. For example, for the 297 mm (approx.

pr -l72 formats for an output on 12 inch printer paper

12 inch) printer paper common in Germany one should choose `num=72`.

Note that one must choose a number of printing lines smaller than the page length unless the option `-t` is used. `pr` uses five lines for the headline and creates the page-feed by using a further five blank lines. Additionally, with the `-f` option the user can force the addition of a form-feed character to the end of each page. In this operation mode, the printer ensures that the headline is always placed at the beginning of the page.

pr uses 5 lines for each headline and each page-feed

Further features of `pr` include adding a blank line after each text line (`-d` option) and numbering each text line (`-n`). By default, the line numbers have 5 digits. A number following directly after `-n` results in "broader" line numbers. `pr -n` adds three blank characters or a hyphen, whichever has been added as final parameter to the option `-n`, between the line number and the text line.

pr -n creates line numbers

Examples

`pr -n -172 pr.c | lpr` prepares the file `pr.c` for printing output page by page. Each line gets a sequential line number. The page length is 72 lines. The result is piped to the print command `lpr`.

`pr -m main.c main.c.org` prints the two files `main.c` and `main.c.org` page by page, and side by side.

pr truncates long lines

6.8.2 Tab Conversion: expand and unexpand

The command

`expand [option]... [file]...`

expand

replaces tab characters by a suitable number of blank spaces. Called without any options, `expand` replaces all the tab characters by the number of blank characters required to obtain a column width of 8 characters. Alternative tab positions are processed by `expand -tab` or `expand -t tab`. The value of `tab` is understood by the program as the width of all the columns in the document.

Backspace characters have the length -1 for expand

If the program is called up together with a list of the form `-tab1,tab2,...` separated by commas, `expand` sets the width

129

of the first column to **tab1** characters, the width of the second column to **tab2** characters, and so on. If an input line includes more tabs than stated in the option, then **expand** replaces the extra tabs by single blank characters.

When called with the option **-i**, **expand** replaces the leading tab characters only, that means it replaces them by blank characters only then when they are at the beginning of the line.

The command

unexpand

```
unexpand [option]... [file]...
```

replaces multiple blank characters in input lines by tabs. It is something like the opposite of **expand**. The algorithm examines successive blank characters to see if they extend up to a tab position and then replaces each of these sequences with a tab character.

By default, **unexpand** generates leading tabs only. The option **-a** instructs the program to examine all character strings that consist of at least two blank characters in a line of text. As with **expand**, the user can specify with **-tab1[,tab2[,...]]** in the command line the tab positions to be considered.

6.8.3 Breaking Text Lines: fold

When there are long lines in the given text files or in the lines of the standard input, the command

fold

```
fold [option]... [file]...
```

fold can prepare texts to be laid out in multiple columns by pr

inserts a line-feed so that the line does not exceed a certain length. Normally, the line has 80 characters (corresponding to the number of columns of a terminal). Alternative line lengths are created by **fold** when the **-num** option is used.

Normally, **fold** can break long lines in the middle of a word. The **-s** option is useful, as instead it places the line-feed in front of the word that extends beyond the allowed line length. Over-long lines that do not contain a blank character before the maximum allowed number of columns are broken in the middle of a word by **fold -s**.

fold -s breaks text lines at the end of the word

Example

`ps -wwwef | fold -s -60` outputs the result of the `ps` call in a line width of 60 characters.

6.8.4 Merging Text Files: `paste`

The command

`paste [option]... [file]...`

creates output lines by writing corresponding lines of input text files (or of the standard input) one after another. This means, it merges text files.

As separator between the elements of the files, `paste` uses the tab character by default. Alternatively, via `-d list` the user can give the program a list of separators, where `paste` places the first delimiter character between the line parts of the first and the second files, the second character between the line parts of the second and the third files, and so forth.

Files prepared with fold and connected with paste get a fixed column format when expand reworks the result

When called with the `-s` option, `paste` successively combines the lines of each file into just a single line. In this operation mode, `paste` first concatenates the lines of the first file, which means it replaces the line-feeds by delimiters. It then indicates the end of the file by a line-feed character. `paste` treats further files to be processed in the same way.

6.8.5 Cutting Columns: `cut`

The command

`cut option... [file]...`

copies parts of text lines of one or more files to the standard output. `cut` expects at least one of the three options `-b` (byte list), `-c` (character list), or `-f` (field list), followed by a range specification. The latter encodes column or field elements that `cut` is to take from the input file.

cut extracts letters or fields

131

Range specifications are either single fields defined by a number or groups of fields, which the user specifies as two field numbers connected with a minus sign. If either a start or an end value or both are not given, cut determines the first element of a line as the start value and the end of the line as the end value. cut extracts several areas if they have been stated as a list separated by commas on the command line.

cut identifies field elements by the separators in the file. As field delimiter, cut uses the tab character (default setting) or a separator given in the command line with -d separator. Wildcards and in particular regular expressions are not allowed to function as field delimiters. When the -s option is given in addition, lines not containing of the field delimiter are left out.

*cut -d " "
processes
words*

The method of operation of cut -b and cut -c is identical at this time. The option -c has been integrated in readiness for the handling of multibyte characters. The option -n is also intended for this purpose, but has no function until the relevant character sets become available.

Examples

*cut -f does not work
here*

ls -l | cut -b -10,29-41,55- creates a part of the result of ls -l in such a way that only the access permission, the file size, and the file name appears in the output.

cut -f 1,3-4 -d ":" /etc/passwd limits the output of the content of the file /etc/passwd to the user name and the respective user and group identifications.

6.8.6   List Processing: awk

The command

awk

awk [option]... file...

mainly searches and replaces text patterns in files, but also makes it possible to use the awk programming language and is thus a multi-purpose tool for processing lists. The name awk comes from the initials of its authors Alfred V. Aho, Peter J. Weinberger, and Brian W. Kernighan; and it represents both a program and a programming language, as described in the document *POSIX 1002.3 Command Language And Utilities Standard*.

In a broader sense, **awk** is mainly used for filtering text files, e.g., formatting the output of other Unix programs or handling small databases. In many cases **awk** is used as a tool for basic system administration tasks.

awk is often used for processing the outputs of other Unix commands

For a comprehensive description of how to use of **awk** see the handbook *AWK Language Programming*, which was written by Arnold D. Robinson and has more than 300 pages. It especially considers GNU **awk**, which was developed by the Free Software Foundation and is included in every Linux distribution. In this book, we only point out a few features of **awk** in order to give a general understanding of its features.

The program awk processes text files line by line and divides the lines themselves into single fields. Fields are separated by spaces or by a separator, which can be given to the program in the command line using the option **-F s**. A certain field element can be accessed by stating the field number with a preceding dollar sign. Internally, **awk** administrates the field elements of the line that is currently being processed in the variables **$1 ... $n** (**n** is the number of fields), and the whole line can be addressed with **$0**. Additionally, **awk** stores the number of fields of a line in the internal variable **NF**.

Field separators are not a part of a field

In the simplest case, the treatment of each field element is controlled by commands put directly in the command line as options. By contrast, complex commands or **awk** programs are combined in files, and **awk** is told with **-f file** to use the content of **file** as an **awk** program.

awk commands consist of a pattern and an action to be executed when the current input line matches the pattern. The result of the action is piped to the standard output. For example, the call

awk commands consist of the components "pattern" and "action"

```
ps -ax | awk '$1 < 100 { print $1 " " $5 }'
```

checks each file in the output of **ps -ax** as to whether or not the process ID (**$1**) is smaller than 100. If this is the case, **awk** prints out the process ID together with the command name (**$5**). **awk** inserts a space between the two output fields.

In this **awk** program, the expression **$1 < 100** is the pattern and the action is the content between the pair of braces. The command itself is put into single inverted commas ´ to prevent an interpretation by the shell.

In the example given, the pattern is a relational expression. Other permissible forms of **awk** patterns are regular expressions, logically connected patterns, and ranges. For example, the call

```
ps -ax | awk ´$1 > 50 && $1 < 60 {print $1 " " $5}
```

limits the output to processes with process IDs between 50 and 60.

A special role is played by the patterns **BEGIN** and **END**, which indicate actions to be executed before or after the output is processed. The empty pattern is special, too, as it matches every input line. The meaning and usage of these patterns is shown in the example on the facing page.

The syntax of the awk commands is similar to that of the shell programming languages

Action components of an **awk** command must be put in braces, and constructs within braces must be formulated in the syntax of the **awk** programming language. Their syntax is similar to the syntax of the shell programming languages. The number of language features, however, suffices to achieve the expressiveness of traditional high-level languages.

Application-defined variables can take character strings or floating point numbers

On the one hand, **awk** offers a number of internal variables that reflect the current **awk** status, among other things. Furthermore, from the application side it is also possible to use non-internal variables. In contrast to most other programming languages, it is not necessary to give a definition of variables to be used; **awk** initializes them when they are first assigned a value. Afterwards **awk** can use their values for comparisons or change them. Variables are available as simple variables for character strings or floating point numbers, or as one-dimensional arrays whose elements can be addressed by indices, as in the C programming language.

awk programs structure branches, loops, and internal and recursive functions

On the other hand, the **awk** programming language provides control commands that, as in traditional programming languages, influence the process of the action part. For example, these include branches (**if-else** statements) and loops (**while, do while, for**). A variety of numeric character string functions and input/output oriented functions complete the range of features.

134

Users can also define their own functions by means of the standard components of the language.

Nevertheless, there are limits on the utility of **awk**, resulting mainly from the fact that all the commands formulated from the user's side are analyzed by an internal interpreter. Therefore, the processing speed is not exactly optimal; furthermore, the size of the **awk** script to be processed has a direct influence on the speed.

A final example of an **awk** script analyzes the result of the call **ps -aux** and thereby determines the current CPU and memory load as well as the number of processes run by the system:

```
BEGIN {
  print "System status:"
}
{
  if ($1 != "USER")
  {
    cpu += $3
    mem += $4
    procs++
  }
}
END {
  print cpu " %CPU " mem " %MEM " procs " PROCS"
}
```

The BEGIN part is executed before the data is processed, the END part is executed afterwards

First, each input line is examined to find out whether or not it is the headline (**$1 != "USER"**). If not, then the value of the respective field elements (**$3, $4**) will be added to the variables **cpu** and **mem** and the number of lines processed will be incremented. After processing the complete list, the script provides a result of the form

awk initializes application-defined variables with 0

```
System status:
34.1 %CPU 71.6 %MEM 52 PROCS
```

If the **awk** script is in the file **pstat.awk** (in the current working directory,) it can be used as follows:

```
ps -aux | awk -f pstat.awk
```

135

tr

6.8.7 Character Translation: tr

The command

```
tr [option]... string1 [string2]
```

copies data from the standard input to the standard output and while doing so removes certain characters or replaces them with others. Additionally, tr can reduce a block of repeated characters to a single character.

When called without any options, tr transforms letters from string1 into letters from string2. This means it expects two character strings as ordered lists of letters that combine to form a set.

If tr is to exchange the minus sign, then this must be placed at the end of the first list

The formats allowed for defining these lists of letters are single letters written directly one after another, ranges (two letters connected by a hyphen), and repeated characters, indicated by [c*n] (c repeated n times). The order of the letters in string1 determines the order tr applies when exchanging letters: the program replaces letters from string1 with those in the same position in string2.

Lists of letters can include the special characters bell, backspace, line-feed, form-feed, and return

The list of letters cannot contain any octally encoded characters. The only control characters accepted by tr are \a (C-g, bell), \b (C-h, backspace), \f (C-l, form-feed), \n (C-j, line-feed) and \r (C-m, return). To prevent the shell from misinterpreting string1 or string2, the strings should be placed in inverted commas. If fewer characters are in string2 than in string1, tr adds the last character in string2 the required number of times.

tr -d list removes all the letters included in list

The following options make alternative or additional operation modes possible: -c tells tr to use the set of characters complementary to string1 (with respect to the extended ASCII character set \000-\377), -s reduces successive repeating letters to a single one, and -d deletes all stated letters during the translation.

Examples

tr a-z A-Z < /etc/passwd copies the contents of the file /etc/passwd to the standard output and changes all the small letters into capitals.

`tr a-z b-za < ~/.bashrc` cycles all the lowercase letters located in `~/.bashrc`. The result is copied to the standard output. `ls` is changed to `mt`, `bc` to `cd`, and so on.

`ls -l | tr -s " " | cut -f 1,5,9 -d " "` limits the output of `ls -l` to access permission, file size, and file name. The `cut` command can process the input data field by field, as `tr` has replaced multiple space characters by single spaces.

6.9 Data Compression

Linux distributions include tools for compressing data with either no or little loss. The latter are used for reducing the amount of data in static and animated image information in cases where the loss of information is limited to details that are largely imperceptible.

For reducing storage space occupied by programs, text files, and data files, methods that work with no loss are required. Programs that serve this purpose work by eliminating the redundancy in the data by encoding sequences of letters that occur repeatedly. When unpacking, they replace the encoded information with the original data by applying the appropriate coding key.

For compressing data and program files, lossless methods are used

We have to differentiate between two methods, both of which are based on the Lempel–Ziv algorithms. One of these is realized by the program **compress** included in each Unix version sold today. Files compressed with it can easily be transferred from one Unix derivative to another. Text files are reduced by 50–60 percent on average. For binary files the reduction ratio is normally less.

Linux distributions additionally include the program **gzip** developed by the Free Software Foundation. The method realized in **gzip** carries out a much better data reduction than that of **compress** (60–70 percent for text files). Only a few other Unix versions include **gzip**. Therefore, the exchange of files compressed using **gzip** with other (Unix) systems is not always possible.

Files compressed with compress are portable in the Unix world

Under Linux, however, `gzip` is in practice the standard compressor. Some Linux distributions consist of a variety of `gzip` compressed `tar` files which bundle individual system and application components into groups. Program packages located on archive servers also tend to be provided in this format in order to allow the quickest possible transfer rate for the downloading process.

the data
compression
reduces the time
needed for copying
processes

Data compression certainly offers the advantage of reducing the space required for archiving data and the time for copying processes of all kinds. However, data compression comes with the risk that one may lose more data when an archive medium is faulty than would occur when files are recorded unencoded. This is because recovering the original data with the available commands **uncompress** and **gunzip** is only possible up to the point where the first mistake occurs.

6.9.1 LZC Compression: compress and uncompress

The command

compress

```
compress [option]... [file]...
```

reduces the space needed by files by compressing data on the basis of a slightly modified version of the Lempel–Ziv–Welch algorithm LZW, often referred to as the LZC method. For the main part, LZC encodes sequential character strings (patterns) as special characters consisting of nine or more bits. A character string so encoded has a maximum bit length of 16 by default. With the **-b bits** option the user can choose a smaller value ($9 \leq$ **bits** ≤ 16), which the program uses, so to speak, as a compression parameter.

compress encodes
character strings
in bit fields

If **compress** has been called up without stating any file name, it takes the information to be compressed from the standard input and copies the result to the standard output. **compress** converts files into a file of the same name and adds the suffix **.z** to the name. Afterwards the original file will be removed from the directory tree. Finally, **compress** checks the compression ratio achieved and replaces the original file by the compressed version

Files compressed
with compress have
the suffix .Z

only when it occupies less space than the original file. The program gives information on the extent of the data reduction when the option −v is given.

If the original file is to be retained, then compress has to be told with the option −c to copy the result to the standard output, and which then needs to be redirected to a file. Note that this method is only successful when compress processes just one file on the time.

compress compresses only normal files that do not yet have the ending .z. When applied to soft links, the program creates a compressed version of the file referred to by the link and stores it by using the name of the soft link together with the usual suffix. The soft link is removed afterwards. Hard links or files whose inode is referred several times in the file system are only compressed by compress when the −c option is used. Files located in subdirectories are considered by compress when it is called up together with the −r (recursive) option.

compress can process normal files and soft links

Example

compress −c file > file.Z creates a compressed version of file; the original file is maintained.

The command

uncompress [option]... [file]...

uncompress

unpacks files that have been compressed with compress. uncompress processes the same options as compress, with the exception of −b. Actually, the latter is not necessary, as files created with compress include the parameter used for the maximum word length. uncompress is entered in the Linux directory tree as a soft link to compress. The command derives its operation mode from the command name used.

When called without a file name, uncompress takes the data to be processed from the standard input and copies the result to the standard output. The action is executed only when the incoming data stream is compressed (indicated by a magic number).

uncompress recognizes compressed files from their magic number

139

uncompress unpacks files only then they have the ending
.z. If a file name given in the command line does not have this
ending, it is completed by uncompress. Restored files are given
their original names and the compressed versions are removed afterwards. When uncompress is called with the -c option, the
result is copied to the standard output, analogously to compress.
In this case the compressed file is maintained.

6.9.2 LZ77 Compression: gzip and gunzip

The command

gzip

gzip [option]... [file]...

gzip replaces
"patterns" by
an index

compresses files by using an LZ77 based method. In this process
a "window" is moved over the input data and patterns that have
already been "seen" in this window are sought. LZ77 replaces the
pattern by an index and the length of the pattern in the window.

Files compressed
with gzip have the
suffix .gz

When called without a file name, gzip expects to get the
information to be compressed from the standard input and then
copies the result to the standard output. Otherwise, gzip converts
the original file to a file of the same name with the suffix .gz. The
original file will then be removed from the directory tree. Alternatively, gzip -c copies the compressed version of one or more
files to the standard output. Hard or soft links are not compressed
by gzip.

If gzip is to create the result file with an ending other than
.gz, it must be called with the -S suf option. Linux users are
recommend to start the character string suf with a dot.

gziped files include
name and time-
stamp of the
original file

Files compressed with gzip usually contain the name of the
original file as well as the relevant time stamps in their data.
Firstly, this prevents a loss of data on file systems that only allow "short" file names, and secondly, it ensures that the original
file is restored to its original state upon unpacking. If gzip is
called with the -n option, these data will not be contained in the
compressed version.

Furthermore, gzip -r also considers files located in subdirectories, and the option -v leads to output of the compression ratio

achieved for each file processed. When called up with -l, gzip also displays the name and size of the original file as well as the size of the compressed version.

With -num the user can control the processing speed and thereby implicitly the compression ratio. The value 1 leads to a high processing speed and little compression, num=9 results in slow compression with maximal data reduction. The default value is num=6.

gzip -9 produces the best data reduction possible

Finally, it is worth noting that gzip can also check the integrity of compressed files (option -t). If gzip finds the environment variable GZIP in its process context, then the program takes its default operation mode from the option stated there. Additional options stated in the command line can override this default setting.

The command

```
gunzip [option]... [file]...
```

gunzip

is the counterpart to gzip and is equivalent to gzip -d regarding its mode of operation. The program unpacks compressed files created with gzip or compress. gunzip recognizes the compression method used by the magic number located at the beginning of the file. It is interesting to note that the operation mode of gunzip -c is identical to the operation of the Unix command zcat. Both gunzip and zcat are soft links to gzip. Like compress, gzip derives its operation mode from the command name used.

gunzip unpacks compress as well as gzip compressed files

gunzip expects to get the data to be processed either from the standard input or from files the user has stated in the command line. The file suffix need not be stated; gunzip adds the endings .z, -z, .Z, -Z, .gz, and -gz to the "patterns" stated and searches for corresponding files. Furthermore, gunzip interprets the identifications .tgz and .taz as compressed tar files, as these suffixes are understood by the program as short forms for .tar.gz and .tar.Z. Files with such suffixes are unpacked by gunzip into files with the ending .tar.

Files with the ending .taz or .tgz are unpacked by gunzip into files with the ending .tar

6.10 Regular Expressions

Regular expression; are complex search patterns

Some basic Unix commands, e.g., `awk`, `cpio`, `diff`, `grep`, and `more`, accept wildcards that offer much more freedom than the common wildcards understood by the shell. In order to distinguish between such constructs and common wildcards, one speaks of regular expressions.

6.10.1 Basic Regular Expressions

*()[]{}$`\ are special characters

Basic regular expressions are constructs describing a single character. The letters of the alphabet, the digits, and most of the special characters refer to themselves. The dot, asterisk, round brackets, square brackets, braces, dollar, caret (ˆ), and backslash are reserved characters (meta characters). If a meta character is to refer to itself then it must be preceded by a backslash.

The dot indicates any character at all

The dot is the wildcard of regular expressions. It indicates any character at all, excluding the line-feed.

If a character string including a space character is sought, the **expression** has to be placed in single (´) or double inverted commas (") to prevent the shell interpreting the space characters. This is also the case if **expression** includes brackets or the backslash \.

6.10.2 Range Information

[A-Z] describes the set of all capitals

Characters put in square brackets (range information) are wildcards that correspond to certain characters. If the first character after the opening square bracket is the caret, the wildcard can take any value not included in the range stated.

*Right: [[ˆ-],
wrong: [ˆ-[]*

Range information consists of either a list of single characters or ranges of characters defined by two characters connected with a hyphen, or both. If a range of letters is to contain the right square bracket, this character must be be set as first element of the list. The caret character must not be put in first place if it explicitly has to be an element of the list, whereas the hyphen or minus sign must be stated as last element if it is not already included in a range of characters.

Most of the Linux tools that process regular expressions use the following range indicators for frequently used range information:

Indicator	Characters included
[:alnum:]	numbers and letters ([0-9A-Za-z])
[:alpha:]	letters ([A-Za-z])
[:cntrl:]	control characters
[:digit]	numbers ([0-9])
[:graph:]	readable characters ([!-~])
[:lower:]	small letters ([a-z])
[:print:]	printable characters ([-~])
[:punct:]	complement of [:alnum:] ([^0-9A-Za-z])
[:space:]	space and tab characters
[:upper:]	capitals ([A-Z]
[:xdigit:]	hexadecimal numbers ([0-9A-Fa-f])

For example, if a wildcard has to stand for any number at all in a regular expression, the range information goes as follows: [[:digit:]]. Instead of [[:alnum:]], the second form \w will be understood as well. Furthermore, \W indicates the range [^[:alnum:]].

Range indicators need to be put in double brackets

6.10.3 Word and Line Limits

Outside a pair of square brackets, the caret character ˆ indicates the beginning of a line, and the dollar sign $ indicates the end of a line. For example, if the user wants to seek all the lines having the character string text at the beginning of the line, the character string ˆtext should be given as **expression**. Similarly, text$ searches for all the lines that end with text.

ˆText\> describes a word located at the beginning of the line "text"

To identify whole words instead of just character strings, the beginning and end of the word have to be marked with \< or \>. For example, the expression ´\<one\>´ searches for one but does not recognize none, oneself, or onerous.

6.10.4 Repetitions

The masked question mark \? has the effect that a preceding character or pattern may occur just once or not at all. For example, with ´\<c\?onc\?e\?\>´ the words on, one, con, cone, and once can all be found. If a preceding character may occur once or more, the masked plus sign \+ should be used.

The asterisk * is used when a character or pattern is allowed to either occur several times or not at all. For example, the regular expression ´\<[Cc][[:alpha:]]*e\>´ for example, matches all the words beginning with a small or a capital c and ending with a small e (change, complete, Claude, etc.).

A minimum and/or maximum number of repeated characters or patterns can be determined as follows:

\{n\}	exactly n times,
\{n,\}	at least n times,
\{,m\}	at most m times,
\{n,m\}	at least n, at most m times.

Character strings in parentheses form a group. Repetition commands \?, \+, and * following immediately afterwards affect the whole character string. For example, (ab)\+ describes the character strings ab, abab, ababab, and so on.

6.10.5 Chaining Regular Expressions

By writing basic regular expressions and range information as well as multipliers one after the other, chained regular expressions are created. For example, ´\<F[A-Za-z]\{3\}\>´ matches all words consisting of exactly four letters and beginning with F.

If a regular expression matches several alternatives, individual "branches" have to be stated and separated by a masked pipe sign \|. A regular expression matching all LATEX commands \begin and \end might go as follows: ´\\begin\|\\end´.

Editors

Editors are without doubt a vital part of every operating system as they help the user to create and modify files. When changing to another operating system, the user is often confronted with an unfamiliar editor which provides features different from those of products already known.

An editor is a standard application for every operating system

To compound matters almost every editor uses its own command set, which means the method of operation is not uniform and one's existing skills are almost worthless. If an operating system includes several editors, the user also has to decide whether he or she wants to learn to using one or more of them.

Features and operation methods are product specific

Editors included in Linux distributions belong to one of three classes:

ed and **ex** are line editors. **ed** was the first standard Unix editor. **ex** is an extended and in parts more powerful version of **ed**. The line editors **ed** and **ex** copy the content of a file into the main memory and, upon commands from the user, carry out changes on a line by line basis. The original file is not overwritten immediately, but rather only when a write command has been given.

Line editors do not immediately display modifications to the text

ed and **ex** include a comprehensive stock of commands. They offer functions for complex operations like searching and replacing, copying, deleting, and moving blocks of text. On the other, hand using these programs is complicated in partieular by the lack of automatic feedback on the effects of each command.

ed and ex have functions for searching and replacing, and for operations within marked areas

sed, the stream editor, uses rules given either on the command line or in a file as a **sed** script to processes a text file. The result is then copied to the standard output. `sed` does not allow a text file to be processed interactively, that is, does not communicate with the user. Nevertheless, in comparison with all other Unix editors, `sed` does offer some advantages: `sed` can process files of any size at all, and functions as a filter by reading data to be processed from the standard input and copying the modified version to the standard output. `sed` is often used when identical modifications need to be made to a large number of files.

The stream editor sed does not work interactively

`vi`, `elvis`, `vim`, `joe` and `emacs` are all screen editors. They can show a part of the file over the whole screen, allow the user to position the cursor within the documents interactively, and reflect any modifications made immediately. Their operation is based on the division of the user dialog into one or more operation modes: "insert mode" provides basic input and delete operations, "command mode" provides access to higher-level word processing functions. Like `ed` and `ex`, they modify a copy of the document located in the main memory; again, the document file is modified only when a write command is given.

Screen editors interact with the user in different operation modes

Today the line editors `ed` and `ex` are only used, if at all, for processing very small files. Nevertheless, there are still some reasons for using these editors. Since they limit their dialog with the user to the bare essentials, they provide satisfactory response times on terminals connected to the computer via slow communication routings.

Line editors are now seldom used

The stream editor `sed`, however, has been an official part of Unix since AT&T Version 7 and has become well established as an indispensable development tool in the course of time. Many application packages subject to the GNU Public License and others commonly declared as public domain (PD) and available in source code form require `sed` in order to build their operational programs.

Many PD products use sed

Among all the Linux screen editors, the standard Unix editor `vi` has a special meaning. Unjustly, it is most unpopular and has even been called the greatest Unix mistake. Nevertheless, anybody who wants to cope fairly well with the demands of the Unix world should at least master the basic **vi** commands, as this editor is sure to be part of every Unix distribution.

elvis is an imitation of **vi**, developed by Steve Kirkendall in the USA. **vim**, mainly programmed by Bram Moolenaar from the Netherlands, is an extended **vi** variant, so to say, the Linux **vi**; in the Linux directory tree **vi** is usually a soft link to **vim**.

The Linux vi is usually a soft link to vim

joe, by Joseph H. Allen, USA, emulates various editors which have become popular outside the Unix world. Depending on the call conventions, it behaves either like WordStar from Micro-Pro, like the Borland Turbo editor, or like GNU Emacs.

joe emulates WordStar and Borland's Turbo editor

GNU Emacs has been developed since 1985 by Richard Stallman, the founder of the Free Software Foundation. Although it is not an official part of Unix, it could establish itself as the preferred tool, especially within developers circles.

Software developers prefer emacs

Some Linux distributions include all Unix editors mentioned, while other do without the line editor **ed**. Every Linux distribution normally includes **sed**, **vi**, and the GNU Emacs. Linux beginners who are accustomed to WordStar or the Turbo editor may choose **joe** as their preferred editor.

The aim of this chapter is to explain the scope of features and operation of the stream editor **sed** and the screen editors **vi** and **emacs**. Explanations of **vi** and **emacs** do not deal with all command sequences, just those frequently used.

For a complete description of all the features of **vi**, see the document **reference.doc** located in **/usr/doc/vim***. A user guide for **emacs** can be found in the directory **/usr/info**, distributed over 26 files with more than 27 000 lines of text in total. Let it also be said that various handbooks in T_EX format, such as the GNU Emacs Manual with about 500 pages, have been added to the GNU Emacs program sources.

Emacs documentation is also available in HTML format

7.1 The Stream Editor **sed**

The stream editor **sed** does not work interactively, which means it does not communicate with the user. Either it takes files to be processed from the standard input or it takes those specified in the command line. **sed** always writes the result to the standard output and creates files only when a redirection operator is used.

sed passes the results of its work to the standard output

147

Commands to be executed by sed are read either from the command line or from a command file. The normal call syntax is

```
sed [option]... command [file]...
```

or

```
sed [option]... [-e command]... \
    [-f command-file] [file]...
```

In the first case, sed carries out the operation command on one or more files. The second case allows several sed commands to be given, where each is preceded with the -e option. Alternatively or additionally, the stream editor takes the operations to be executed from the command-file.

sed editing commands operate on a pattern space

The input files are processed by sed line by line. In the first step, sed copies one or more lines of text to an internal "pattern space". Next, it applies the editing commands, supplied either in the command line or from a sed command file, to the data stored in the pattern space. After the operations have been carried out, the result is piped line by line to the standard output.

Generally, a sed command consists of an optional address, a command name, and possibly command arguments, according to the format

3,4d or s/[.,:]/!/

```
[address [,address]] command [argument]
```

sed command sequences given in the command line should be put in single quotation marks to prevent the shell interpreting any special characters they may include.

7.1.1 sed Addresses

Address patterns determine the range for the sed commands

By specifying address ranges, the user can instruct sed to apply the commands only to particular parts of the files. If there are no address patterns at the beginning of a sed command, the program considers all lines in the files. If only one address is specified, sed interprets the value stated as both the start and end address. This means it carries out the desired operation for one line of the document only.

If the address range includes two values and the end address occurs in the file before the start address, then **sed** only considers the line of the file specified by the start address. By adding an exclamation mark **!**, the user can instruct **sed** not to apply the operation to the address range stated.

Addresses are either line numbers or context addresses formed as regular expressions. An exception to this rule is the dollar sign, which indicates the last line of an input file.

Two address formats: line numbers and context addresses

Context addresses need delimiters, which are placed before and after a regular expression. In general, a context address has the format

    \?expression?

/expression/ is also allowed

beginning with the escape character \ and followed by a delimiter. The delimiter can be any character at all, provided it is not part of the regular expression. The end of the regular expression is signalled by the second occurrence of the delimiter.

If the delimiter has to be part of the regular expression, it must be preceded by an escape character. For example, **sed** is told by the context addresses

    \TPA\THT,\T\TERMT

\?\<text\$? and /\<text\$/ describe the word text located at the end of the line

to execute the desired operation beginning at the line containing the character string **PATH**. The line including the character string **TERM** is the end of the address range.

7.1.2 sed Commands

The **sed** commands consist of a single letter representing the function to be executed. The function operates on the pattern space, that is, either on one or more input lines or on a portion thereof. For example, the call

    sed ´2,3d´ test.txt

removes the second and third lines of the file **test.txt**, and

```
sed ´s/[a-z]/./g´ test.txt
```

replaces all small letters by a single dot. Capital letters A–E are converted into lowercase letters with the call

```
sed ´y/ABCDE/abcde/´ test.txt
```

The hold pattern space is a temporary storage

To support complex operations, sed internally administers a "hold pattern space" that can store parts of the input file for later use. Input and output functions, command groups, and minimal flow control complete the range of sed features.

The following list states each sed command and explains how it works. The preceding numbers in parentheses indicate the maximum number of address specifiers accepted.

Line Commands

*Line-feed characters within text need to be masked with *

(1) a\\
text...

adds one or more lines to the end of either the line stated or each input line. An escape and a line-feed character must follow directly after the command a. The following arguments *text* can then extend over several lines.

(2) c\\
text...

replaces one or more lines by the argument *text*.

(2) d

removes one or more lines. E.g., the call

```
sed ´11,$d´ test.txt
```

suppresses the output from the 11th line onwards. The result is equivalent to that from the call head test.txt.

(1) i\\
text...

adds *text* to the beginning of the input line stated.

(2) n

copies the content of the pattern space to the standard output and replaces the pattern space by the next line.

The meaning of the command n is illustrated by an example. The following sed script outputs two successive lines of a file and then adds a line containing five hyphens:

```
    n
    a\
    -----
```

*Without address
indicators the
whole file will be
treated the same
way*

Replacing Character Strings

(2) `s/RegExp/String/[Flags]`

replaces the regular expression **RegExp** with the character string **String**. Both components are separated with a slash. The optional argument **Flags** determines how the **s** command works:

*If the option Flags
is missing, sed only
replaces the first
character string of
the pattern space
that matches the
RegExp*

g (global) replaces every recognized regular expression by **string**. Without the switch **g**, only the first element in the pattern space matching **RegExp** will be replaced.

n exchanges the **n**th character string in the pattern space matching **RegExp**.

p prints out the pattern space if an exchange has been carried out.

w file copies the pattern space to a file if the contents of the pattern space have been modified.

The character string **String** will not be interpreted as a pattern, so special characters according to regular expression syntax are not expanded. Nevertheless, the **&** character has a special meaning: **sed** replaces **&** with the character string that matches the pattern.

s/[A-Z]/&*/g
writes a star before
and after each
capital letter*

(2) `y/string1/string2/`

replaces all characters from **string1** with the corresponding character from **string2**. Both character strings must contain the same number of characters.

Input and Output

(2) **p**   displays the addressed range of text on the standard output.

r and w have to be followed by a space character

(2) **w file**
   writes the given address range to a file.

(1) **r file**
   adds the contents of a file at the given address.

Pattern Space

(2) **N**   adds further lines of the input file to the contents of the pattern space.

If the pattern space contains only one line, D behaves in the same way as d and P behaves in the same way as p

(2) **D**   removes the first line from the pattern space. If the pattern space is then empty, **sed** loads the next line from the input file.

(2) **P**   copies the contents of the first line of the pattern space to the standard output.

Hold Pattern Space

(2) **h**   copies the contents of the pattern space to the hold pattern space. Any existing contents of the hold pattern space will be overwritten.

1h
1s/.//*
1x
G
s/\n//

(2) **H**   adds the data from the pattern space to the contents of the hold pattern space.

(2) **g**   is the reverse function of **h**. The pattern space receives the contents of the hold pattern space.

adds the first word of the first line to the end of each line

(2) **G**   is the reverse function of **H**. The contents of the hold pattern space are added to the end of the pattern space.

(2) **x**   exchanges the contents of the pattern space and the hold pattern space.

(2) `!`   is executed by the given command only for the lines
that are not located in the address range stated.

(2) `{...}`

groups commands into a command sequence. Data   *sequences are*
located in the pattern space are modified according   *allowed to contain*
to the given commands before the result is displayed.   *sequences*
Each command must appear on a line of its own.

(0) `: mark`

sets a mark within a command sequence. Marks are
character strings consisting of 8 or fewer characters.

(0) `b mark`

branches to the given mark, then **sed** carries out the
commands in the command sequence.

(0) `t mark`

branches to the given mark only when the pattern space
has been modified.

Miscellaneous

(1) `=`   writes the current line number to the standard output.   *The line number*
                                                                        is followed by
(1) `q`   writes the contents of the pattern space to the standard   *a line-feed*
output and finishes processing.

7.2   The Screen Editor `vi`

Early Unix systems consisted of a central processing unit and
a number of ASCII terminals. The manufacturers' own interests   *Each type of*
dictated that each terminal used its own command set for standard   *terminal uses its*
actions like positioning the cursor and inserting or overwriting   *own command set*
characters. Therefore, while developing screen editors for Unix,
developers had to bear in mind the need to of support a wide range
of terminals with different characteristics.

The problem was solved with the introduction of a "terminal capabilities database". BSD Unix stores descriptions of a few hundred terminal types in the plain text file `/etc/termcap` and there links terminal functions to machine specific control sequences.

/etc/termcap links
functions to control
sequences

System V's terminfo mechanism, on the other hand, encodes the terminal features in a binary format. Each type of terminal is described in a file in `/usr/lib/terminfo/?/*`. The program `infocmp` transforms the description data into plain text in either termcap or terminfo format. `tic` converts the terminfo source code into binary, and `captoinfo` translates termcap files into equivalent terminfo source code.

The editor `vi` deduces the type of the terminal to be served from the environment variable `TERM` and, based on that, loads an entry from `/etc/termcap` describing the features and abilities of the terminal. This information is vital for operating all Unix screen editors. If the screen display or the translation of the keys are incorrect, it is often due to a wrong value for the environment variable `TERM`.

7.2.1   Starting and Quitting `vi`

The usual call syntax of the `vi` is

```
vi [option]... [file]...
```

Frequently used command line options work as follows:

`+[num]` places the cursor either at the beginning of the line `num` or at the beginning of the last line if no value for `num` is given.

`+/string` puts the cursor to the beginning of the first line of the document containing the character string `string`.

`-b` sets some options that make it possible to process binary files.

`-o[num]` divides the screen into `num` windows. If there is no `num` argument, `vi` opens a window for each file given.

-s script loads the file **script**. Character sequences in the script are interpreted and executed by **vi** as keyboard commands.

-t tag searches through a tag file **tags** for the entry **tag**, loads the file stated, and carries out an operation if also stated. **ctags** creates the tag files.

ctags creates tag files in vi format

-v opens a document in the view mode. The user can see the file but cannot alter it.

Figure 7.1 shows as an example the screen structure of **vi** when it has been started up with **vi -o ~/.bashrc ~/.bash_profile**. In the upper section, **vi** shows a part of the first file and a status line forming the boundary. The lower section shows a part of the second file. When called without the **-o** option, **vi** only shows the file stated first, using the whole screen, and does not display a status line.

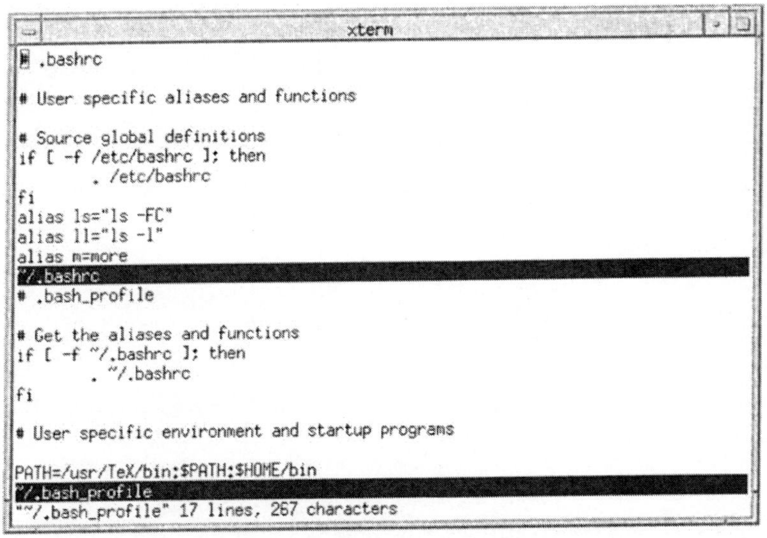

Fig. 7.1
The screen editor vi

The program can be terminated by entering **ZZ** to save and quit. The command sequences **:x**, **:q** close **vi** after saving the text and **:q!** closes **vi** without saving the text. The commands are completed with the return key.

The **:q** command will only close **vi** if either the file has not been modified or the user has already saved any changes with **:w**.

In the multi-window mode :qall! RETURN closes vi without saving

If c-z is entered, the program will be suspended. Typing **fg** will cause the process to continue again.

7.2.2 **vi** Operation Modes

How the input made at the keyboard is interpreted depends on which mode **vi** is in at the time. **vi** distinguishes between

command mode,
input or replace mode, and
ex mode.

Directly after **vi** starts, it will be in command mode. In this mode it expects one-letter commands which move the cursor within the document, search for character strings, delete, replace or copy text lines, or switch **vi** to another operation mode.

The text input is
carried out in the
input or replace-
ment mode
Text is normally input in the input or replace modes. In these modes **vi** adds each character to the document or overwrites already existing characters directly. Pressing the escape key switches **vi** back to the command mode.

ex commands
process command
parameters
The third operation mode is **ex**. In this mode, the cursor is located in the status line just after a colon, which is the **ex** prompt, and **vi** waits for one-line, **ex**-like commands to be given. The **ex** mode offers some higher-level commands that accept additional parameters.

7.2.3 Input and Replacement Modes

vi will change to the input or replace modes upon pressing the following keys:

i	inserting in front of the cursor,
I	inserting at the beginning of the line,
a	inserting behind the cursor,
A	inserting at the end of the line,
o	inserting after the current line,
O	inserting before the current line,
r	overwriting a single character,
R	overwriting text,

The escape key
ends the input or
replace mode

| c | deleting to the end of the line, then inserting, |
| s | deleting a line, then inserting. |

The r command replaces just one character and switches vi to the input or replace modes. In all other cases, it is necessary to press the escape key to switch back to the command mode.

If the user presses one of the keys u or U. While vi is in command mode, vi re-establishes the state of the text before the last change. u undoes the last change, U restores the current line.

U and u re-establish the state before the last change

In the input or replace modes, the cursor can only be moved with the arrow keys, character by character or line by line. In the command mode, the cursor will "jump" conveniently within the document.

7.2.4 Moving the Cursor

In the command mode the user can move the cursor by screen units (characters, lines, and pages), by objects (words, sentences, paragraphs, sections), or by searching for text patterns:

Cursor movements are based on screen units (character, line, page), objects (word, sentence, paragraph, section), or text patterns

character by character

→, l, BLANK
one character to the right,

←, h, DEL
one character to the left.

word by word

w	to the right to the next special character or to the beginning of the next word,
W	to the right to the beginning of the next word,
e	to the right to the next special character or word end,
E	to the right to the next word end,
b	to the left to the preceding special character or beginning of a word,
B	to the left to the beginning of the word.

157

line by line

↓, j	down one line,
↑, k	up one line,
^	to the first visible character of the line,
+	down one line to the first visible character,
−	up one line to the first visible character,
$	to the end of the line,
0	to the beginning of the line,
C-y	scrolls the screen down one line,
C-e	scrolls the screen up one line,
G	to the end of the document,
nG	to the nth line.

BLANK and TAB are invisible characters

page by page

H	to the beginning of the screen,
M	to the middle of the screen,
L	to the end of screen,
C-d	down half a page,
C-u	up half a page,
C-f	down one page,
C-b	up one page.

When entering C-d or C-u the cursor will stay in the same screen line

by object

)	next sentence,
(	preceding sentence,
}	next paragraph,
{	preceding paragraph,
[[	next section,
]]	preceding section.

/**pattern** forward to the next **pattern**,

?**pattern** backward to the preceding **pattern**,   *patterns are*

n   carries out the last context search again, going   *regular expressions*
           forward,

N   carries out the last context search again, in the
           reverse direction.

With the exceptions **0**, **M**, and **^**, **vi** executes the commands for moving the cursor multiple times if the user enters a number before the actual command. For example, the key sequence **12j** moves the cursor down 12 lines, and **3C-u** scrolls down three pages.

According to **vi**, words are strings of characters, and word delimiters are space characters or special characters (such as **. , ! ***). A sentence is a sequence of words where dots, question marks, or exclamation marks form the bounds.

A new paragraph starts after a blank line or after an **nroff**   *nroff macros* macro. An **nroff** macro is a sequence at the beginning of the   *consist of a point* line consisting of a point followed by a maximum of two let-   *followed by* ters. The **vi** internal variable **paragraphs** stores a list of **nroff**   *maximum of two* paragraph delimiters. **vi** recognizes a form-feed character or an   *letters* **nroff** macro as the beginning of a new section. This **nroff** macro must be listed by the **vi** internal variable **sections**.

7.2.5 Deleting, Replacing, Copying

The **vi** commands for deleting, replacing, and copying parts of a document consist of a letter indicating the function and of one or two additional letters determining the scope of the command.

c   replaces an object,

d   removes an object, and   *dd deletes a line*

y   copies an object to a temporary buffer.

When pressed twice, the command affects the whole line. Other object indicators stand for

BLANK		following character,
w		to the end of the next word, with a **BLANK** or a special character forming the bounds,
W		to the end of the next word, with a **BLANK** forming the bound,
b		to the end of the preceding word, with a **BLANK** or a special character forming the bound,
B		to the end of the preceding word, with a **BLANK** forming the bound,
0		to the beginning of the line,
^		to the first visible character at the beginning of the line,
$		to the end of the line,
(		to the beginning of the sentence,
)		to the end of the sentence,
{		to the beginning of the paragraph,
}		to the end of the paragraph,
[[		to the beginning of the section,
]]		to the end of the section.

objects are characters, words, lines, sentences, paragraphs, and sections

If the cursor is located in the middle of a word, dw deletes from the cursor position on to the end of the word

Numbers preceding or following the command result in the operation being executed repeatedly. For example, **6dw** and **d6w** remove the following 6 words.

The replacement command **c** deletes the object stated, then **vi** switches to input mode. When the user switches back to the command mode using the escape key, the replacement of the objects is considered to be finished.

P inserts in front of the cursor, p behind the cursor

There are two steps involved in copying. In the first step, the desired region is copied to **vi**'s temporary buffer. Next, the cursor is moved to the target position. Then the content of the temporary buffer is inserted in front of the cursor position with **P** or after the cursor position with **p**.

vi has one unnamed and 26 named registers (a-z)

For copying, **vi** provides an unnamed buffer and other buffers bearing the names **a** to **z**. The named buffers are addressed by double quotation marks. For example, a **vi** command that copies the 8 lines following the current cursor position to the register **w** goes as follows:

```
"w8yy
```

7.2.6 Marks, Keyboard Sequences, Abbreviations

The mark concept of **vi** makes it possible to conveniently jump back to a position within a document. The **m** command followed by a letter in the range **a** to **z** stores the current cursor position in a mark register. At a later point in time, the user can address a stored position using:

'x	to jump to the mark **x**,
' '	to return to the last jump address,
' [	to jump to the beginning of the line containing **x**,
']	to jump to the end of line containing **x**,
´x	to jump to the first visible character of the line containing **x**.

Marks set are displayed by the **vim** after entering the **ex** command **:marks** (the leading colon switches **vi** from command mode to **ex** mode). Similarly, the **ex** command **:jumps** provides a list of the last jumps made.

Marks can also be used as reference positions. For example, when **y'a** is entered, the contents between the mark **a** and the current cursor position are copied to the temporary buffer.

When y'a is entered the cursor jumps to the mark a

A further feature of **vi** is the ability to administer command sequences in registers. In this case, **vim** helps the user by providing the "record" command **qx**, where **x** stands for a register name in the range **a** to **z**. In command mode, keyboard sequences up to the next **q** are copied by **vim** to the register **x**. The keyboard sequence stored in the register **x** can be repeated by the user with **@x** at any chosen place.

vim offers a record function for storing sequences

Finally, we mention the possibility of automatically replacing parts of the text. With the **ex** command

161

```
:ab abbreviation text
```

the abbreviation **abbreviation** will be stored. After entering **abbreviations** in the input or replacement mode, **vi** replaces the abbreviation with **text**. A list of the defined abbreviations is display by the command **:ab**.

The user can combine frequently used abbreviations, without a leading colon, in the start-up file **$HOME/.exrc**. They will then be available immediately after **vi** is started.

The vi start-up file is $HOME/.exrc

7.2.7 ex Commands

After a colon (:) is entered in the command mode, **vi** switches to the **ex** mode and waits for a command line to be entered. The cursor jumps to the last line of the screen and accepts an **ex** command after the colon (the **ex** prompt). The most important commands:

The vim help function gives an overview of commands

help   displays a list of commands (**vim** only),

w [file]
       saves the document in **file**,

b,ew file
       saves the lines **b** to **e** in **file**,

wq   save and quit,

x   save if the document has been modified and quit,

q!   quit without saving,

q   quit,

e file   load a new file,

e!   forget the changes, load the file being processed again,

n   process the next file,

N   process the preceding file,

r file   insert the content of **file**,

!command

    execute the **command** in a sub-shell,

r!command

    execute the **command** in a sub-shell, insert the result in the document,

sh   open a sub-shell as active child process. After the shell is terminated the user can continue to work with **vi**.

3,5!command pipes lines 3-5 to command, replaces the region by the result of command

7.2.8 Searching and Replacing

For exchanging parts of the text in a document, **vi** has a convenient replacement command in the **ex** mode. Its syntax is

    `[address [,address]] s/RegExp/string/ [flags]...`

If no address ranges are stated, the **s** command searches forward for the pattern **RegExp**, beginning at the current cursor position, and replaces the first pattern found with the character string **string**. If an address range has been stated, **vi** replaces the first found pattern in each line within the range.

    With **flags** the user can modify the operation of the replacement command: **flags=g** (global) instructs **vi** to replace all patterns occurring on the line, beginning at the current cursor position, or in the address range stated. If **flags=c** has been set, **vi** asks for confirmation before carrying out the replacement.

Addresses are line numbers or context addresses (/text/)

7.2.9 **vi** Options

The mode of operation and the appearance of the **vi** are controlled by special options. They can be accessed by the user via **vi** internal variables. **vim** provides about 100 internal variables storing logic, numeric, or character string values. The following list gives some variable names, their abbreviations if necessary, the variable type in parentheses (l logic, n numeric, z string), and their purpose. In the case of logical variables, the explanation describes the behavior of **vi** when the variable value is "true".

There are about 100 variables controlling the operation modes of vim

163

autoindent ai (l) When starting a new line, it will be automatically indented the same amount as the preceding line.

backup bk (l) Creates a backup of the original, with the suffix .bak, before saving the file.

ignorecase ic (l) Searches will not differentiate between upper and lowercase letters.

magic (l) Search patterns are treated in the same way as regular expressions.

number nu (l) Line numbers are displayed on the left hand side.

paragraphs pa (z) Holds a list of **nroff** delimiters for paragraphs.

sections sect (z) Holds a list of **nroff** delimiters for sections.

Tab-stops have a fixed number of spaces in between

tabstop ts (n) Sets the number of space characters between tab-stops.

wrapscan ws (l) If the end of the file is reached during a search, the search will be continued from the beginning of the file and vice versa.

The variables of **vi** can be manipulated with the **ex** command **set**. As with other **ex** commands, the colon is required for switching to **ex** mode. The general calling convention is

```
:set [option[=value]]...
```

set all displays the overview page by page

When called up without an argument, **set** displays the names and values of the variables that have values differing from the default setting. **set all** gives a general overview and **set option?** displays the value of the variable **option**.

Values are assigned to numeric and character string variables with **set option=value**. There are three different ways of setting the state of a logical variable:

`set option`	sets `option` to "true",
`set noOption`	sets `option` to "false",
`set invOption`	inverts the value of `option`.

The `set` command also allows several options to be set with a single call: `set ai bk nu` sets the values of the variable `autoindent`, `backup`, and `number` to "true".

set nu displays line numbers

Options differing from the default setting are set by `vi` as the program starts, by first interpreting the content of the environment variable `EXINIT` and then translating `ex` commands located in the user's own `vi` start-up file `$HOME/.exrc`.

7.3 GNU Emacs

GNU Emacs is a multipurpose tool for creating and manipulating text files. It also processes binary files. Emacs is not an editor for processing documents in the desktop publishing style.

In development circles especially, Emacs enjoys great popularity. This is due to its comprehensive range of commands and its flexibility in allowing the user to configure each operational feature individually. The most striking features of the program are the integrated online documentation and the ability to extend the number of functions. For beginners there is an online tutorial.

Emacs includes online documentation

In comparison to `vi`, Emacs has only insert and replace modes. Files loaded for processing are stored in internal buffers. The screen, or more precisely a window region, is assigned to a buffer and displays a section of that buffer. Some windows can display not only different parts of a file but also parts of other files. Each window manages its own cursor position. Input from the keyboard, provided it does not contain control characters, is inserted directly in front the current cursor position. Emacs recognizes control characters or sequences as editing commands.

Various text windows display the context of one or more files

Another difference between Emacs and `vi` (and most other editors) is in the architecture of Emacs. The program is written completely in C, but has an internal Emacs Lisp interpreter (elisp). All the editing functions are written in elisp. The user can extend the number of commands by writing additional elisp functions.

The editing functions of Emacs are written in elisp

The standard system includes about 300 files of elisp source code. In addition to the editing functions, elisp also makes it possible to utilize the operating system services. For example, in a new window the user can start a command interpreter, read or send electronic mail, or exchange files with remote systems without terminating the editor. He or she can also run a compiler directly, instruct the cursor to jump to faulty program lines, and even test executable programs.

7.3.1 Starting and Quitting Emacs

When run on the console Emacs fills the complete screen. When started from an **xterm** application of the X Window System (see Chap. 11), the editor opens in a X window. In this case, the X server is the interface between the editor and the user. The general call syntax is

```
emacs [option]... [file]...
```

Emacs includes an
X11 connection

X Window System users should start Emacs as a background process by ending the command line with an **&**. At the console or on an ASCII terminal, the program must run in the foreground. In both cases, the screen content has the structure shown in Fig. 7.2.

Fig. 7.2
The screen content
after starting
emacs

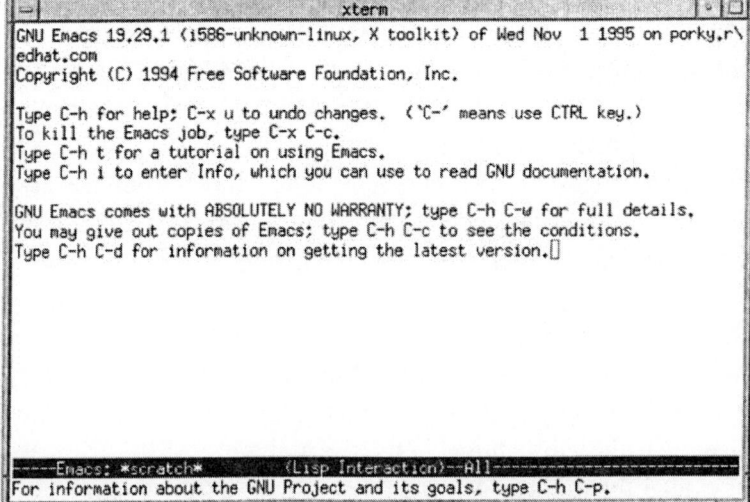

A status line displayed in inverse video forms the lower bound of the text window. In the status line, Emacs gives information on the name of the file displayed in the text window.

A status line forms the boundary of text windows

The last line of the screen (or frame) has two purposes. On the one hand, this line is used as an "echo region" by Emacs, for transferring program information to the user. On the other hand, this region serves as the "minibuffer" for receiving commands and command arguments from the user.

When called without a file name, the initial "frame" appears as shown in Fig. 7.2. The text screen shows the version number of the program and displays some of the help functions available, including the keyboard sequences to be entered for this help.

If the program call has been supplied with an argument, Emacs loads the file and positions the cursor at the beginning of the file. If it has been called with two file names, Emacs divides the frame into two texts windows and displays the first file at the top and the second file at the bottom.

The user can start Emacs with files to edit

When starting up with more than two file names, the screen of text will also be divided, but in this case the last file stated on the command line is displayed at the top. When using this kind of call, Emacs presents a "buffer list" in the lower region. For each file there is a line listing the buffer name, the file size, the Emacs mode, and the complete file name. The cursor is in the buffer list and the echo region shows a list of valid commands. Especially for beginners, it is advisable to start Emacs with at most two files (the keyboard sequence C-x o switches between the two screens of text).

When called with more than two files Emacs makes a buffer list

The keyboard sequence C-x C-c terminates Emacs. The editor checks whether or not the user has saved the contents of all modified buffers before it terminates. Files are saved either one by one with C-x C-s or interactively by entering the command M-x save-some-buffers. If not all modified buffers have been saved, Emacs asks whether or not the unsaved files should be saved. The program can be quit only when all processed files have been saved or when the user asks Emacs to terminate without saving by answering the question exit anyway with yes.

C-x C-s saves a file, C-x C-c terminates Emacs

Modified versions of file that have not been saved will nevertheless be saved by Emacs as #file#. If Emacs has to process `file` in a later session and finds a directory entry `#file#` with a newer time stamp than `file`, an appropriate message will be displayed to the user. Entering `M-x recover-file` will tell Emacs to replace the buffer contents `file` with the backup version. The backup will be removed by the editor after `file` is saved with `C-x C-s`.

Emacs creates backups periodically

The key sequence `C-z` will temporarily suspend the program. The user can then interact with the shell. Entered the internal shell command `fg` will active the editor again. Note that when `emacs` is called again while it is in the suspended state, a second Emacs will be started, which will consume more system resources.

7.3.2 Basic Commands

Like `vi`, Emacs provides functions for moving the cursor as well as for deleting, replacing, and copying text regions. Most of the functions can be used directly via control sequences. The most important functions are usually bound to the keyboard's function keys. All the functions can be activated by entering their function name. The user does this by switching to the minibuffer with `M-x` and entering the function name. Inputs to the minibuffer and active operations are aborted by Emacs if it receives `C-g` (`keyboard-quit`).

Emacs carries out editing commands when given a control sequence or a function name

7.3.3 Moving the Cursor

Sequence	Name	Function
`C-f`	`forward-char`	character to the right
`C-b`	`backward-char`	character to the left
`M-f`	`forward-word`	word to the right
`M-b`	`backward-word`	word to the left
`C-a`	`beginning-of-line`	to the beginning of the line
`C-e`	`end-of-line`	to the end of the line
`C-n`	`next-line`	down one line
`C-p`	`previous-line`	up one line
`C-x ]`	`forward-page`	one page forward
`C-x [`	`backward-page`	one page backward
`M-<`	`beginning-of-buffer`	to the first line

Sequence	Name	Function
M->	end-of-buffer	to the last line
C-v	scroll-up	down one screen of text
M-v	scroll-down	up one screen of text
C-x <	scroll-left	screen of text to the left
C-x >	scroll-right	screen of text to the right
C-1	recenter	center current line

In the syntax of Emacs, the bounds of a word are marked by a separator (space character, tab, minus sign, dot, etc.). The bounds of a page are marked by the form-feed character ^L.

The "vertical" scroll functions move the view down (C-v) or up (M-v) a number of lines. The number of lines is the height of the screen of text minus the value of the variable scroll-next-context-lines, whose default value is 2.

The functions scroll-left (C-x <) and scroll-right (C-x >) move the screen of text either to the left or to the right. If these sequences are preceded with Escape and a number, emacs moves the text by the number of columns given, otherwise by the number of columns displayed.

Horizontal scrolling moves the screen of text either to the left or to the right

s well as the character, word, line, and page oriented operations already mentioned, Emacs offers several sentence and paragraph oriented functions, such as backward-sentence or forward-paragraph. When M-x goto-line is entered, the cursor jumps to the line stated.

M-x goto-line jumps the cursors the line specified

Emacs recognizes the end of the sentence by a dot, a question, or an exclamation mark followed by two space characters. Paragraph delimiters are controlled by the internal variables paragraph-start and paragraph-separate. The values of these Emacs variables are regular expressions ("^[\t\n\f]" and "^[\t\f]*$", see Sect.6.10).

The end of a sentence is marked by two blanks following a ., ?, or !

7.3.4 Deleting

Sequence	Name	Function
C-d	delete-char	delete character to the right
Del	backward-delete-char	delete character to the left
M-d	kill-word	delete word to the right
M-Del	backward-kill-word	delete word to the left
C-k	kill-line	delete to the end of the line

Some of the delete operations listed include the character string **delete**, others contain **kill**. The different names indicate the operation mode of the command: the former remove a single letter, the latter remove a region from the buffer and copy the data to the "kill ring". Data located in the kill ring are recalled by Emacs when the user enters the **yank** commands (**C-y**, yank and **M-y**, yank-pop). **C-y** pastes the last entry from the kill ring in front of the current cursor position, **M-y** (to be executed directly after **C-y**) replaces the last text segment inserted with the next element from the kill ring.

The kill ring stores deleted words, lines, and regions

Each **kill** operation adds an entry to the kill ring. The maximum number of entries in the kill ring is controlled by the variable **kill-ring-max**. The default value is 30. If the user carries out several **kill** functions directly one after another, **emacs** adds the respective object to the last entry in the kill ring. If other commands have been carried out between the two **kill** operations, say, if the cursor has been moved, then **M-C-w** (append-next-kill) will cause the subsequent **kill** command to append data to the last entry in the kill ring.

7.3.5 Marking

Sequence	Name	Function
C-SPACE	set-mark-command	sets a mark
C-x C-x	exchange-point-and-mark	move the cursor to the last mark

C-@ sets a mark, C-x C-x jumps to the mark

Emacs assigns to each buffer the two positions "mark" and "point". The user sets the mark within the buffer by entering **C-SPACE** or **C-@** (set-mark-command). The point is the current cursor position. The current position of the mark can be seen by using the keyboard sequence **C-x C-x**, which will swap the point and the mark.

C-w deletes the region between the mark and the point, M-w copies the region to the kill ring

The user sets marks mainly for the purpose of defining regions to be copied or deleted. The function **kill-region** (**C-w**) kills the region between the mark and the point from the buffer, whereas **kill-ring-save** (**M-w**) copies the region between the mark and the point to the kill ring, leaving the buffer unaltered.

For each file being edited, or rather, for each buffer, Emacs administers a mark ring which can store 16 positions. Each time a mark is set, the mark ring is extended. The user can use old mark positions by entering `C-u C-SPACE` or `C-u C-@`. Additionally, Emacs always stores the last mark position before changing to another buffer in a "global mark ring". The cursor jumps to addresses stored there when `C-x C-BLANK` is entered.

7.3.6 Searching

Sequence	Name	Function
C-s	isearch-forward	search forward
C-r	isearch-backward	search backward
M-C-s	isearch-forward-regexp	search forward
M-C-r	isearch-backward-regexp	search backward

Emacs searches either for character strings (`C-s` and `C-r`) or for regular expressions (`M-C-s` and `M-C-r`). When the respective command is executed repeatedly, the next occurrence of the last search string entered is sought. If during the search the beginning or end of the file is reached, then the search is continued from the end or beginning of the file, respectively.

M-C-s and M-C-r search for regular expressions

By default, character string oriented search operations only differentiate between upper and lowercase letters when the character string sought contains capitals. If the value of the internal Emacs variable `case-fold-search` is `nil`, Emacs will only search for character strings that match the given search string exactly.

Regarding the search, there is no distinction made between upper and lowercase letters

7.3.7 Replacing

Sequence	Name	Function
M-%	query-replace	replace character strings

Emacs offers various commands for replacing character strings. The function used most often is `M-%`. After the keyboard sequence or function name is entered, the program asks the user to enter two character strings in the minibuffer, both of which

M-% asks the user before an exchange is carried out

are to be ended with **RETURN**. The cursor then jumps to the next position in the buffer, where the first string (the search string)) is located, and asks the user to enter a key code.

SPACE replaces and jumps to the next position where the search string is located,

Del jumps to the next position of the search string without replacing,

RETURN terminates the function,

C-g terminates the function too

, replaces and displays the result (the minibuffer prompts for a further command),

˜ jumps back to the last position of the search string,

! replaces each following search string without further query.

replace-string and replace-regexp replace without querying

Global replacement is made by calling the function **replace-string**. It replaces each search string found, without query, from the position of the point up to the end of the file. Other replacement commands allow a regular expression to be entered for the search string and replaced with or without confirmation (**query-replace-regexp**, **replace-regexp**). Usually these commands are not bound to keyboard sequences.

If the variable **case-replace** has a value other than **nil**, then capitalization is retained during replacement:

query-replace-string operates analogously

M-x replace-string RETURN x RETURN y RETURN

replaces **x** with **y** and **X** with **Y**. The variable **case-fold-search** also influences the replacement commands. If it has the value **nil**, Emacs only replaces character strings matching the search string exactly.

7.3.8 Restoring

Sequence	Name	Function
C-_	undo	undo the last change

Emacs stores all executed operations in a command list for each buffer. The length of each list is determined by the variable **undo-limit**, whose default value is 20000. When **C-_** is entered repeatedly, the last changes will be canceled one after the other.

7.3.9 Loading and Saving Files

Sequence	Name	Function
C-x C-f	find-file	load file
C-x i	insert-file	insert file
C-x C-s	save-buffers	save buffer
C-x s	save-some-buffer	save several buffers
C-x C-w	write-file	save file

With the exception of **save-buffer**, the commands stated prompt the user to enter a file name in the minibuffer, specifying a file to be loaded or created. If the file name has the format **/host:file** or **/user@host:file**, Emacs will try to establish a connection to the remote system via **ftp**. In this case, to validate the access permission, it will prompt for a password.

Emacs can process files located on remote systems as well

During entry of a file name, Emacs attempts to complete the name automatically if the user presses the space or tab keys. Of course, this will only succeed if the desired file already exists. If several files matching the entered pattern already exist in the directory, Emacs will display a list of possible completions.

File and function names entered in the minibuffer will be completed by Emacs if space or tab are entered

Copies of files for which the user has write permission are loaded by Emacs into a buffer in the insert mode. The user can then modify the buffer as he or she wants. If the user has read permission only, then the buffer content cannot be modified. The function **find-file-read-only** (**C-x C-r**) specifically loads a file in the read-only mode.

Files loaded with C-x C-r cannot be modified

While saving a file, Emacs creates a backup, if the value of the variable **make-backup-files** is not **nil**. The default value is **t**. The user can usually recognize backups by a tilde character ~ appended to the file name. Multiple numbered backups are create by Emacs if the value of the variable **version-control** is **t** or if the program finds the environment variable **VERSION_CONTROL** with the value **t** in its context.

Emacs creates numbered backup files if the variable version-control has the value t

7.3.10 Switching Buffers

Sequence	Name	Function
C-x b	switch-to-buffer	switch buffers
C-x C-b	list-buffers	display a buffer list
C-x k	kill-buffer	remove buffer

As already mentioned, Emacs copies each file to be processed into a buffer and the user modifies the copy of the file in the buffer. There is only ever one active buffer, which can be identified by the cursor located in the corresponding text window.

C-x b prompts for a buffer name, C-x C-b displays a buffer list

When **C-x b** is entered, Emacs activates another buffer. **C-x C-b** displays a list of all buffers currently stored in memory, and **C-x k** removes a buffer. The function **vc-toggle-read-only** (**C-x C-q**) switches a buffer in or out of read-only mode.

7.3.11 Window Commands

Sequence	Name	Function
C-x 0	delete-window	remove window
C-x 1	delete other-window	remove window
C-x 2	split-window-vertically	split window
C-x 3	split-window-horizontally	split window
C-x o	other-window	switch window

C-x o activates the next text window in the window stack

Working with multiple windows enables the user to look at different parts of a file or parts of different files. The cursor can be moved from one text window to another with **C-x o**. It is also possible to copy a part of the text to the kill ring using **C-x w** and to insert the "cut" text into another text window with **C-y**.

Screens of text can be split horizontally or vertically

Emacs allows text windows to be split horizontally (**C-x 2**) or vertically (**C-x 3**) into two windows of the same size (if the screen of text has an even number of lines or columns). The window where the cursor is located is removed with the key sequence **C-x 0**, whereas **C-x 1** removes all other windows and lets the active buffer occupy the whole screen or frame. It is also possible to enlarge or reduce the window size. In the vertical direction, **M-x enlarge-window** enlarges the window and **M-x shrink-window** shrinks it (changing the number of lines). In the horizontal direction, `M-x enlarge-window-horizontally` widens the window and `M-x shrink-window-horizontally` narrows it.

7.3.12 Command Sequences

Sequence	Name	Function
C-x (	start-kbd-macro	start recording
C-x)	end-kbd-macro	end recording
C-x e	call-last-kbd-macro	carry out the last recorded sequence

The key sequence `C-x (` makes Emacs carry out all following commands and store them in parallel in a command buffer until the user enters `C-x )`. The sequence `C-x e` repeats the last command sequence stored. The sequence `C-u C-x (` allows the command sequence stored last to be extended, and `C-x )` ends the recording.

C-u C-x (allows the key sequences last stored to be extended

The user can assign a function name to a command sequence recorded (`M-x name-last-kbd-macro`); calling up the function name later causes the stored sequence to be carried out.

It is also possible to store a named command sequence in a file. Normally, the Emacs start-up file `$HOME/.emacs` is loaded and the command `M-x insert-kbd-macro` executed for this purpose. After the function name is entered, Emacs copies an elisp function to the file. Then, after the modified `$HOME/.emacs` file is saved, the new command will be available again under the function name given.

Emacs can copy named key sequences as elisp code to a file

7.3.13 Repeat Execution

If the user puts a numeric argument in front of an Emacs command, the command will be executed repeatedly. For example, the sequence `M-5 C-n` moves the cursor down five lines, `M-64 a` inserts the character **a** in front of the current cursor position 64 times, `M-20 C-x e` carries out the last defined command sequence 20 times, and so on.

Negative numeric arguments often result in the chosen operation being executed repeatedly in the "opposite direction".

A multiplier created with M-num or C-u num results in the following command being executed repeatedly

Besides the sequence `M-num` defining the multiplier `num` for the subsequent command, Emacs also provides the function `universal-argument` (`C-u`). If `C-u` is not followed by a numeric argument, the subsequent command is carried out 4 times. Repeating `C-u` quadruples the already defined multiplier. For example, `C-u C-u C-d` deletes the following 16 characters. If `M-num` or `C-u num` is mixed up with `C-u`, no multiplier will be defined.

7.3.14 Abbreviations

sequence	Name	function
`C-x a g`	`add-global-abbrev`	define abbreviation
`C-x a e`	`expand-abbrev`	expand abbreviation

Abbreviations are only expanded by Emacs in the abbrev-mode

Abbreviations are only processed by Emacs in a special operation mode called the **abbrev** mode. The user can toggle the **abbrev** mode on or off by entering `M-x abbrev-mode`. The character string `Abbrev` in a buffer's status line indicates whether or not the **abbrev** mode has been activated for the buffer.

Defining abbreviations requires two steps. First, the text to be abbreviated is entered in the buffer. Then, after the key sequence `C-x a g` is entered, Emacs prompts the user to specify a short form for the text standing in front of the cursor.

Normally, Emacs copies a single word from directly in front of the cursor to the **abbrev** buffer. It will copy several words into the buffer if the user specifies the number of words forming the abbreviation. The number of words can be defined by entering `C-u num` before `C-x a g`.

As well as globally valid abbreviations, Emacs supports mode-specific abbreviations. These will only be expanded in a particular Emacs mode (see Sect. 7.3.16). Such local abbreviations are defined in the same way as general abbreviations, but instead of `C-x a g`, the sequence `C-x a l` is used.

Emacs automatically expands abbreviations if the user enters an abbreviation as a word followed by a space character. The sequence `C-x a e` expands an abbreviation standing directly in front of the cursor, and **M-x expand-region-abbrevs** expands each abbreviation between mark and point.

The command **M-x list-abbrevs** shows a list of the defined abbreviations, **M-x edit-abbrevs** allows the defined abbreviations to be edited interactively, and **M-x kill-all-abbrevs** deletes all local and global abbreviations.

The user can store the currently defined abbreviations with **M-x write-abbrev-file**. When **M-x read-abbrev-file** is called in a later session, the stored abbreviations will be available once again.

7.3.15 Online Help

Conceived as a self-explanatory text editor, Emacs offers a wide range of functions allowing the user to access online help. This includes the online tutorial already mentioned, which in particular displays a text file explaining to the user step by step how to handle basic commands.

The online tutorial is activated with the sequence C-h t

The actual online help consists of various functions displaying, for example, a short description of an individual editing function, an Emacs variable, or a command linked to a control sequence. Additionally, Emacs includes an **apropos** function that creates a list of all the command names containing a certain character string (regular expression), and a short description of each. The most important help functions are:

The apropos function shows a list of commands containing a certain character string

Sequence	Name	Function
C-h a	apropos	displays command names including a character string
C-h b	describe bindings	displays a list of key bindings
C-h f	describe-function	describes a function
C-h C-h	help-for-help	creates a list of the help commands
C-h k	describe-key	describes a key sequence
C-h v	describe-variable	explains the meaning of an Emacs variable
C-h w	where-is	shows the key sequence for a command

177

7.3.16 Modes

The modes of Emacs make it possible to match the behavior of the editor with the layout of certain file types. C, C++, and Pascal programmers, for example, like block structures to be indented automatically. When writing Lisp programs and TEX documents, it is desirable to highlight the corresponding opening parenthesis when a closing parenthesis is entered, and so on.

If the editor is started without a file name it will be in the unspecified "fundamental" mode. When the user loads a file, Emacs can normally see from the file identification or from the first line of the file whether it is a programming language and, if so, which one it is, and whether or not the file includes a document format. The appropriate "major" mode is then assigned to the buffer. Furthermore, each major mode adds further functions to the fundamental Emacs functions.

In some cases, some function keys will be given a new meaning. For example, the tab key does not insert a tab character in the C mode, but instead indents the line according to the surrounding context. Figure 7.3 shows a list of Emacs' major modes.

Buffer-menu-mode	emacs-lisp-mode	pascal-mode
LaTeX-mode	f90-mode	perl-mode
TeX-mode	fortran-mode	plain-TeX-mode
ada-mode	fundamental-mode	prolog-mode
asm-mode	help-mode	scheme-mode
awk-mode	icon-mode	scribe-mode
bibtex-mode	indented-text-mode	sgml-mode
c++-mode	lisp-mode	slitex-mode
c-mode	mail-mode	tar-mode
command-history-mode	nroff-mode	text-mode
completion-list-mode	objc-mode	vi-mode
edit-abbrevs-mode	occur-mode	wordstar-mode

The user can assign a major mode to a buffer by stating the mode name in the minibuffer. Major modes are exclusive; a buffer can only be linked to one major mode. Additionally, the user can switch on various "minor" modes, for example the `abbrev-mode` (explained in Sect.7.3.14), the `auto-fill-mode` (automatic line-feed), or the `line-number-mode` (displays the current line number in the status line). Figure 7.4 lists the minor modes of Emacs. The function `M-x describe-mode` displays the features of the major mode currently in effect.

abbrev mode	font-lock-mode
auto-fill-mode	iso-accents-mode
auto-lower-mode	ispell-minor-mode
auto-raise-mode	line-number-mode
auto-save-mode	menu-bar-mode
auto-show-mode	outline-minor-mode
binary-overwrite-mode	overwrite-mode
compilation-minor-mode	pending-delete-mode
delete-selection-mode	scroll-bar-mode
double-mode	toggle-rot13-mode
enriched-mode	transient-mark-mode
fast-lock-mode	

Fig. 7.4
Emacs'
minor modes

7.3.17 Application Packages

In the standard GNU Emacs distributions there are some additional Lisp programs that form complete application packages. These include the directory editor `dired`, the `rmail` package for looking at received electronic mail, the `mail` subsystem for producing electronic mail, a calendar `calendar`, the `gnus` system controlling access to news groups in the worldwide usenet, and the `info` system, which displays a special document format and can also follow cross references. Interfaces to services of the system, for example comparing buffer contents with `diff`, spell checking with `ispell`, printing output with `lpr`, or emulating a terminal (`shell`) round off the range of application programs for the Emacs.

The application packages also include the games dunnet and gomoku

Some application packages, namely `dired`, `info`, `mail`, and `shell`, have their own special major modes. They are not designed for processing user files. The task of these special Emacs modes is to link application-oriented functions to each buffer used. An explanation of the packages `rmail`, `news`, and `calendar` is outside the scope of this book.

dired, info, mail and shell are special modes

Dired

The directory
editor dired makes
it possible to
delete, copy, and
print files as well
as change the
access permissions

The purpose of **dired** is to edit directories. After entry of **C-x d** or **M-x dired**, Emacs displays the contents of a directory, or a list of files within a directory that fit a mask stated, in a **dired** buffer. Within a **dired** buffer, the user can load a file in a normal text buffer (**f**), mark files with **d** and delete the marked files with **x**, send to the print spooler **lpr** (**P**), or change access permissions (**M mode**). If the **f** command is applied to a directory name, **dired** changes the respective subdirectory. **dired** is automatically loaded if the user gives a directory name as argument to the command **C-x C-f**.

Info

Strictly speaking, the **info** system belongs to the group of help commands. The sequence **C-h i** loads the **info-mode** and initially displays the root of the **info** hierarchy (the content of the file **dir** from the directory **/usr/info**). Menu items in an **info** file are indicated by a star at the beginning of the line. When **m**

info files have a hypertext structure

or **return** is entered, the **info** system displays the menu topic located beneath the cursor. **n** jumps to the next page and **p** to the preceding one, **u** changes to the next page up in the hierarchy (directly above the current page), and **d** displays the table of contents (the root). Linux distributions usually include various **info** files, for example containing explanations of the **tar** command or **bash**.

Mail

The mail package helps the user to write an email, rmail process received email

After **C-x m** or **M-x mail** is entered, Emacs creates a mail-mode buffer. For the most part, the mail mode works like the normal text mode, with some exceptions. Firstly, the system presents two fields where the email recipient and a subject for the mail have to be entered, and secondly, a number of special mail commands are installed. The actual message has to be typed after a dividing line. Finally, when **C-c C-s** or **C-c C-c** is entered, the message is sent to the addressee. During text entry the usual Emacs editing commands are available. In particular, it is possible to insert text lines from another buffer or file. The message can be checked for spelling by entering the **M-x ispell-message** command.

Shell

Like **vi**, Emacs can call up a system program (**M-! command**) or pipe the area between a mark and a point to another program (**M-| command**). In both cases, Emacs only adds the result of the program call to the current buffer when the user puts an argument in front of the call (e.g., with **M-1**). Otherwise, the editor copies the result to an "output" buffer. Text areas that have been piped to another program for "filtering" are replaced by the result of the program call if a numeric argument has been used.

M-| pipes a text area to a filter program

Furthermore, Emacs can run an interactive shell in a buffer of its own (**M-x shell**). A second command interpreter will be available in another buffer if the user renames the first shell buffer ***shell*** with **M-x rename-uniquely**, so that the editor can create a new ***shell*** buffer. The type of the command interpreter loaded by the shell is specified by the variable **shell-file-name**. In the shell mode, the commands **M-p** and **M-n** allow scrolling through the command history.

Passwords are not displayed by Emacs when the user enters their character string after calling M-x send-invisible

7.3.18   Miscellaneous

The aim of this section is to list other Emacs functions which are either useful for everyday work with the editor or which help to adapt the system to individual demands.

Multiple space characters are removed by the sequence **M-**, and **M-SPACE** reduces multiple space characters to a single one. Similarly, the key sequence **C-x C-o** reduces several blank lines to a single blank line.

Tabs are also considered to be blank characters

Word by word conversion of capital into small letters and vice versa (`case-fold`) are carried out by the keyboard sequences `M-u` (uppercase letters), `M-l` (lowercase letters), and `M-c` (capitalize initial letter).

M-, repeats the search for the last search string given

Special `tag` functions operate on file groups. Calling up the system command `etags file...` creates a tag file used for this purpose. After the tag file is created, the user can search through the whole file group for a character string or a regular expression with `M-x tags-search`. The function `M-x tags-query-replace` allows the user to interactively replace a sought string with a character string. In this case, Emacs examines each file in the file group in order.

If the minor mode `auto-fill` is active, Emacs automatically makes a line-feed when entering continuous text. The line length is determined by the variable `fill-column`, whose default value is 70. Emacs allows this value to be altered by assigning a new numeric value with `M-x set-variable` or by positioning the cursor in the desired column and entering `C-x f`. A text area can be adjusted to the line length set with the function `M-x fill-region`.

In the hexl mode the structure of the left and middle column corresponds to the result of the command od -x

For processing binary files, the program provides the hexl mode. Files loaded with `M-x hexl-find-file` are displayed in the buffer as hexadecimal numbers with an offset column on the left-hand side. Each line represents 16 bytes of the file. An additional column on the right-hand side displays the ASCII characters included in the file. The function `C-q` allows any byte codes at all to be entered, either as control characters or as octal values. It is also possible to insert the latter in normal text buffers.

Control and meta characters are to be entered as C and \M

Key bindings are set by the commands `M-x global-set-key` and `M-x local-set-key`. Normally, the user sets his or her individual key bindings in Emacs' start-up file `$HOME/.emacs` by adding Lisp commands to it in the form

```
(global-set-key [f1] `call-last-kbd-macro)
```

In this case, the function stated is bound to the function key `F1`.

If a major mode is to be linked to one or several minor modes per default, then a hook must be entered in the start-up file. For example, the line

```
(add-hook 'tex-mode-hook' turn-on-auto-fill)
```

causes the `auto-fill` mode to be switched on automatically when the user loads a TEX document.

7.3.19 The GNU Emacs as an X Application

In comparison to the ASCII version, as an X application the GNU Emacs additionally integrates mouse support. The current Version 19 additionally includes a menu bar, multiple frames (i.e., several independent X windows), multiple fonts, and colorization of text elements.

Mouse support includes the capability to position the cursor anywhere place at all by moving the pointer to the desired position and pressing the left mouse button. A scrollbar at the right-hand side makes it possible to scroll back and forth within the document (left mouse button, right mouse button) and to scroll fast (middle mouse button). A menu bar at the top allows some basic editing operations to be activated with the mouse.

Pressing the middle mouse button in the buffer carries out the yank command at the pointer position

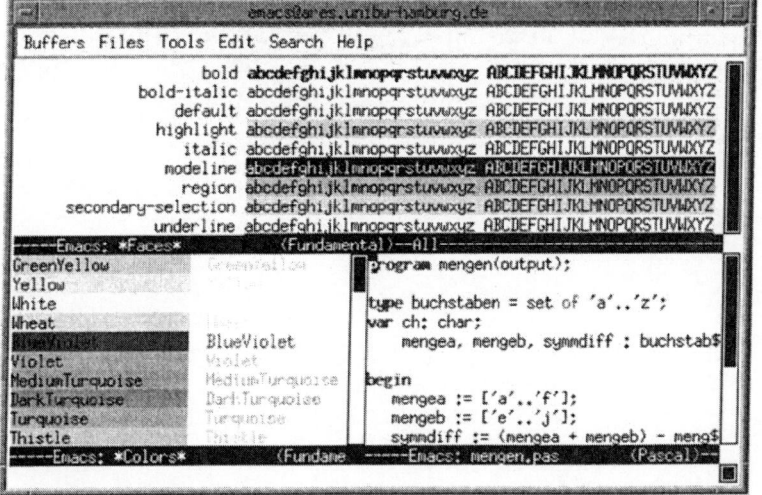

Fig. 7.5
Faces in the
GNU Emacs

Face fonts have to have the same height as the default font

Colors and fonts are administered by Emacs as "faces" linked to a buffer by the editor. For example, some major modes define faces for highlighting the reserved words in the respective programming language in a program text. Figure 7.5 shows an Emacs frame giving an overview of the available font faces in the upper area and a color table in the lower left area. In the lower right area, some Pascal program code includes reserved words highlighted by color assignments.

set-face-font asks for a face identifier and a font name

The font list is created by **M-x list-faces-display** and the list of colors is displayed by **M-x list-colors-display**. The function **M-x set-face-font** assigns a font to a buffer, and functions **M-x set-face-foreground** and **M-x set-face-background** set colors. The Lisp program **hilit19.el**, which is loaded with **M-x load-library**, is responsible for coloring the reserved words of the Pascal program.

Some Linux distributions alternatively or additionally include the program **xemacs**. This is a variant of GNU Emacs, originally developed by Jamie Zawinski and Richard Mlynarik as "Lucid Emacs", based on an early alpha version of GNU Emacs Version 19.

xemacs can also redirect frames to a remote display

xemacs is operated in almost the same way as GNU Emacs. Vertical scrollbars and a configurable tool bar that displays functions as graphic icons are also in **xemacs**. An HTML browser that can also show graphics is included in **xemacs**. In addition, the program features an appealing tool for processing electronic mail. By way of an example, Fig. 7.6 shows the graphical interface of **xemacs**.

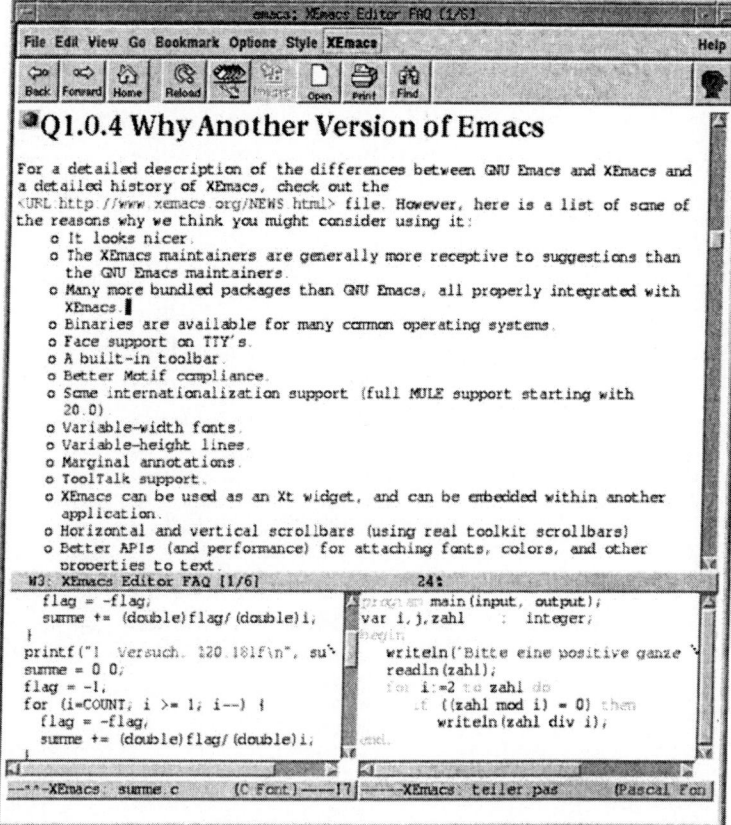

Fig. 7.6

xemacs as editor

and HTML browser

Shell Programs

The command interpreter (shell) is the direct interface between the user and the operating system. Its task is to analyze command lines, to expand or replace some command line values, if necessary, and then either to execute an action or to start a program. The shell reads individual command lines either from a terminal or from a file.

Additionally, the shell provides a command language enabling to the user to define application oriented commands by using already existing service programs. Like traditional standard languages, the shell programming languages include the basic concepts "variables" and "running structures".

Shell programs use variables and running structures

Following up Sect. 3.3, this chapter presents a detailed explanation of the language and operation of the internal shell programming languages. Sections 8.2 and 8.3 deal with the Linux command interpreters **bash**, **ksh**, and **tcsh**, and subsections explain such elements of the shell programming languages as shell variables, in/output, branches, loops, functions, and comments.

At first, the **bash** will be prominent. It is the standard shell of each LST distribution. As most of the language tools listed for the **bash** are also available in the **ksh**, this section is also directed to **ksh** users. Possible differences between **bash** and **ksh** are accordingly brought out in the text.

The bash is the Linux standard shell

Next, the language tools of the **tcsh** are explained. Some of these differ considerably from those of **bash** and **ksh**. The explanations are limited to additional possibilities of the **tcsh** and to language tools differing from those of the other shells treated before.

8.1 Linux Shells

Linux distributions are supplied by default with the Bourne Again shell **bash**, the TENEX-style C shell **tcsh**, and the public domain Korn shell **ksh**.

The bash integrates features of csh and ksh

bash is an AT&T-**sh** compatible command interpreter with various extensions. It was developed by the Free Software Foundation, mainly by Brian Fox. The aim of the project was to translate the guidelines of the IEEE POSIX Shell and Tool Specification 1003.2 and to integrate some useful features of **csh** and **ksh**. The programming language of the **bash** is largely compatible with **sh**.

The syntax of the tcsh language is based on the programming language C

tcsh is an extended version of the C shell developed by William Joy within the framework of Berkeley Unix. The C shell was especially widespread in the academic field, as in comparison to the Bourne shell **sh** used then, it already integrated a command line memory, an alias name, a completion of file names, and job control functions. The **tcsh** additions include command name completions and a command line editor. Its internal shell programming language is based on the language of the C shell, with a great similarity to the programming language C.

The Korn shell is the standard command interpreter of SVR4

ksh, as public domain version, provides a nearly complete implementation of the AT&T Korn shell, named after its author David Korn. As conceptual part of System V Release 4, the **ksh** can be found in each SVR4 operating system, where it is often the standard shell. It shares the main features of **bash** and **tcsh**. Its programming language follows the **sh** syntax.

Alias definitions introduce short names for complex commands

Each of the three types of shell processes commands from the command line or from files (shell scripts). They provide a number of internal shell commands, such as **cd**, **echo**, **kill**, **set**, and **test**, and various tools for controlling background processes (job control, **jobs**, **bg**, **fg**). The alias substitution makes it possible to call up commands or command sequences by using abbreviations. Further features include a command line memory (history), the completion of command and file names, and the ability to edit the command line.

Though, in the course of time, many Unix users preferred to use the C shell as command interpreter, shell programs have mainly been written in the **sh** syntax. Therefore, the majority of Unix operating systems are still supplied with both shell variants. Their successors **bash** and **tcsh** integrate largely corresponding concepts, at the level of the interactive command interpreter. Nevertheless, the **bash** is the preferred variant, especially among Linux users. Finally, the **ksh** differs only slightly from the **bash**, at least in comparison to the **tcsh**.

Existing shell programs are mainly written in the sh-syntax

8.2 **bash** and **ksh**

Shell programs or shell scripts are mainly command sequences combined in a file. Their central meaning for Unix is e.g. expressed in that way that a large part of the system initialization is achieved by running the shell scripts located in the **/etc/rc.d** directory.

During initialization, the operating system executes the shell scripts located in /etc/rc.d

The shell programming languages use two different kinds of variables: predefined ones and application-defined ones. The internal shell language tools for run control allow command sequences to be structured within a shell program. For this purpose, **bash** and **ksh** offer the following tools:

#

initiates comments. The shell ignores following character up to the end of line.

Comments explain the program text

{ *command sequence* **}**

corresponds to a **begin...end** block in which the list of commands is carried out in sequence.

(*command sequence* **)**

causes the shell to process a command sequence in a sub-shell.

if *command sequence1* then *command sequence2* fi
    carries out *command sequence2* only when *command sequence1* has terminated with status 0.

for *variable* do *list of commands* done
    repeatedly carries out the list of commands stated.

bash and ksh provide three loops: for, until, and while

while *list of commands1* do *list of commands2* done
    alternately carries out *list of commands1* and *list of commands2*, until the former terminates with a status other than 0.

until *list of commands1* do *list of commands2* done
    alternately carries out *list of commands1* and *list of commands2*, so long as the former terminates with a status other than 0.

case *variable* in *pattern*) *list of commands* ;; esac
    provides a kind of multiple branching.

Command sequences are linked together by ; or && or ||

Command sequences can be several commands or command sequences (see Sect.3.3.6). In particular, it is possible to run background processes and to use redirection operators.

Lists of commands are command sequences that may extend over several lines. Unlike command sequences, they also allow single commands to be separated by a line-feed.

Command sequences set in parentheses are carried out in a sub-shell. For example

Command sequences put in () are carried out in a sub-shell

    (cd /tmp; rm core)

changes the current working directory of the sub-shell and deletes the core file there, whereas the working directory of the active shell remains unchanged. The latter will not be the case if the command sequence is set in braces.

The if branching also allows if...else..fi (twofold alternative) and if...elif...else...fi (multiple branching) constructs.

With case, multiple branchings result from repetition of the constructs standing between in and esac.

8.2.1 Variables

Both **bash** and **ksh** provide a set of internal (predefined) shell variables. The user can also increase the number of shell variables. One must distinguish between local and global shell variables, where the shell bequeathes the latter to the process context of child processes. A shell variable's indicator consists of a letter followed by letters, numbers, or an underscore.

The shell bequeathes global variables to programs

Values of **bash** or **ksh** variables are always of character string type. Some commands, e.g., **expr**, allow them to be treated as numeric or logic values. For example, if two variables **a** and **b** include numbers, possibly with a leading character, the call

Values of bash and ksh variables are of the character string type

```
c='expr $a + $b'
```

will define a new variable **c** whose value is the sum of of **a** and **b**.

User-Defined Variables

A (**bash** or **ksh**) user may create new shell variables by assigning values with the syntax

```
variable=value
```

No spaces should be set before and after the equals sign

The shell understands **value** here as a character string. The latter must be set in apostrophes within parentheses if it includes space or tab characters. The shell variable can be removed with the call

```
unset variable
```

One can access a shell variable value by prefixing a dollar character. For example

```
echo $variable
```

displays the value of **variable** as a character string. If the value of a shell variable is to serve as a parameter and is directly followed by further letters or numbers, the variable name must be set in braces:

Variable indicators set in braces can be used as parameters

191

```
${variable}a
```

outputs the value of **variable** with the letter **a** directly after it.

Other than protected variables, such as the predefined variables **EUID**, **PPID**, and **UID**, the value of a defined variable can be

Read-only variables cannot be modified

modified by making another assignment:

```
readonly [-f] [name]...
```

tells the shell not to allow any modifications of the **name** variable. Protected shell variables cannot be deleted and cannot be translated into common shell variables.

Predefined Variables

Variables with command-wide validity include the components of the command line

The command interpreter uses some predefined variables with determined meaning, partly set by the command interpreter itself. One must distinguish between command-wide and session-wide validity shell variables (i.e., variables with command or session scope). Command-scope variables are only valid while a command is executed and mainly provide access to the command line content:

$0   provides the name of the program or shell script running,
$#   provides the number of program parameters,
$n   provides the value of the nth program parameter (n=0...9),
$*   outputs each program parameter as a character string,
$@   outputs each program parameter as a list of character strings,
$?   provides the final status of the command carried out last,
$!   provides the PID of the background process started last.

Note that the command-scope variables **$n** only separately include the first nine parameters. When the internal shell commands **shift n** are called, **$1** outputs the value of **$n**, **$2** the value of **$n+1**, and so on.

/etc/profile defines shell variables with system-wide validity

When it is initialized, the **bash** loads some session-scope shell variables from the system file **/etc/profile** and from the user-specific files **$HOME/.bash_profile** (**bash** Login) and **$HOME/.bashrc** (**bash**). The Korn shell **ksh** loads its configuration from **/etc/profile** and **$HOME/.profile**.

Furthermore, the command interpreter automatically sets a variety of variables. The most important predefined shell variables have the following meaning:

CDPATH	search paths for the cd command,
EUID	effective user identification,
HOME	standard directory for cd,
IFS	hyphens for command line elements,
PATH	search paths for commands,
PPID	PID of the shell's parent process,
PS1	first prompt sign of the shell,
PS2	prompt sign for following lines,
PWD	current working directory,
UID	user identification.

When called up without any argument, cd will change to $HOME

CDPATH and PATH

The variables **CDPATH** and **PATH** usually include directory lists, where the entries are separated from each other by colons. Before a program is called, the directories are searched one after another by $PATH until the program is located. When changing the directory, cd analogously searches through the $CDPATH paths if the target path stated cannot be reached directly.

CDPATH and PATH include a list of directory names

If the command interpreter refuses to call up a program, this will usually be because the **PATH** variable does not contain the directory where the desired command has been set. It would help to extend the lists of $PATH with

```
export PATH=new_path:$PATH
```

or

```
export PATH=$PATH:new_path
```

When setting a variable again, one has to use the "old" value

The call stated first will replace the content of the environment variable **PATH** by the old value with an additional path put in front. In the second case, the new path will be added to the list. The order of the search paths is important in so far as the shell always calls the first program found.

Prompt Variables

The ksh does not support any prompt formatting sequences

The **bash** includes some formatting sequences for conveniently configuring its prompt. However, the **ksh** prompt's appearance must be configured essentially with shell-variables and command sequences. The only "meta command" provided by the **ksh** is the exclamation mark, which creates a running command line number.

Formatting sequences **bash** must be preceded with the escape character \. The following character then tells the shell to incorporate the current date, working directory, user name, host name, and so on as part of its prompt sign. Figure 8.1 lists the most important formatting sequences.

Fig. 8.1 Sequences for formatting the prompt

Sequence	Result
`\u`	login name
`\h`	host name
`\t`	current time (HH:MM:SS)
`\d`	current date (day month year)
`\w`	working directory
`\n`	line-feed

To configure the **bash** prompt, one has just to assign a character string consisting of letters, variables, and formatting sequences to the **PS1** variable. For example, the definition of a **bash** prompt with a first line including the login name, followed by @, host name, space character, and the current time, and in a second line including the working directory and a angled bracket, can go as follows:

```
export PS1="\u@\h \t\n\w>"
```

The **ksh** prompt will get a similar appearance using

ksh prompts often contain program calls

```
export PS1=`${USER}@'/bin/host name' \
   'date "+%T"'${IFS}${PWD}>`
```

The sequence for forming the **ksh** prompt includes two command calls and uses three shell variables. Furthermore, note that three kinds of quotation marks are used for the assignment.

Braces with Quotation Marks

Sometimes it is necessary to formulate variables containing character strings as well as space characters and variables accessing them implicitly. The way the shell treats variable indicators is influenced by the braces chosen.

Variables put in double quotation marks " will be expanded, which means replaced by their value. This will not be the case if the user employs single quotation marks ´. With

```
PS1=´${PWD} >´
```

ksh users can make the shell prompt include the character string `´${PWD} >´` and ensure that the latter always outputs the current value of the PWD variable (the current working directory) when displaying the shell prompt. When changing the working directory, the PWD value alters. The shell prompt changes too, and mirrors the current working directory. If the expression has been put in double quotation marks, the shell will expand `${PWD}`, and the PS1 variable will then contain the character string included in PWD when assigned to PS1.

Values framed by ' are executed, and the shell replaces the expression put in braces by the result of the program call. For example, the command line

```
HOSTNAME='/bin/hostname'
```

sets the value of the HOSTNAME variable to the result of the /bin/hostname command. But let it be noted here that the shell replaces expressions put in such braces by the result of the command call located there. For example

```
ls -l 'which bash'
```

causes the shell first to carry out which bash and then to call up ls together with the -l option and /bin/bash as argument (the result of the expression put in braces). Figure 8.2 gives an overview of the shell's masking mechanism.

*"${PWD}"
provides the
current working
directory,
'${PWD}' provides
the character string
${PWD}*

meta character						
	´	"	'	\	$	*	key
´	T	N	N	N	N	N	T: terminator
"	N	T	J	J	J	N	J: interpretation
'	N	N	T	J	N	N	N: no interpretation

Fig. 8.2
Interpretation of
meta characters
put in braces

Global Variables

Even defined shell variables are primarily local variables in the sense that the shell does not transfer them to programs. In contrast to this, environment variables are global. The shell exports them to programs started by the shell. After

```
export variable
```

is called, **variable** will be a global one. The shell exports the variable to programs started afterwards. If no value has been assigned to **variable** before, the shell will export a variable without any value. To make things easier, the shell syntax allows the single call

```
export variable=value
```

to set global variables including a value.

After calling up
set -a, all newly
created variables
are automatically
global

Freshly set shell variables are automatically global if the internal shell command **set** has previously been called up with the **-a** option. Called up without an additional argument, **set** displays a list of the local and global variables. **printenv** reduces the output to global variables. **unset variable** deletes shell variables, local ones as well as global ones.

8.2.2 Input and Output

Complex shell scripts often require a dialog with the user, on the one hand, to ask for additional parameters needed, and on the other hand, to present the user with both provisional and final results. For this purpose, the command interpreter includes special input/output functions that among other thing facilitate the construction of query menus.

Default input and output channels are the standard input and output. When using redirection operators, the functions stated after them operate on file channels.

bash and ksh Input

The internal shell function **read** waits for an input line from the keyboard or reads a line from the standard input. Its general syntax,

```
read [-r] [variable] ...
```

causes a single line to be read from the standard input. A redirection operator directly after it allows a line to be read from the file:

```
read [-r] [variable] ... < file
```

Note that this method only considers the first line of **file**. If successive **read** functions are to read out an input file line by line, the input channel of the processing shell must be redirected.

If **read** is to assign values to several variables in one call, the function assigns all the characters up to the first separator (a character of the **IFS** variable) to the first variable, the following keyboard codes up to the second separator to the second variable, and so on. Successive separators are treated by **read** in the same way as a single separator.

If the number of separators is greater than the number of variables to be occupied by **read**, the variable stated last additionally receives all remaining characters on the line. Conversely, in case the input line includes fewer separators than variables to be occupied, **read** instead assigns the blank character string to variables standing at the end of line.

The **-r** option causes **read** to see the escape character \ as part of the input. Otherwise, the **read** function removes the escape character \:

```
read a
x\ny
```

replaces the variable **a** with **xny**, and

```
read -r a
x\ny
```

does so with **x\ny**.

If "variable" is lacking, the shell copies the result read to the variable REPLY

By default, IFS includes space, tab, and line-feed characters

Called up without -r, read removes each escape character from the input line

197

bash and ksh Output

e(ho -e
interprets the
control sequences
\a, \b, \c, \f, \n,
\r, \t, and \v

For the data output the **bash** and the **ksh** include the internal shell command **echo**. Additionally, the **ksh** includes an internal **print** function that carries out a default interpretation of control characters (\n creates a line-feed, \t a tab character, and so on). The **echo** command of **bash** and **ksh** only does this when it is called up together with the **-e** option.

By using redirection operators, **echo** and **print** perform an output to files. Referring to Sect. 3.3.5, we note that the operator > sets a new output file and >> either sets a new output file (if one does not already exist) or extends an already existing output file.

8.2.3 Branches

For commands or command sequences that are to be carried out on certain conditions only, the shell programming language provides branching commands **if...then...fi** and **case... esac**. The former operate on logical values (0 or not 0) and are usually only applied when there are just one or two alternatives, although a greater number of alternatives can be created by nesting the branch constructs. The **case...esac** construct evaluates an expression and performs multiple branching based on the character string value of shell variables.

if...then...fi

if-constructions
branch on logical
values, 0 is "true"

The general conditional branching

```
if   command sequence1
    then   command list1
[elif   command sequence2
    then   command list2]...
[else   command list3]
fi
```

carries out *command sequence1*. If the exit status of the last *command sequence1* command is 0, the **then** part will be carried out. Otherwise, the shell evaluates the following (optional) *command sequence2* initiated with **elif**. The corresponding **then** part will also be processed only if *command sequence2* provides the exit status 0. If an **else** command is put on the end of the sequence (in front of **fi**) then *command list3* will be carried out in case none of the queries performed returns 0.

The else-part will be carried out if none of the preceding conditions are met

The following example checks whether or not the password file **/etc/passwd** exists (should always be "true"), and counts the number of characters of **/etc/passwd** if the following condition is true:

```
if ls /etc/passwd
    then wc /etc/passwd
fi
```

For evaluating logic expressions, the shell includes an internal **test** command to be applied to **expression**, which outputs the result 0 if **expression** is true, otherwise 1. Furthermore, the shell allows just the syntax [**expression**] to be used for **test expression**. Figure 8.3 shows some often used one-digit **test** expressions, Figure 8.4 some often used two-digit expressions.

The internal shell test function creates the values 0 (true) and 1 (false)

Expression	True if...
–b file	file exists as block device file
–c file	file exists as character device file
–d file	file exists as directory file
–e file	file exists
–f file	file exists as normal file
–L file	file exists as soft link
–r file	file exists and is readable
–w file	file exists and is writable
–x file	file exists and is executable
–z string	string has length 0
string	string has length greater than 0
!expression	expression is not true

Fig. 8.3
One-digit test expressions

Expression	True if...
`file1 -nt file2`	`file1` is a newer file than `file2`
`file1 -ot file2`	`file1` is older than `file2`
`string1 = string2`	the character strings are identical
`string1 != string2`	the character strings are not identical

Fig. 8.4
Two-digit
test expressions

For example, the following `if` construction checks whether or not the file `/usr/X11R6/lib/X11/XF86Config` is a regular file. If this is not the case, `/etc/XF86Config` will be checked. The file that meets the condition will then be output together with its inode. Note that directly after the opening and before the closing square bracket a space character must be inserted.

After [and before]
a space character
must be inserted

```
if [ -f /usr/X11R6/lib/X11/XF86Config ]
    then ls -i /usr/X11R6/lib/X11/XF86Config
elif [ -f /etc/XF86Config ]
    then ls -i /etc/XF86Config
fi
```

As an alternative to `elif`, the shell also allows conditional branchings to be nested by inserting a further `if...then...fi` construction directly after `else`. In practice, though, it is more common to use `elif` instead.

`case...esac`

Multiple branching

```
case variable in
    pattern1)  list of commands1;;
    [pattern2)  list of commands2;;]...
esac
```

case branches
on patterns

is carried out by the first list of commands whose *pattern* fits the character string *variable*. The `;;` signs directly in front of `esac` are optional, and may be omitted.

The patterns stated can also include wildcards understood by the shell, especially `?`, `*`, and `[...]` for information on ranges. Note that a single `*` matches every variable.

Furthermore, in front of the bracket there can be several patterns separated by |. The shell interprets the list so derived as an or-connected pattern and carries out a list of commands if *variable* matches the corresponding patterns.

Patterns linked by the pipe character are interpreted as or-link by the shell

`case...esac` constructions are especially suitable for evaluating program parameters. For example, if a shell script `dir` includes the sequence

```
case $1 in
    /[Ww]) ls -C $2 ;;
    /[Pp]) ls -l $2 | more ;;
    *) ls -l $1
esac
```

its mode of operation basically corresponds to the DOS command `dir` with a permitted parameter and the target path as (optional) argument. When called up without any option, `dir` displays the contents of the current working directory or of a stated one, together with file type, access permissions, and so on. The `/P` (`/p`) option results in displaying the information page by page, and `/W` (`/w`) displays the file names column by column. The shell script `dir` is directly executable when execution permission has been set and the program is located in a directory included in the search path `PATH`.

8.2.4 Loops

The Bourne Again shell `bash` and the Korn shell `ksh` provide three different loops:

`for`loops take the number of loop flows to be executed from a list of words at the beginning;

`while`loops will be repeated until a condition stated at the beginning is broken;

The cancel condition always stands at the beginning of the loop

`until`loops are dual to `while`-loops; they will be repeated until a condition stated at the beginning is met.

for-loops

The number of loops corresponds to the "length" of the list

The construction

```
for variable [in list]
    do command list
done
```

assigns, in order, the elements of *list* to *variable* and then carries out *command list* as loop parameter with *variable*. The number of loop flows corresponds to the number of elements of *list*.

Within the loop, each element of the list can be accessed in order as variable

If the **in** *list* part is lacking in the construction, the command interpreter will replace *variable* by the arguments with which the shell script was called up, namely **$1** to **$n**. In this case, the number of loop flows will be **$#**.

In the following example the shell script requires a data file **$HOME/phones** containing the names and telephone numbers of each member of an organization line by line. Called up with a list of names, the sequence outputs the corresponding private data:

```
for i
    do grep $i $HOME/phones
done
```

If **list** contains wildcards, the shell first creates a list of all files from the current working directory matching the pattern stated. In Sect. 3.2 (p. 24), an example was given of a **for** loop using this technique (renaming a list of files).

while **and** until **loops**

For while and until loops, the result of a com- mand is controlled by the repetition

Whereas the number of loop flows of the **for** loop depends on the length of a parameter list, the execution of **while** and **until** loops is controlled by a command's exit status. The general syntax of the **while** loop is

```
while command list1
    do command list2
done
```

Having this construction, the shell will execute *command list2* only if the last command of *command list1* has provided the exit status 0. After each loop flow, the shell again carries out *command list1*.

An `until` loop is processed in nearly the same way, with the only difference that the loop will be repeated so long as the last command of the first list of commands outputs an exit status other than 0. Its syntax is

```
until command list1
     do command list2
done
```

`while` and `until` constructions can also be used to make infinite loops. This mode of operation is supported by the operating system with the commands `true` and `false`, which always provide the exit status 0 and 1, respectively. Additionally, `bash` and `ksh` include an internal `:` command that always provides the exit status 0. This command enables one to create interval-controlled daemons.

/bin/true and : output the exit status 0. /bin/false creates the exit status 1

8.2.5 Functions

Comprehensive shell programs can easily become confusing. Additionally, they sometimes contain identical program fragments at different places. Self-defined shell functions allow reuse of program fragments and construction of modular structured shell scripts.

Shell functions support the structure of modular structured shell scripts

A shell function consists of a function name and a list of commands with the syntax

```
name ()
{
     command list
}
```

When using `name` during the further shell script processing, the command interpreter carries out the `name` function's list of commands.

The exit status of a function is the exit status of the last command called up from the function

Like shell scripts, shell functions can process parameters. With $1, $2 and so on, the parameters can be accessed within the function. The number of parameters is $#. The $0 variable contains not the function name but the shell script name.

Unlike shell variables, shell functions are always local, which means they will not be exported and will therefore not be known in a sub-shell. In an interactive shell, shell functions work like the alias mechanism.

8.2.6   Starting Shell Programs

Shell scripts are carried out from a sub-shell

If a file includes command sequences, possibly structured with language tools from the shell programming language, and if this file is marked as executable in the file system, then the user can directly initiate their processing by entering the file name together with the program parameters required. Then, the command interpreter starts a sub-shell and the latter interprets the file line by line.

By means of a meta-comment, one can additionally determine which command interpreter will process the shell script. This meta-comment must be placed in the first line of the shell program. For example, the entry

A preceding meta-comment determines the shell to be executed by the shell script

```
#!/bin/ksh
```

ensures that the shell script will be processed by a Korn shell.

In any case, the user can start a shell script by entering the command line

```
sh [option]... script [parameter]...
```

where **script** can also have the status of a common (readable) file. Any meta-comments will be ignored when using this call convention. Of course, the line can also start with **ksh** instead of **sh**.

If a command within a shell script has an unusual end, the processing shell outputs an error message and continues processing with the next command. If the command interpreter discovers syntactic errors, the shell script terminates immediately.

8.2.7 Signals

Active shell programs also react on signals. The user can finish a shell script running in the foreground by entering C-c (SIGINT) and stop it with C-z (SIGTSTP). So, in this context, shell scripts behave in the same way as common programs.

C-c creates SIGINT,

C-z creates SIGTSTP

Sometimes it is desirable to protect shell programs against unscheduled termination or, before a signal-controlled kill, to carry out certain clear-up operations such as deleting temporary files. For this purpose, the shell includes the internal **trap** command allowing signals to be linked to actions. Its syntax goes

trap allows interception of exceptional situations

```
trap ´command sequence´ signal...
```

If a shell script running in the foreground has to remove all /tmp/vsx* files, say, before the user kills with C-c, then

```
trap ´rm /tmp/vsx*; exit 1´ 2
```

does the job. For this purpose, the internal shell command **exit** must be entered, as otherwise the shell continues processing the program. Additionally, the generic shell gets the **exit** parameter 1 as exit status.

Another **trap** application makes it possible to lock signals:

```
trap ´´ 1 2 3 15
```

After calling up trap 1 2 3 15, the shell again reacts on the signals locked earlier

within a shell-script running in the background, will be translated by the sub-shell into an independent process (see also Sect. 4.4).

8.2.8 Shell Internal Functions

The **bash** includes nearly 50 internal commands and the **ksh** about 40. For a complete explanation of all internal commands see the relevant manual pages. The following list explains internal shell commands that are used often and also form reserved words in the shell programming language.

. script performs the shell script **script** and is used for example to load variables and functions.

: provides the exit status **0**.

alias [name[=value]...] defines abbreviations for command sequence or shows the list of alias definitions.

bg [job] translates a program stopped with **C-z** into a background process.

break n finishes the surrounding **for** or **while** loop. If **n** has been stated, **break** finishes **n** layers.

cd [directory] changes the current working directory.

continue [n] jumps to the beginning of the surrounding **for** or **while** loop and continues the processing with the next variable value (**for**) or checks the kill condition (**while**). If **n** has been stated, the nth higher loop will be continued.

echo [option]... [variable]... outputs character strings and/or variable values.

enable [option]... [command]... switches on or off the usage of internal commands.

eval [Arg]... combines the parameters **Arg** in one command call and executes it.

exec [command [parameter]...] executes **command** without starting a child process (the shell process is replaced).

exit [n] terminates the shell with exit status **n**.

export [variable[=value]]... shows a list of exported variables, translates shell variables into environment variables, or defines environment variables.

fg [job] continues a stopped or a background process as a foreground process.

history [option]... [file] shows the contents of the command history, stores the list in a file, or reads a history from a file.

`jobs [option]... [job]...` provides information on all or some stopped and/or background processes.

`kill signal PID` sends a signal to the process with the number **PID**.

`logout` finishes a login shell.

`pwd` outputs the current working directory.

`read [-r] [variable]...` reads a line from the standard input and copies single words to **variable**. If the input **variable** is lacking, **read** copies the line to an internal variable **REPLY**.

`return [n]` finishes a shell function with exit-status n. If n has not been stated, **return** returns the exit status of the command carried out last.

`set [option]... [argument]...` sets one or more shell options or shows a list of defined shell variables,

set -o vi switches the command line editor to the vi mode

`shift [n]` reorganizes the command-scope valid shell variables. Afterwards, **$1** displays the value of the nth command line parameter, **$2** the value of **$n+1**, and so on.

`test expression` assesses conditional expressions.

`times` outputs the user and system time so far used by the shell and the processes started by the shell.

`trap [´ command ´] [signal]...` installs an exceptional function **command** that will be carried out when the shell receives **signal**.

`type [command]...` displays the position within the directory tree of each command located in the search path. Furthermore, **type** displays whether **command** is included in the alias list or whether it is an internal shell program or a shell function.

After calling up ulimit -c 0, no more core files will be created

`ulimit [option... [value]]` shows (option **-a**) or sets upper limits for maximum allowed file sizes, number of user processes, and so on.

207

`umask [-S] [modus]` shows or sets the mask for access permissions given when setting files.

`unalias [-a] [name]...` removes entries from the alias list or deletes its content (option `-a`).

`unset [name]...` removes each shell variable or shell function `name`. Removal of `PATH`, `IFS`, `PPID`, `PS1`, `PS2`, `UID`, and `EUID` is prevented by the shell.

`wait [n]` waits for process or job `n` to be finished. If `n` is not stated, the shell waits until all child processes are terminated.

8.2.9 External Help Programs

In addition to the internal shell commands, Linux distributions are supplied with some further commands preferential used for shell programming. These are in particular:

`basename name [ending]`

*basename deletes
leading directory
names from a path*

deletes all parts ending with `/` from the character string `name`, which limits pathnames to file or directory names by deleting leading directory names. If a second parameter `ending` has also been stated, `basename` will remove any matching ending. For example, the program

```
for i in *.c
   do mv 'basename $i .c'\
      'basename $i .c'-alt.c
   done
```

renames each `*.c` file in `*-alt.c` located in the current working directory.

`dirname name`

has, so to speak, the opposite effect as `basename`, which means it removes the file or directory on the last layer.

expr **expression...**
> evaluates or estimates **expression** and copies the result to the standard output. **expression** consists of terms (numbers, character strings, and operators) separated by space characters. Special shell characters (**|**, **&**, **>**, **<**, *****) must be masked. The following operators are allowed:

shell variables within expression will not be expanded if expression was set in single quotation marks

> **expression1 | expression2**
>> outputs **expression1**, if its value is not **0**, otherwise **expression2**.

> **expression1 & expression2**
>> outputs **0**, if one of the two expressions is blank or **0**, otherwise **expression1**.

> **expression1 {< <= = != >= >} expression2**
>> displays the result of a comparison. If the operands are numbers, **expr** carries out a numeric comparison, otherwise a lexicographic comparison.

> **expression1 {+ - * / %} expression2**
>> outputs the result of an arithmetic link. If **expression1** or **expression2** is a character string, **expr** creates an error message.

The % operator works like the modulo function

> **expression1 : expression2**
>> compares the character string **expression1** with a regular expression **expression2**. If **expression2** does not match, the result is **0**, otherwise **expr** returns the length of the character string.

> **(expression...)**
>> puts expressions into parentheses divided in groups.

false
> outputs the exit status **1**.

getopt options string
> expands options from the character string **string**. The **options** argument is a joined string of one-digit option characters (without the space character). If a colon follows after an option character, **getopt** will be told to interpret the following character string in **string** as the option

value. As result, **getopt** returns a newly prepared list of parameters, where the end of the option is indicated by the character --:

getopt can also
"take apart"
-l 66 -n

```
getopt nl: -n166 file
```

analyzes a list of the parameters sent to **pr** (creating line numbers, 66 lines per page) and outputs the result

```
-n -1 66 -- file
```

The **getopt** command can only process option lists beginning with a hyphen.

printf format [argument]...

printf formats
numbers of
character strings
according to a C
format string

outputs the arguments according to a format description. The latter must be put together from directives consisting of the percent sign **%** and following format information in the syntax of the C function **printf**. Control commands beginning with the escape character \ will also be interpreted (\n, \t, and so on). In most cases, it is necessary to put the format description in quotation marks.

sleep [time[smhd]]

creates a stack. The following command will be carried out **time** seconds (**s**, standard), minutes (**m**), hours (**h**) and days (**d**) later.

8.3 **tcsh** Programs

The syntax of tcsh
programs roughly
corresponds to the
programming
language C

Shell programs in the **tcsh** syntax use language tools quite similar to those of the programming language C. Conditions evaluating branchings or loops are put in parentheses. Blocks within a running structure do not require a preceding **do**, and only the end of the block is marked by **end**, **endif**, or **endsw**.

There is no thing like a **read** function in the **tcsh**. Input commands are carried out by assigning the predefined variables **$<** to a user-defined variable. Characters following **#** on a line are interpreted as comment by the shell **tcsh**. Shell-functions can be made compatible via the alias mechanism only.

In comparison, however, the variable concept of the **tcsh** is powerful. In addition to common character string variables, the user can also define numeric variables and field variables. When assigning values to a variable, an expression can also be stated that, like to the argument to the **expr** command, consists of operands and operators.

The user can initialize tcsh variables with expressions

The stock of **tcsh** internal commands is to a great extent identical to the **bash** and **ksh** internal functions. So, for an excerpted overview see Sect. 8.2.8.

8.3.1 tcsh **Variables**

In contrast to **bash** and **ksh**, the **tcsh** user creates local variables by entering

```
set variable = value or @ variable = value
```

and global (character string) variables are created with

```
setenv variable value
```

Variables declared with @ (followed by a space character) can include numeric values only. Conversely, accessing such variables results in a numeric value. Conversion with **expr** is not therefore necessary. The sum from **a** and **b** to **c** can be assigned with the call

Variables declared with @ include numeric values

```
@ c = ( $a + $b )
```

Spaces can be set before and after the equal sign

In this definition, not a single value but an expression will be assigned to the (numeric) variable **c**. Expressions will be allowed with numeric, logic, and bit operations (analogous to those of the programming language C).

Array Variables

The **tcsh** also allows fields (one-dimensional arrays) to be declared with

```
set field = (a_1 a_2 ... a_n)
```

or with `setenv` instead of `set`. The expression `$field` outputs each element of the variable, `$#field` the number of field

$#field provides the number of elements of an array variable

elements, `$field[n]` the nth field element, `$field[n-k]` the values of the elements n, n+1, ... k, `$field[-k]` the first k elements and `$field[k-]` all elements from the kth index on.

Fields that are to contain values must be declared in advance with `set` or `setenv`, with in the field size desired. With

$$\text{set field} = (\text{\$field a\_n+1 ... a\_n+k})$$

the field size can be extended at a later point in time, where the fields added can also be entered at the beginning or in the middle:

$$\text{set field} = (\text{a\_0 \$field[-3] a\_4 \$field[4-]})$$

Numeric arrays must be defined as normal field variables and occupied with numbers component by component

Afterwards, numeric values can be assign to the elements of the field variable using

$$\text{@ field[2] = 4711}$$

As an alternative to the explicit assignment of values, the operators `+=`, `-=` `*=`, `/=` and `%=` are also allowed to modify existing variable values.

Furthermore, the `tcsh` allows protection of local variables (`set -r`), after which it is not possible to give a new definition or to delete (`unset`).

Predefined Variables

In contrast to `bash` (and `ksh`), small letters are used for the predefined `tcsh` variables. In the `tcsh`, the variable `cwd` (current working directory) takes the place of the `bash` variable `PWD`, and the `tcsh` prompt variable `PS1` is called `prompt`. There are further differences between `bash` and `ksh` variables and `tcsh` command-scope variables.

the tcsh copies command line arguments to the array variable argv

`$argv`	outputs the complete command line,
`$#argv`	outputs the number of program parameters,
`$argv[0]`	outputs the name of the program started,
`$argv[n]`	outputs the value of the nth program parameter,
`$argv[*]`	outputs each program parameter,
`$$`	outputs the PID of the running shell.

When accessing the **nth** command line argument, **n** can be any number at all from **0** to **$#argv**. So, in principle, the function **shift** needed for **bash** and **ksh** programs is not needed to enable the program to use internally the values of the 10th and following arguments. Nevertheless, the **tcsh** includes an internal function

```
shift [variable]
```

Called up without an argument, the **shift** function deletes the element **argv[1]** and shifts each following field element one position to the left. Otherwise, **shift** applies this treatment to the field variable stated.

The predefined session-scope shell variables include

cdpath	search paths for the **cd** command,
cwd	current working directory,
gid	the user's group identification,
home	standard directory for **cd**,
owd	last working directory,
path	search paths for commands,
prompt	first shell prompt,
prompt2	prompt for subsequent lines,
status	exit status of the last command,
uid	user identification,
user	login name of the user.

owd of the tcsh corresponds to OLDPWD of the bash

cdpath and path

The **tcsh** variables **cdpath** and **path** are field variables, hence, they contain a list of pathnames. The shell links the contents of **path** to a common environment variable **PATH**; the contents of both variables are automatically compared by the shell. When accessing **path** it is possible to enter a new path in a certain position:

The tcsh links the array variable path to a common variable PATH

```
set path = ( $path[-3] . $path[4-] )
```

inserts the current working directory **.** after the third search path.

213

Prompt Variable

Like the **bash**, the **tcsh** provides a number of formatting sequences for defining variable prompts. The quit symbol is the percent sign %. Figure 8.5 summarizes the most important **tcsh** prompt format sequences.

Fig. 8.5

Sequences for

tcsh prompt

formatting

Sequence	Result
%n	login name
%!	running command number
%M	complete host name
%m	host name without domain name
%P	current time (HH:MM:SS)
%T	current time (HH:MM)
%D	current day (dd)
%W	current month (mm)
%y	current year (yy)
%Y	current year (yyyy)
%/	current working directory
\n	line-feed
%?	exit-status of the last command

8.3.2 Input and Output

The **tcsh** command for reading in a text line from the standard input is **$<** and is normally used directly with a variable initialization thus

```
set variable = $<
```

With this call convention, **variable** will get each character up to the first separator. If an input line consists of several "words", the user can assign each word of the line to a field variable by using

```
set variable = ( $< )
```

As with **bash** and **ksh**, the internal shell command **echo**, which normally copies to the standard output, serves the purpose of creating an output. Output to files can be achieved by using redirection operators.

The interpretation of control characters within a list of **echo** parameters is controlled by the variable **echo_style**. If its value is **sysv** or **both**, **tcsh-echo** translates the character string **\t** into a tab, creates a line-feed at **\n**, and so on.

echo_style deter-mines the way control characters are treated by tcsh-echo

8.3.3 Branches

The **tcsh** includes language tools for branchings to one, two, or more directions.

```
if ( expression ) command sequence
```

carries out a one-line command sequence, if **expression** evaluates to 0.

tcsh if-constructs branch on the logical value of an expression

```
if ( expression )
    then
        command list
    endif
```

is an extension of the conditional command consisting of one line. Commands standing between **then** and **endif** can be displayed between line-feeds.

```
if ( expression )
    then
        command list1
    else
        command list2
    endif
```

is the split-branching. If **expression** evaluates to 0, the **tcsh** processes *command list1*, otherwise *command list2*. Nested **if** branchings additionally require **if...endif** constructions as part of a list of commands.

The tcsh does not contain an equivalent to bash-elif

Branches to different directions within a **tcsh** program is enabled by the following **switch** construction:

breaksw within a
case branch
terminates the
switch construction

```
switch ( text )
    case pattern1: list of commands1 [; breaksw]
    [case pattern2: list of commands2 [; breaksw]]...
    [default: list of commands]
endsw
```

The shell examines each pattern in turn and executes the respective list of commands, provided `text` fits the pattern. In contrast to the `case` command of `bash` and `ksh`, the comparison will be made for each pattern stated. If the shell should not examine further patterns after a list of commands has been executed, a `breaksw` command must be entered as the last command of a `case` block. The latter terminates the `case` branching. Then, the shell executes the command following `endsw`.

8.3.4 Loops

Like `bash` and `ksh`, the `tcsh` provides three different kinds of command loops.

The component
(list) of a foreach
loop is absolute
necessary

```
foreach Index ( list )
    command list
end
```

repeats *command list* according to the number of elements from `list`. Within the loop, `Index` (as local variable) successively represents the elements from `list`.

```
while ( expression )
    command list
end
```

The number of
loop runs of a
while loop can be
controlled with
numeric values

before each loop run, analyzes `expression` (similar to the `expr` command) and repeats *command list*, until `expression` provides a value other than 0. The `while` loop is used for stating a determined number of loop runs:

```
@ a = 5
while ( $a > 0 )
    echo $a; @ a -= 1
end
```

executes the loop five times; the parameter used for the kill condition is modified within the loop.

```
repeat n command
```

executes a single command exactly **n** times. The parameter **n** can be a positive whole number or the value of a numeric or a character string variable. If the **repeat n** command is followed by a command sequence, only the first command of the sequence will be carried out a second time. If a command sequence is set in parentheses, **repeat** creates an error message.

repeat only repeats some commands

8.3.5 Jump Command

The jump command makes it possible to continue a **tcsh** program at a place indicated by a mark. The command

```
goto mark
```

causes the shell to search for a program line including the expression

```
mark:
```

The program is then continued with the next command.

The tcsh carries out forward and backward goto jumps

8.3.6 Signals

Like the **bash** and the **ksh**, the **tcsh** includes a mechanism allowing a special treatment in case of incoming signals.

```
onintr mark
```

tells the shell to jump to a mark when a **SIGINT** signal occurs and to continue processing the program there. If the argument to **onintr** is the hyphen **-**, the shell ignores the **SIGINT** signal. If **onintr** stands alone, the **tcsh** does not carry out a special treatment on receiving **SIGINT** signals.

On receiving a SIGINT signal, the tcsh jumps to a goto mark

217

Networked Systems

Unix was developed with the aim of supporting the teamwork and communication of several programmers. Furthermore, based on services, the operating system in its present form can integrate remote systems. While terminal service, file service, and electronic mail (email) have become part of the popular services of almost all operating systems, Unix stands out against most competitors because of its ability to export performance to foreign systems.

Networked Unix systems can exchange messages and services

Linux integrates almost all mechanisms for communicating with remote workstations known from other (Unix) systems. The relatively new operating system kernel was able to integrate the most recent developments practically from the outset.

Linux integrates almost all common net services

To communicate with each other, systems first of all need to link computers, by connecting two or more workstations via a transmission medium. Usually, the latter is either a common cable, a light wave conductor, or a radio contact. Each terminal within a computer network forms a node. The physical and logical map of a computer network, the network architecture, follows a topological structure (network topology).

In a computer net each end device forms a "node"

The actual exchange of information between networked systems is controlled by software components. The task of the operating system kernel is to embed send commands from the user in a protocol and to relay it to the physical transmission interface or to send incoming messages to an application.

The kernel acts as mediator between the network hardware and the applications

For this purpose, in the course of time, various protocol families have been specified. Independently of industrial standards by producers influenced, the International Standards Organization ISO developed the Open Systems Interconnect

Unix systems communicate via TCP/IP protocols

Reference Model OSI with the aim of creating a basis for uniform communication in heterogeneous systems. However, actual communication, especially between Unix systems, is based on the "DoD standard" TCP/IP.

The nodes are identified with logical and physical addresses

A further precondition for data transfer within a computer network is the addressing scheme, which has to ensure an unambiguous identification of the data stations linked with each other. Here, one has to distinguish between logical and physical addressing. While the transmission medium uses hardware addresses that cannot be changed (Ethernet address, telephone number), the systems operate among each other on the basis of configurable logical addresses.

9.1 Network Topologies

With the basic equipment, a PC is only partly suitable for networks

Computer networks are mainly created by connecting two or more computers via electrical or optical cables or radio waves. For establishing such connections, PCs contain serial and parallel interfaces as basic equipment. In addition, plug-in cards are available for supporting a computer connection via Ethernet, FDDI (Fiber Distributed Data Interface), modem (modulator/demodulator) or ISDN (Integrated Services Digital Network).

Local networks are often constructed in an uniform technology

Equipped with these components, several systems can be connected to a local area network (LAN), and it is possible to establish a connection to a wide area network (WAN). To clarify the terminology: a LAN needs little space, has a uniform technology, a high transfer rate, and a limited number of users, whereas WANs are created by connecting different network technologies and are not subject to any space limits. In principle, the number of users in a WAN is unlimited, the transfer rate between different systems is rather low.

Each computer network structure follows a network topology. Today, the main ones used are bus, star, ring, and tree nets.

In a bus topology, the systems use a common cable for communicating. A star topology has a point-to-point connection from a central point (concentrator) to each network node. In a ring topology the systems are linked up to the cable network in a closed ring. A tree topology can be created by cascading several concentrators. Figure 9.1 illustrates these topologies.

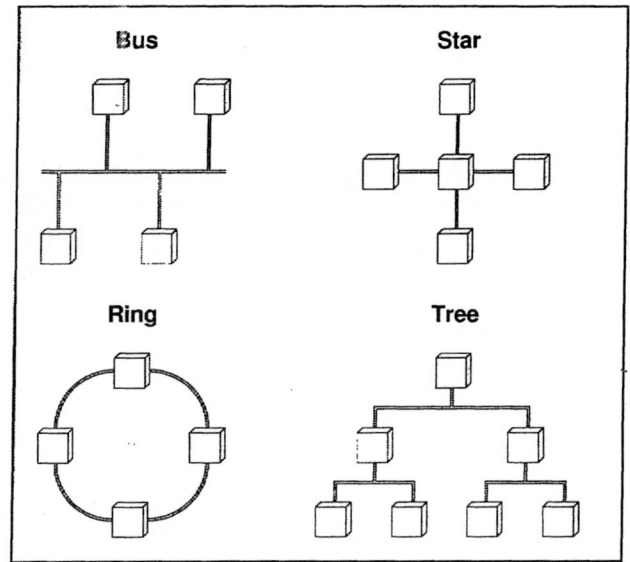

Fig. 9.1
Bus, star, ring, and
tree topologies

Larger networks often result from hierarchically connecting single subnets representing different topologies (hybrid network topology). For example, in a larger enterprise with several buildings, the systems in a department are linked with each other via a bus net. Within the building, the departments' subnets flow together in a star configuration. The buildings are connected with a ring net.

Large networks are produced by connecting several subnets

Usually, average-sized or large networks use some further hardware components. Ethernet-based networks often include a transceiver, which adapts the Ethernet signal to a special type of wire (Thin-Wire 10Base2, Thick-Wire 10Base5, Twisted Pair 10BaseT). Repeaters work in effect as boosters and used whenever relatively long wires are needed for connecting two or more systems.

A concentrator, also called a hub, forms the link within a star net. There, several "rays" meet. Bridges connect two nets of the same kind in such a way that local data transfer within one segment does not load the second segment (they will carry only data addressed to systems outside the local segment).

Bridges connect subnets of the same kind

A gateway connects any subnets at all

A router, on the other hand, connects two similar or different networks (of different topology) and also carries out a protocol transformation, if necessary. Furthermore, the router delimits address areas from each other. Gateways, finally, are computer systems connecting any networks at all with each other. Besides converting protocols, they also transform addresses.

Modem and ISDN adapter make it possible to access WANs

For the private network user, it will normally be enough to connect the accessible computers via local Ethernet in a bus topology. Then, Wide Area Networks can be accessed via a system providing a modem (analog data transfer) and/or an ISDN adapter (digital data transfer), which so to speak forms the gateway.

9.2 Protocol Families

From the user's sight, the physical information transfer from one (Unix) computer to another is successful only just because of a connecting medium (copper wire, optical fiber or radio channel), and the logical component of the communication is realized by a program translating the service desired.

Proprietary network applications use unstandardized protocols

The first computer networks may have been operated on the basis of this theory. At the very beginning, producers each implemented their own ideas for computer networks, and communication between systems from different computer worlds was mostly possible only with additional technical effort.

Influenced by university and commercial developments, a variety of network protocols emerged in the course of time to determine the structure of an electronic message. Many great number of these protocols, still used today, were developed for a certain network architecture and for the services it offered.

The OSI model is internationally standardized

The first steps to unify computer based message transfer were taken by the International Standards Organization ISO in 1977. Under the working title "Open Systems Interconnect Reference Model", the ISO developed the 7-layer model OSI (ISO 7498) with the purpose of ensuring an error-free exchange of information between any network applications at all. The first documentation of this work was published in 1982.

So far, however, the OSI standard has served mainly as a theoretical model. Although today some products are available that include OSI plus all protocols and applications defined there, OSI was not as successful on the market as had been hoped. Instead, further protocols and interface definitions were developed later.

Only few producers have translated the OSI standards

AppleTalk controls communication between Macintosh computers and peripheral devices linked to them, and NetBIOS, an integral part of IBM's OS/2 operating system, connects PCs. For Windows NT and Windows for Workgroups, Microsoft declared NetBEUI as the standard protocol, and Novell developed IPX for controlling communication within NetWare based networks.

AppleTalk, NetBIOS, NetBEUI, and IPX are widespread within the PC world

Popular network protocols mainly found outside the PC world include SNA, DECnet, X.25, UUCP, and TCP/IP, all developed long before personal computers appeared.

Since 1974, SNA (Systems Network Architecture) has been developed as a hierarchically oriented network for controlling terminals, suitable for the demands of IBM mainframe systems. Up to now, SNA has been constantly extended. When personal computers became available end devices, the APPC (Advanced Program to Program Communication) concept was added to the SNA. APPC provides a convenient interface for communicating transaction programs.

SNA serves the purpose of connecting terminals with an IBM mainframe

DECnet is a group of hardware and software products for controlling communication between systems from the manufacturer Digital Equipment. Development began in 1975 and now consists of five stages. Each stage is compatible with its predecessor. In stage III, X.25 and extended routing mechanisms were added. In stage IV, Ethernet was integrated. Besides coupling DEC systems, it is also possible to connect PCs and to address public networks. Stage V realizes the ISO/OSI (DECnet/OSI, 1994) standards.

Originally, DECnet was intended for coupling DEC systems

Since 1977, under the supervision of the French Comité Consultatiy International Télégraphique et Téléphonique CCITT, the protocol X.25 has been developed. It defines an interface controlling access to public networks (Public Data Network PDN). An example of an X.25 network is DATEX-P (Datex Packet Switching Network) run by Deutsche Telekom. X.25

X.25 describes packet based data transfer in a public PDN

223

describes packet based data transfer between devices connected to the PDN. Each data packet consists of an address part and a data part, encoded as 128 bytes.

Furthermore, X.25 formed the foundation for developing the amateur packet-radio link-layer protocol AX.25. Here, the communication medium is a radio channel. Data transfer is carried out packet by packet in the form of analog modulated UHF/VHF signals.

AX.25 packages
are sent by radio
amateurs

UUCP (Unix-to-Unix-Copy) was developed in the Bell Laboratories in about 1977. The aim was to establish communication between existing Unix systems. UUCP combined a collection of programs enabling data transfer and initiation of remote applications via a serial connection. UUCP based networks are hardly used any more, but this protocol was a milestone on the way to global networks. For example, the first Netnews system, in a way the predecessor of today's Usenet, was realized by using UUCP tools.

UUCP was
developed for
serial communi-
cation between Bell
Laboratories Unix
systems

The most popular standard protocol for Unix operating systems became the Transmission Control Protocol/Internet Protocol TCP/IP. Since 1983, TCP/IP has been an official part of Unix. TCP/IP combines several application programs developed within the framework of the first packet-switching network ARPANET (in 1969 ARPANET was established under the overall control of the American Department of Defense). One of the TCP/IP protocol family members is the Telnet protocol, proposed as early as 1971. In LAN networks, TCP/IP connections usually communicate via Ethernet.

TCP/IP combines
several protocols
in a family

Today, TCP/IP is available not only for Unix operating systems, but also for practically all important hardware platforms. Furthermore, TCP/IP is the basis for exchanging messages within the Internet. For further details on TCP/IP see Sect. 9.4.

Based on TCP/IP, the Serial Line Internet Protocol SLIP has been developed to meet the demands of communicating via serial routings. In 1984, first implementations for 4.2 BSD and SunOS were realized. At the latest when it was included in 4.3 BSD, SLIP was considered to be a *de facto* standard. Additionally, Compressed SLIP (CSLIP) handles compressed files. Parallel Lines IP (PLIP), on the other hand, controls com-

SLIP and CSLIP
control the
exchange of IP
packets via serial
routings

munication between two systems connected via parallel interface (printer port).

SLIP and its variants require that two systems be directly connected and that the computers affected know their network addresses (IP addresses) for routing purposes. Furthermore, SLIP has no error identification and only allows IP datagrams to be send.

In 1988, the Point-to-Point Protocol PPP was defined as a kind of successor to SLIP. PPP includes error control, supports the establishment of connections via dial routings, and can encode several protocols (IP, IPX, DECnet, AppleTalk).

PPP is a multi purpose and safe protocol for serial connections

Linux supports the following network protocols: UUCP, TCP/IP, SLIP, CSLIP, PLIP, PPP, AppleTalk, IPX, and AX.25. In future, one can expect compatibility with DECnet. Operating all these protocols under Linux requires the corresponding modules to be integrated into the operating system kernel and suitable device drivers for the interface hardware.

9.3 OSI

The ISO/OSI model is practically the only international standard guideline for linking open communication systems. Though it is strongly criticized for largely following traditional telephone engineering, OSI, as a producer-independent model, claims to form the basis for future developments regarding the whole of data communication.

OSI is a producer-independent model

OSI uses a 7-layer model to define LAN protocols and applications. Each layer communicates with the layers directly above and below. The first 4 "transport-oriented" layers define the data transport. Starting at the top, they control the structure and maintenance of a connection, the coupling of the transport nets, the segmentation of data packets, and the transfer of bit sequences using any medium at all. The components of the three remaining "application-oriented" layers are communication control, data representation standardization, and the application operated by the user. Figure 9.2 represents the OSI model layers.

OSI consists of 4 transport oriented and 3 application-oriented layers

225

Fig. 9.2
The seven OSI
model layers

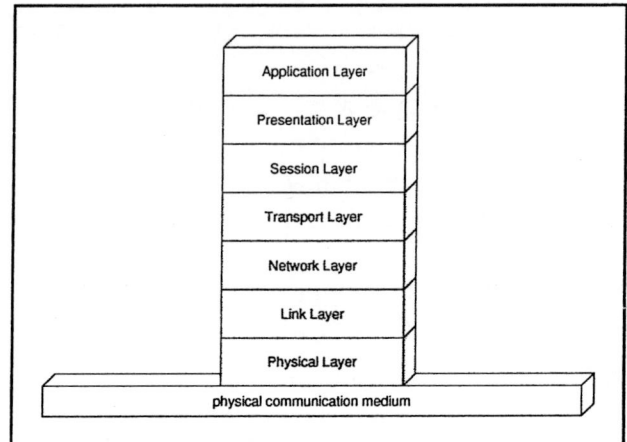

Layer 1 defines
hardware
parameters

On the lowest level, the physical layer defines mechanical and electrical specifications for interface cards and connection routings.

The data link layer above it establishes the connection of end systems and controls data transfer. There, data packets are encoded in chunks including not only the actual data but also control information (sender and recipient addresses, packet size) and the protocol used in higher layers. A further task of the data link layer is to handle transfer errors occurring in the physical layer.

The network layer
carries out the
routing

The network layer determines the network routing and dials the transport net addressed, e.g., with Internet Protocol IP. Additionally, in this layer the information to be transferred is dismantled into datagrams.

In the last level of the transport-oriented layers, the transport layer is responsible for data integrity, and also controls data transfer.

On the lowest application oriented level is the session layer. Its task is to establish, close, and control sessions and to synchronize dialog units.

The presentation
layer is created by
an architecture-
independent
data format

The presentation layer located above it converts received data, so that it can can be understood by the applications, or transforms data from the application side into a uniform format.

Finally, the application layer defines the specific applications that can be used by the levels below. These include, for example, mail programs and file transfer programs.

9.4 TCP/IP

The Transmission Control Protocol/Internet Protocol TCP/IP arose from the need to ensure secure data exchange between systems linked together in the experimental ARPANET (Advanced Research Projects Agency Network) developed by the Department of Defense. ARPANET was intended for connecting computers used for military purposes. Also involved in this project were industrial and university research institutions, such as the Massachusetts Institute of Technology (MIT).

TCP/IP was the first used in ARPANET

TCP/IP, since 1983 an official component of Unix, was proposed in 1974 by Vinton G. Cerf and Robert E. Kahn (MIT). It is a collection of several protocols that complement one another. It was intended to be used for different media and computers, and can mediate between any subnet regardless of the computer hardware, operating system, and network architecture used. Figure 9.3 is a schematic presentation of some TCP/IP components.

TCP/IP is an official part of Unix

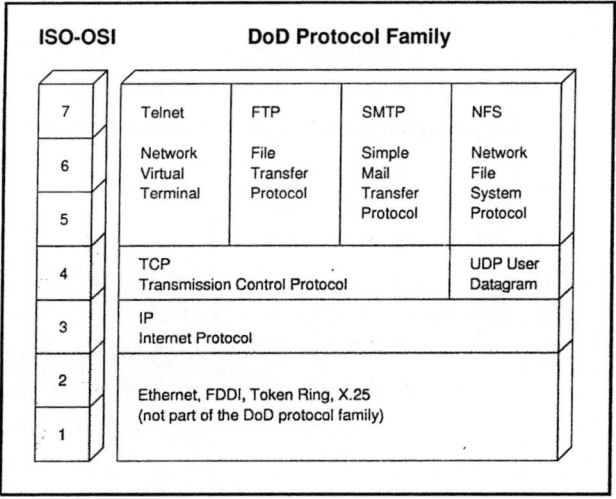

Fig. 9.3 Components of the DoD protocol family

IP forms a link-less protocol that packs data into packets (datagrams), addresses the recipient (by transforming a logical Internet address into a physical network address), and transfers the data.

IP defines packet oriented data transport

A datagram consists of an address component and a data component. The packet must have at least 576 and at most 65 535 bytes. Referring to the OSI model, IP realizes the network layer. A number of interface descriptions control IP compatibility with various transfer media, such as Ethernet, FDDI, X.25, and serial connections.

A datagram consists of an address component and a data component

TCP is a link-oriented protocol based on IP. TCP ensures that IP datagrams reach the recipient in the right order. This will always be necessary when IP datagrams are sent in parallel via several media and individual packets arrive at the recipient in a different order than they were sent. Additionally, TCP is designed to inform the sender whether or not the transfer was successful. If transfer errors occur, TCP asks for the data to be resent. TCP corresponds to the fourth layer of the OSI model (transport layer).

TCP controls data transport

Additional TCP/IP elements include various application programs. These make basic services possible, such as remote login (controlled by Telnet or Rlogin), file transfer (File Transfer Protocol FTP,), and electronic mail transfer (Simple Mail Transfer Protocol, SMTP).

Today, several other protocols are based on TCP too, such as the Network News Transfer Protocol NNTP (controls access to Usenet) or the External Data Representation Protocol XDR. The latter was developed by Sun Microsystems. XDR defines a hardware-independent data format, meaning it realizes the demands of the OSI reference model's presentation layer (OSI Level 6). Protocols using XDR include the Remote Procedure Call RPC and the Network File System NFS.

XDR defines an architecture-independent data format

Another linkless TCP/IP protocol is the Address Resolution Protocol ARP (locating physical addresses) and the Internet Control Messages Protocol ICMP. As a link-oriented protocol, the User Datagram Protocol UDP has been added to the collection. This forms in effect the "check free" equivalent to TCP. Following the OSI model, the UDP is parallel to TCP.

ARP changes Internet addresses into Ethernet addresses

In local networks, the receiving order of IP datagrams usually corresponds to the sending order. With regard to Ethernet as transfer medium, high reliability is ensured and just a minimum protocol specification is required. So, essentially it is possible to operate applications reliably using UDP. Protocols defined on top

X terminals and diskless clients use either BOOTP or TFTP

228

of UDP include, for example, the Trivial File Transfer Protocol TFTP and the Bootstrap Protocol BOOTP.

A variety of documents on protocols belonging to the TCP/IP family and on topics somehow connected with computer net- works, and in particular with the Internet, are collected in the "Request For Comments" document series RFC, which com- menced publication in 1969. The documents are published at irregular intervals and can be found on many FTP servers.

Furthermore, protocols in the DoD protocol family are de- fined as MIL-STD military standards. Figure 9.4 shows the RFC numbers and the MIL-STD numbers under which the network protocols stated here are documented.

Protocol	RFC	MIL-STD
ARP Address Resolution Protocol	826	
BOOTP Bootstrap Protocol	951	
FTP File Transfer Protocol	765	1780
ICMP Internet Control Message Protocol	792	
IP Internet Protocol	791	1777
NNTP Network News Transfer Protocol	977	
PPP Point-to-Point Protocol	1661	
SMTP Simple Mail Transfer Protocol	821	1781
SUN-NFS Network File System Protocol	1094	
SUN-RPC Remote Procedure Call Protocol	1057	
TCP Transmission Control Protocol	793	1778
TELNET Telnet Protocol and Options	854	1782
TFTP Trivial File Transfer Protocol	783	
UDP User Datagram Protocol	768	
XDR External Data Representation	1014	

Fig. 9.4
TCP/IP RFC
documents

9.5 System Addresses

If several computers are connected, successfully addressing a certain system requires that each system be unambiguously identified. Ethernet encodes each packet with the sender's and the recipient's identification.

*Ethernet addresses
are unchangeable
physical addresses*

Ethernet addresses consist of six two-digit hexadecimal numbers. Within Unix it is common to write Ethernet addresses according to the format

```
aa:bb:cc:dd:ee:ff
```

In the Internet, the system identification is defined by four two-digit hexadecimal numbers, written as four decimal numbers divided from each other by dots, thus:

```
aa.bb.cc.dd
```

(dotted quad notation). The unambiguous distribution of Internet addresses is controlled by a central committee, the Network Information Center NIC.

*Internet addresses
and domain
addresses are
logical system
identifications*

To simplify the addressing of special systems it is common to address a host by stating its host name, possibly extended by the network name (domain name):

```
ftp.informatik.uni-erlangen.de
```

Systems outside the LAN can be addressed in that way, too.

Each kind of addressing presupposes, that existing hardware components and a logical structure over them have been configured. The latter determines for the local operating system kernel which net participants the hardware run by it constitutes and how it can reach other systems.

9.5.1 Internet Addresses

*The assignment of
network addresses
is controlled by the
Network Informa-
tion Center NIC*

An Internet address encodes a network address in the leading numbers and a host address in the remaining area. The number of figures (or rather, the number of bits) of the host address depends of the LAN size. There are three predefined classes of local networks:

large networks (class A) encode the network address in the leading eight bits and reserve 24 bits for the host address. Addresses of large networks range from `1.0.0.0` to `127.0.0.0`, and each net can address up to 1.6 million hosts (in subnets), middle size networks (class B) use 16 bits for the network address and the same number for the host address. From `128.0.0.0` to `191.255.0.0` there is space for 16 320 networks, each of which can include up to 65 024 hosts,

small networks (class C) use eight bits for the host address (254 hosts) and encode network addresses in 24 bits. The latter are located between `192.0.0.0` and `223.255.255.0` (about two million network addresses).

192.168.2 is a "free" network address

The remaining area from `224.0.0.0` to `254.0.0.0` is reserved for experimental and future networks.

The network address `127.0.0.0` plays a special role. It is used for host local IP communication. Normally, the host address `127.0.0.1` is linked to the loopback interface. Thereby, it is possible to use and test network software without concrete a physical nection to other systems. For example, with

The loopback device is a software interface

```
telnet 127.0.0.1
```

the user can initialize a Telnet session with the local host.

In each subnet, host addresses with the values `0` or `255` in each column are additionally reserved. Addresses with host bits set to `0` represent the subnet itself. The address with host bits all set to `1` is the broadcast address.

A message addressed to a subnet's broadcast address is received by each host there. For example, if one wants to send an inquiry to each host located in the network `192.47.11.0`, the relevant datagram should be addressed to the broadcast address `192.47.11.255`.

Messages addressed to the broadcast address are received by each subnet host

In an Ethernet based network, a particular data station can only be addressed via its Ethernet address. According to the address conventions of the Ethernet protocol, the operating system's IP component must replace the Internet address of the target system by its Ethernet address.

The key to locating the target system's (physical) Ethernet address is provided by the Address Resolution Protocol ARP. The latter sends a datagram to the broadcast address of the subnet where the searched computer system is located. There, each host then compares the IP address received with its own, and the

ARP sends a datagram to the broadcast address

system that "matches" the IP address sends back its Ethernet address. The "broadcast host" then stores the remote Ethernet address in its ARP cache, but discards it after a while.

Conversely, the Reverse Address Resolution Protocol RARP makes it possible to get IP addresses from Ethernet addresses. For example, RARP is necessary when a diskless client (a system without local hard disk) consults a remote host for system initialization.

9.5.2 Domain Addresses

A domain address includes the host name as well as the organization and a place identification

Without a doubt, it is laborious and also old-fashioned to identify a computer system with a sequence of numbers. The alternative is to address individual systems by their host name, possibly extended by the domain name. The host name usually consists of several letter combinations separated by dots, which build up place names and organization names. For example,

```
ftp.informatik.uni-erlangen.de
```

indicates the ftp server of the computer science faculty of the Erlangen University, Germany. The contraction `de` (top-level domain) is the name of the country.

Country codes follow the ISO standard 3166

Each country outside the USA has a two-letter code as top-level domain according to ISO 3166. Top-level domains in the USA use the identifications `edu` (universities and educational institutions), `com` (commercial enterprises), `org` (non-commercial organizations), `gov` (official administration), or `mil` (military).

The resolver translates domain into IP addresses

As the addressing in TCP/IP networks expects 32-bit Internet addresses, the domain addressing needs a kind of translator, converting domain addresses into IP numbers. This is done in the operating system "resolver", which consists of a handful of library functions. In the simplest case, the resolver takes a host name or a host address and creates a structure containing both. For this purpose, it is only necessary to analyze the host name database located in `/etc/hosts`.

If the searched system is not included in the local host table, the resolver asks the name server's name daemon to resolve the domain address.

In small LANs, it is usual to install identical host tables in each system. From time to time, a system will also be configured as name server. In middle-size networks, however, the Network Information System NIS (developed by Sun Microsystems), will often be used. A NIS central master host provides the host table and, when asked, supplies a NIS client with all the data needed.

The name server will only be consulted if /etc/nsswitch.conf contains the entry dns in the hosts field

9.6 Network Services

In Sect. 4.6 some network-wide daemons are mentioned that support certain services. In particular, daemons analyze incoming (IP) datagrams and send back locally created information to the sender. In this context, the terms "server" and "client" are normally used:

the client is the system or program initiating an action in order to use a service.

the server is the system or program receiving incoming service demands and processing them accordingly.

On the target system, some server programs have to be active continuously (as daemons, started in `/etc/rc.d/rc.inet2`), others are activated by the Internet superserver `inetd` if needed. The latter plays the key role for often used basic services, as it receives incoming inquiries from the network and uses any service code included to start a subdaemon.

Unix daemons reply to a client's service demands

The majority of the network services are therefore available on demand only. Conversely versa, this technique reduces the need for system memory, as only those subdaemons are active that are responding to a request.

Clients or network applications, on the other hand, ask the server for a service. The dialog-oriented network applications of a Linux distribution support terminal emulations,

file transfer,

Some tools include

electronic mail (email),

a convenient

dialog with other users, and

graphics interface

access to information systems.

Furthermore, the Linux distribution's range of features includes several "batch services", such as remote printing, remote execution, a name service, network analysis, and a network file system. The batch and dialog-oriented Linux network applications are dealt with in Chap.10.

9.7 Network Configuration

Normally, the Ethernet interface is configured by the installation script (e.g., `lisa`, see Sect. 5.6.9). Ethernet-based TCP/IP communication with other systems located in the LAN should therefore succeed practically right from the start. If a serial connection to remote systems is planned, the time needed for the configuration depends on the kind of connection intended.

sz and rz make it
possible to transfer
data during a login
connection

If it is planned to use the local system as a terminal of a remote computer, then in practice it is usually only necessary to address the target system. Of course, the system administrator can also enable remote systems to login serially on the local system. With some limits, these kinds of operation also allow copying processes, e.g., by using the commands `sz` (Send ZMODEM) and `rz` (receive ZMODEM).

SLIP and PPP
configure a serial
routing for general
network services

A more convenient connection to a remote system via serial routings is provided by SLIP and PPP connections. In these modes of operation, several local applications can address, more or less in parallel, the general TCP/IP services of a remote system, and vice versa. After a connection has been established, the operating system runs SLIP or PPP device drivers (`sl0`, `sl1`, ..., `ppp0`, `ppp1`, ...) for this purpose. PPP can run TCP/IP, IPX, or AppleTalk connections, but SLIP can only offer TCP/IP communication.

9.7.1 Serial Login

It is relative easy to establish a common terminal connection via a modem routing. In practice, one just has to call up a program operating a modem routing (e.g., **kermit** or **seyon**). The connection will be established after a dial command is entered: **ATDP*number*** causes pulse dialing and **ATDT*number*** causes tone dialing of the telephone number **number**. If the modem is connected to a local telephone exchange that does not support tone dialing by default, the user first has to tell the modem with **ATX3** to ignore the tone dialing.

Some local telephone exchanges only allow pulse dialing

After the connection is successfully established, the remote system asks for an access permission to be entered, indicated by a login prompt. If the user afterwards enters a valid user identification and the password, the remote system will load a command interpreter. In this mode of operation, the local system functions as an ASCII terminal.

Configuring the local system as n login server is also relatively easy. With reference to Sect. 5.6.7, we simply mention that only a common **getty** process operating on a serial routing has to be entered in **/etc/inittab**. If one additionally wants to receive fax messages, one should use **mgetty+sendfax**, developed by Gert Döring.

Local terminals are to be linked via a null modem cable

9.7.2 SLIP Connections

To configure a SLIP connection, one normally uses the **dip** program (Dialup IP), which must work with the superuser's rights. **dip** includes an interpreter analyzing a language similar to Script. Normally, the user creates a **script.dip** file summarizing the commands needed and then The User calls up **dip script.dip** to establish a SLIP connection to a remote system via modem (in the **/etc** directory, the LST distribution contains an example file **sample.dip**).

With the slattach program, an existing connection can be switched to the SLIP mode

Conversely, the system administrator can configure the local system as a SLIP server. Then, for each authorized user, the administrator successively enters into **/etc/diphosts** the user name, a password, the host names or IP addresses of the remote

235

and the local system, the netmask, a comment (optional), and the protocol to be used, separated by colons.

New dip versions can also establish PPP connections

The protocol field must include two components separated by a comma, namely the protocol name (SLIP, CSLIP or PPP) and the maximum permitted packet size MTU. The following entry enables the user `mf` of the system `jeannie` to get SLIP access to the local computer `ares`:

```
mf:dip-pwd:jeannie:ares:255.255.0.0::SLIP,296
```

In a second step, the authorized users in `/etc/diphosts` must be entered in the `/etc/passwd` password file. As login-shell, `/usr/sbin/diplogin` must be entered, for example

```
mf:*:501:100:SLIP:/home/mf:/usr/sbin/diplogin
```

diplogin is a soft link on dip

If the user `mf` tries to access `ares` from `jeannie` via a serial routing, the `/usr/sbin/diplogin` login shell analyzes the `/etc/diphosts` file, asks for the decoded `diphost` password, and configures the serial routing as a SLIP connection following successful validation.

9.7.3 PPP Connections

Many providers and computer centers support PPP

PPP is a standard protocol, today offered as dial-in possibility by the majority of the Internet providers and by universitary computing centers. In contrast to SLIP, PPP allows the systems involved to exchange information while a connection is being established. So, it is possible to allocate IP addresses dynamically. In particular, a PPP server can assign an IP address to a PPP client (the system establishing a connection). Authentication mechanisms integrated into PPP serve the purpose of protecting against unauthorized establishment of a PPP connection.

Addresses used often are entered in the local host table

Before establishing a PPP connection, it is helpful to enter identifications used by the remote system as domain names and name server in the resolver file `/etc/resolv.conf`. Furthermore, it is recommended to add addresses used often to the local host table, to limit the demand for inquiries to the name server. If the local system has no Ethernet interface, one should additionally ensure that the loopback interface is configured.

A connection is actually established with two programs, the **pppd** daemon and the **chat** dial-up program. To kill an existing PPP connection, one just has to quit the daemon process with **kill**.

*A connection is
established with
pppd and chat*

chat usually analyzes a **chat-script**, but it can just as well get the parameter needed for establishing a connection from the command line. For example,

```
chat -v ATZ OK ATDT4711 CONNECT \
     ogin: mf word: ppp
```

sets aside the modem (**ATZ**), waits for the **OK**, and then dials the number **4711** using tone dialing. After receiving the **CONNECT** character string, **chat** waits for the **ogin:** string, answers with the user identification **mf**, and then (after receiving **word:**) sends the password. Note that in the command line, **CONNECT** must be followed by two space characters. Finally, the **-v** option causes **chat** to inform the syslog daemon about its activities, and the latter registers them accordingly. Incidentally, it is not advisable to enter the options to **chat** in the command line, as each user can have a look at the command line parameters when calling up **ps** and so, among other things, can see the user identification and the password.

*chat addresses the
target system and
carries out the
login*

An additional capability of **chat** is that the program can abort a connection if the routing is occupied or an error occurs. Furthermore, **chat** will terminate if the modem creates a character string that the user has previously told **chat** by means of the keyword **ABORT**. Several abort conditions require several **ABORT** commands. Figure 9.5 shows a **chat** script for aborting the connection when one of the four character strings stated is received.

```
ABORT "NO CARRIER"
ABORT "NO DIALTONE"
ABORT BUSY ABORT ERROR
"" +++ATZ
OK ATDT4711
CONNECT ""
ogin:--ogin: \qmf
word: \qppp
```

*Fig. 9.5
A chat script
as example*

`ogin:--ogin:` is a subexpect-subsend string: if the modem does not receive the `ogin:` character string, `chat` sends a return signal and again waits for `ogin:`.

The escape sequence `\q` in front of the user's identification and password causes `chat` not to pipe the character strings to the syslog daemon, which means the corresponding data will not be entered in the `/var/log/debug` file.

pppd connects the serial routing with the kernel's PPP driver

When `chat` has established a connection with a remote system, the PPP daemon `pppd` can link the serial routing to the PPP kernel driver. `pppd` must work with superuser rights, which means it must belong to `root` and include the set user ID bit in its list of attributes. For example,

```
pppd /dev/cua1 38400 crtscts modem defaultroute
```

With transfer rates over 9600 baud, hardware handshake will be necessary

converts the device driver `/dev/cua1` into PPP mode and establishes an IP connection to the system previously addressed. The communication routing operates with a transfer rate of 38 400 baud and uses hardware handshake (RTS/CTS). Additionally, the `pppd` will be told to enter the target system as the standard route in the routing table. At this call, the IP address of the target system is gathered from the local host table by `pppd`.

`pppd` can also call up `chat` implicitly. For this purpose, one just has to enter the `connect` option in the command line and to add a suitable `chat` call.

IP addresses to be used can be set or called up by pppd

Furthermore, `pppd` can cause the computers involved to use special IP addresses. If the command call includes the option `local_addr:remote_addr`, the PPP connection of the local system operates on the address `local_addr`, and the remote computer can be addressed with `remote_addr`. If the user just sets the value for `local_addr`, `pppd` will ask the target system for the `remote_addr` value. If `local_addr` is set on `0.0.0.0`, the target system assigns a "dynamic" IP address to the local computer.

Figure 9.6 summarizes the steps necessary for establishing a PPP connection with dynamic address allocation in a shell script. The `/etc/ppp/ppp.chat` file used there contains a `chat` script, such as that in Fig. 9.5.

Options to be used by **pppd** can also be summarized by the superuser in the **/etc/ppp/options** file. The PPP daemon loads this file before analyzing the command line options. The latter must exist in any case, but may also be empty.

```
LOCALIP=0.0.0.0
REMOTEIP=
DEVICE=cua1
PPPFLAGS="9600 modem debug defaultroute"
chown root /dev/$DEVICE
chmod 666 /dev/$DEVICE
exec /usr/sbin/pppd lock connect \
     '/usr/sbin/chat -v -f /etc/ppp/ppp.chat' \
     /dev/$DEVICE $PPPFLAGS $LOCALIP:$REMOTEIP
```

Fig. 9.6
Establishing a PPP
connection with
pppd and chat

If additional authentication is desired, the PPP option file must include the keyword **auth**. PPP supports two methods: the Password Authentication Protocol PAP, which works like the login mechanism and the Challenge Handshake Authentication Protocol CHAP. In contrast to PAP, CHAP also makes security queries at regular intervals for PPP connections that are already active. If the **auth** option is set, PPP tries to make first a CHAP, and then a PAP authentication. If neither method is successful, PPP aborts the connection.

CHAP offers high
security for PPP
connections

The files responsible for the authentication are called **pap-secrets** and **chap-secrets**. They are to be deposited in the **/etc/ppp** directory. The two files have an identical structure. Each line contains the names of the target system and of a server (which carries out the authentication), a security key (as character string), and optionally the name of the system to which PPP is to establish a connection.

Finally, we briefly repeat the steps for structuring a PPP server. To do so, the superuser just enters a PPP user in **/etc/passwd** and assigns the **/etc/ppp/ppplogin** shell script as login shell to the user. Figure 9.7 shows an example of a **ppplogin**.

```
#!/bin/sh
mesg n
stty -echo
exec /usr/sbin/pppd -detach silent modem crtscts
```

Fig. 9.7
Login script for
an external PPP
access

TCP/IP Applications

The aim of this chapter is to give an overview of the variety of application programs that enable Linux users to access network services. To get a general idea of the network services supported under Linux, see the enumeration of network daemons in Sect. 4.6.2.

An introductory section explains some tools that generally serve the purpose of testing the network interface. The following next sections explain how to handle `telnet` and the "Berkeley r Utilities". The latter were originally developed for TCP/IP-based access on BSD Unix systems.

The Berkeley r Utilities have been developed for BSD Unix

Next, some dialog-oriented applications using the TCP/IP protocol are discussed. Sections deal respectively with terminal emulators, data transfer, email, news, and applications allowing communication in real time with other LAN or Internet users. Some applications of these categories include appealing graphical interfaces, although these can only be used over the X Window System (see Chap. 11).

Some dialog-oriented TCP/IP applications include graphical interfaces

A final section deals with accessing information systems. In particular, applications will be presented for searching for programs, files, or special documents over the Internet.

The World Wide Web is a global information system

10.1 Network Analysis

The commands responsible for configuring a TCP/IP connection were mentioned in Sect. 5.6.9 (Ethernet configuration, `ifconfig`, `route`) and 9.7 (SLIP and PPP configuration, `dip`, `pppd`, `chat`). There, the meaning of the local host table

The resolver converts a domain name into an IP address

/etc/hosts and the task of the resolver library that converts domain addresses into IP addresses were discussed: the configuration files /etc/host.conf, /etc/nsswitch.conf and /etc/resolv.conf control the resolver's mode of operation. In the following, some tools are listed that allow the configuration to be tested.

The hostname command displays the host name and hostname -d outputs the domain name

The hostname command outputs the local system's host name. In addition, the call hostname -d displays the name of the domain to which the local system belongs. This information is also provided by dnsdomainname; the latter usually is a hard link on /bin/hostname. The host name will be set during the boot process. The superuser can change it while the system is running. By default, the host name of the local system will be stored in the /etc/HOSTNAME file.

When called up without any option, netstat outputs each active network connection

route and netstat -r display the routing table entered in the kernel. The superuser can modify the routing table with the route command to add new entries or remove existing ones. route add creates a route either to a host or to a network. The /etc/networks file links network names to network addresses, and in effect forms the network equivalent of the file /etc/hosts.

ping checks whether or not a remote system can be addressed

With ping host, the user can check whether or not a connection to the host system is possible. In particular, the ping localhost command shows whether or not the loopback interface of the local system can be addressed, and ping 'hostname' checks the connection to the IP address standing in front of the local system's host name in the /etc/hosts file. ifconfig displays a list of locally configured IP addresses and the corresponding network interfaces.

nslookup and host pipe an inquiry to the name server

Information on the IP address and domain name of a remote system is provided by host and nslookup. These need either an IP address or a domain name as argument. As a result, host and nslookup display the IP address as well as the target system's domain name.

traceroute displays each gateway passed by a datagram on its way to a target node

The traceroute command, too, processes an IP address or a domain name. traceroute additionally outputs a list of all the gateways passed by a protocol packet on its way to the target. Each entry in this list contains the domain name and the IP address of each node passed as well as the time (in milliseconds) needed by a datagram to go from one node to the other.

Finally, we mention the `tcpdump` program, which can display all incoming datagrams starting from a TCP/IP interface. The program is often used for analyzing a local network.

10.2 `telnet`

The `telnet` program is a network client including a user interface for accessing the Telnet protocol. The call syntax goes

`telnet [option]... [[-l user] host [port]]`

`telnet` mainly serves to establish a login connection to a remote system by using the TCP/IP protocol. The values of the environment variables `TERM` and `DISPLAY` are piped to the target system's shell by `telnet`.

DISPLAY and TERM of the removed shell receive the values set locally

Called up without host identification, `telnet` switches to the command mode and asks the user to enter a `telnet` command. Commands available in this operation mode are displayed by `telnet` after a question mark `?` is entered. During the period of a connection, the user can switch back to the command mode with `^]`.

If a host identification (in the form of a host name or an IP address) was stated in the command line, `telnet` tries to establish a connection to the address stated, i.e., it automatically carries out the `telnet` command `open host`. Then, the target system asks the user to enter a user identification and the corresponding password.

Before authenticating, the remote telnet daemon copies the file /etc/issue.net to the local standard output

The user identification will not be asked for if `telnet` is called up together with the option `-a` (automatic login) or `-l user`. In both of these cases, `telnet` gives its own option (option `-a`) or a special user identification to the target system while the connection is being established.

By default, `telnet` addresses port 23 of the target system and asks for the Telnet service of the addressed host. By stating a port number `port` the user can contact an alternative service.

For example, `telnet host 13` provides the current system date of `host` and thereby creates a similar result as the command `rdate host` (see Sect. 10.3).

Some servers offer games, sports reports, weather reports, etc.

On some servers accessible via the Internet, special services have been set up that can be accessed via free port numbers. A survey of such services is included in the `internet.services` document, which can be found for example on the `ftp` server `ftp.uni-augsburg.de` in the `/pub/info/DOCs` directory.

10.3   Berkeley r Utilities

rlogin, rsh, and rcp are a part of every Unix version today

The Berkeley **r** utilities make it possible to transparently access remote systems on which the user has access permission. They mainly support the establishment of a TCP/IP-based login connection (`rlogin`), allow execution remote service programs (`rsh`), and offer access to remote files (`rcp`). Today, `rlogin`, `rsh`, and `rcp` are supplied with BSD as well as with AT&T Unix derivatives.

$HOME/.rhosts includes a list of trusted user

A special feature of these three commands is that the user can access a remote system without entering the password. For this purpose, a `$HOME/.rhosts` file just has to be set on the target system listing host and user names of trusted users line by line. If no user name is given, a user with identical user identifications on the trusted host stated as well as on the target system will get access.

In addition, the superuser can set a system-scope file `/etc/hosts.equiv` analogously containing a list of trusted hosts, possibly combined with their user names. Another possibility for `rhosts` authentication is to bar certain users or hosts free access. If an entry in `/etc/hosts.equiv` or `$HOME/.rhosts` starts with a minus sign, the user so specified must always enter the password.

rusers shows a list of each active LAN user

In the course of time, some further programs have been added to the Berkeley **r** command family. These commands ask a target system for special status information (`rdate`, `ruptime`, `rusers`, `rwho`), send messages to each active user in the net (`rwall`), or create information on one or more users (`finger`).

The latter is useful for getting personal information on a certain user:

```
finger mf@ares
```

displays parts of the user's password entry `mf` (login name, comment, home directory, login shell) and gives information on whether or not the user `mf` is currently active on the system `ares`. Furthermore, the finger daemon of the target system searches through the user's home directory `mf` for the files `plan` and `.projects`. If these files exist, the finger daemon copies their contents to the standard output of the calling system.

finger @host creates a list of the users active on host

The commands `rdate`, `ruptime`, `rusers`, `rho`, `rwall`, and `finger` do not use the `rhost` authentication. Instead, they send an inquiry to the target system's `inetd` that checks, by analyzing the `/etc/inetd.conf` file, whether and how the service required must be executed. If a system refuses one or more services, the superuser must comment out the corresponding entry from `/etc/inetd.conf`.

The user has to remove undesired services from /etc/inetd.conf

10.3.1 `rlogin` Remote Login

The command

```
rlogin [option]... [-l user] Host
```

rlogin

establishes a login connection to a remote system `host`. If the `-l user` option has been stated, `rlogin` uses the user name `user` to establish the connection. In both cases, the user gets free access to the remote system if he or she is registered as trusted user there.

The `rlogin` command passes on the environment variable `TERM` to the target system. Remote applications using the termcap or terminfo mechanism (e.g., `vim`), should therefore run faultlessly right from the start.

The `rlogin` connections can be terminated with either the `logout` or the `exit` command. Furthermore, the user can temporarily stop the `rlogin` connection. To do so, one enters the `rlogin` escape character (ASCII tilde ~) and then `C-z` on the keyboard. In the command line, the user can set the `rlogin` escape character to be used with the `-e` option.

A temporarily terminated rlogin connection is reactivated by entering fg

245

10.3.2 rsh Remote Shell

The command

```
rsh [option]... [-l user] host [command]
```

carries out an application **command** on the system **host**. It pipes local (keyboard) inputs to the remote system and redirects remote outputs to the local standard output or the local standard error channel. **rsh** requires that the user is registered as a trusted user on the target system.

Command sequences must be put in quotation marks

Command can be either a single command with command line parameters or a command sequence. Command sequences are to be put in single or double quotation marks. Note that the shell interprets meta characters put in double marks and pipes meta characters put in single marks (see Sect. 8.2.1, p. 195). **rsh** terminates after the remote command has terminated. If **rsh** is called up without the argument **command**, it establishes a login connection to the **host** system.

Examples

rsh jeannie ls -l /tmp displays a comprehensive list of the files located in the **/tmp** directory of the system **jeannie**.

rsh ares "cd /home/mf; tar cf - ." | tar xvf - switches to **ares** in the **/home/mf** directory and copies the directory hierarchy located there to the standard output using the **tar** format. A locally running **tar** command extracts the **rsh** call result to the current working directory.

10.3.3 rcp Remote Copy

The commands

```
rcp [option]... file1 file2   and
rcp [option]... [-r] file... directory
```

copy files between two systems, if the user is registered as trusted user on the target system. In any case, **rcp** can only set a target file if the user has write permission in the directory addressed. Similarly, `rcp` can only copy source files for which the user has read permission.

Files located on remote systems must be stated in the format `[user@]host:path`. If `user@` is missing, `rcp` accesses the remote system under the local user identification. If `path` is not initiated with `/`, then `path` describes a file relative to the home directory of `user`. Otherwise, `rcp` interprets the `path` argument as an absolute path statement.

When linked with the `-r` option, `rcp` copies a list of source files or directories together with the subdirectories located there. The last argument to `rcp` must then be a directory name.

rcp -r copies complete directory hierarchies

If a file name is to include wildcards, then either the wildcard must be masked with a backslash `\` or the file name must be put in quotation marks to prevent interpretation by the local shell.

Examples

`rcp -r ares:/tmp/a\* /tmp` copies each file `/tmp/a*` of the host `ares` to the `/tmp` directory of the local system.

`rcp -r ares:/tmp /tmp` copies the `/tmp` directory located on the host `ares`, together with all the files and subdirectories included there, to the local `/tmp` directory. Each source file is then located in the `/tmp/tmp` directory.

`rcp -r "marion@ares:/.[A-z]*" .` copies each dot-file of the user `marion` of the host `ares` to the local directory.

10.4 Terminal Emulators

In Sect. 7.2 it was mentioned that the first Unix version had to be operated via external terminals. It was also mentioned that it is no problem now to connect any terminal at all, because the termcap or terminfo mechanism sees that ASCII-oriented applications can operate without hitch on nearly every ASCII terminal.

External terminals can be operated without any problems under Linux

In addition to the ASCII terminals intended for processing text information only, graphics-capable terminals were linked to

Unix systems later on. These terminals were the only way to use graphics applications under Unix until workstations became available.

Terminal emulators on the other hand, are programs copying the behavior of an ASCII or graphics terminal to a (virtual) console or to a Window system's window. Combined with an additional communication program, they allow a login connection to be made with a remote system. For example, the UUCP program cu (call Unix) has been developed for communicating via serial routing, and telnet establishes a login connection via a TCP/IP communication routing.

A terminal emulator is software copying the behavior of an external terminal

To users of the X Window Systems, xterm forms a terminal emulator controlling a session either with the local or with a remote system (see Sect. 11.4.2). xterm includes a DEC VT-102 and a Tektronix 4014 emulator (monochrome graphics).

xterm emulates DEC VT-102 and Tektronix 4014 terminals

From an xterm application, the user can establish a connection to a remote system with cu, telnet, rlogin or rsh. For ASCII-oriented applications a DEC VT-102 emulation is provided, and graphics applications can be controlled by the Tektronix 4014 emulator. xterm stores all the ASCII outputs in an internal buffer. A user who has activated the scrollbar can scroll back to earlier screen contents.

Trying to access a remote system from the console via cu, telnet, rlogin, or rsh can cause some problems. The reason is that some operating systems do not contain a suitable termcap or terminfo entry for the terminal type linux, and therefore, screen-oriented applications, like the vi or emacs, cannot be used at present. Explicitly setting the environment variables TERM to vt100 helps a little. It is true that the terminal type linux is not completely compatible with vt100, but the most important basic functions use identical control sequences. A terminal emulator that can do graphics is still not available for making a connection to remote systems from the console's side.

The basic functions of the Linux console are compatible with the DEC VT-100 terminal type

As an accessory for Linux, the popular product kermit is freely available. kermit is a communications program which, in the course of time, has been adapted to nearly every computer platform. Remote systems can be accessed via a serial routing as well as via a TCP/IP connection. kermit emulates the terminal

kermit emulates a DEC VT-102 terminal

type DEC VT-102. A Tektronix 4014 emulator exists in part, but there is no access to the Linux version. `kermit` is not supplied with the Linux distributions by default.

The `seyon` telecommunications package exclusively supports modem-based access to remote systems. Normally, an `xterm` application serves as terminal emulator there, so that `seyon` can emulate either an ASCII terminal of the type DEC VT-102 or a Tektronix 4014 graphics terminal via a common login connection. Appealing menus offer comprehensive control of the serial routing to be operated. A user-specific telephone book allows a connection to be established just by pressing a certain key.

seyon is a telecommunications program using an xterm window as terminal emulator

As an alternative to `xterm`, the XView toolkit includes the products `cmdtool` and `shelltool` which can also be used only over the X Window System. They emulate the terminal types `sun` and `sun-cmd`, and can for example be used as `sun` or `sun-cmd` emulators in connection with `cu`, `telnet`, `rlogin`, `rsh`, `kermit`, or `seyon`.

The XView toolkit includes the cmdtool and shelltool Sun emulators

Like `xterm`, `cmdtool` provides a scrollbar allowing the user to access earlier screen contents. Unlike `xterm`, however, `cmdtool` offers further useful functions such as menu-based searching for character strings, saving the text buffer in a file, and activating an internal editor. While the system is running, from the menu bar the user can switch off the scrollbar and so change to the operation mode `shelltool` (in the Linux directory tree, `shelltool` is a soft link to `cmdtool`).

cmdtool offers some useful editor functions

Furthermore, within X11 applications, Linux includes the `x3270` program, which can establish a Telnet connection to the local system or to a remote one. This product was developed in particular for communicating with IBM mainframe computers. `x3270` emulates various 3270 models displaying 80 or 132 columns in 24, 27, 30, or 43 lines (IBM 3278-4, IBM 3279-4). A connectable "keypad" provides access on function keys. Figure 10.1 shows the `x3270` emulator together with the corresponding keypad.

x3270 is designed for communicating with IBM mainframes

Fig. 10.1
The x3270
emulator with
graphical keypad

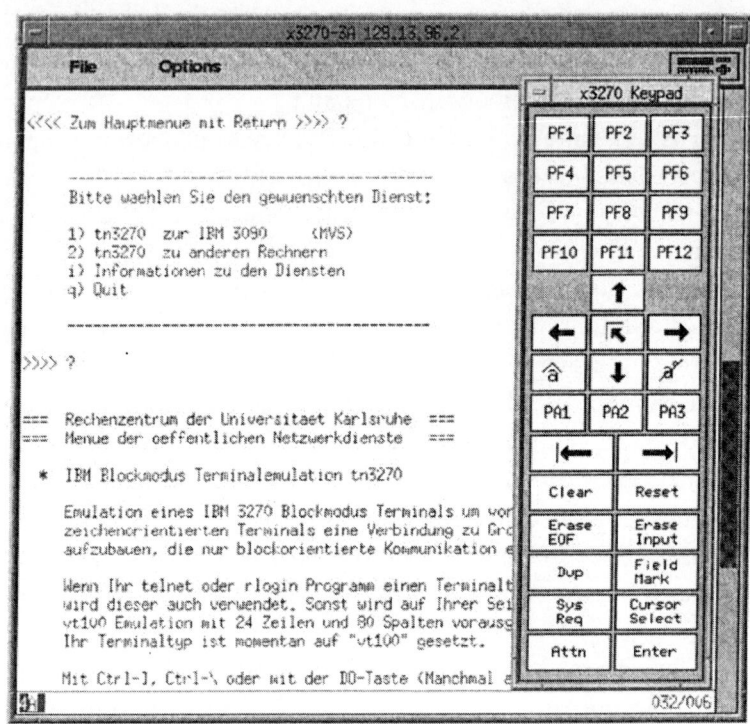

10.5   File Transfer

kermit and seyon
allow data transfer
during a login
connection

Some of the terminal emulators that have been mentioned in Sect. 10.4, namely **kermit** and **seyon**, include a mechanism allowing the data transfer during a login connection. **kermit** provides this service via the internal commands **get**, **getc**, **send**, **resend** and **transmit**. The **seyon** program makes it possible to transfer data with the Unix commands **sx**, **sb**, **sz** (Send X, Y, ZMODEM) as well as **rx**, **rb**, and **rz** (Receive X, Y, ZMODEM).

Checksums protect
against loss of data

To protect against loss of data during the transfer, the methods stated use protocols splitting the data in individual data packets, provide them with checksums, and ask the recipient for confirming the proper transfer. If an error occurred, the recipient again asks for sending the respective packet.

TCP/IP-oriented file transfer applications, like **rcp** (see Sect. 10.3.3) or **ftp** (File Transfer Protocol), do not need any internal program mechanisms for ensuring data integrity, as the latter is already guaranteed by the TCP-IP protocol. In a local Ethernet-based network, the Trivial File Transfer Protocol TFTP, which uses UDP, also can be considered as a save method (see also Sect. 9.4).

rcp and ftp use the TCP/IP protocol

Another safety measure when transferring data from one Unix system to another, is to protect against unauthorized file access. There, Unix already takes suitable precautions with its access permission scheme. The user has access on readable files only. Additionally, accessing a remote system usually requires the respective authentication. For example, `rcp` allows trusted users only, to access a special system. Merely the TFTP-service allows accessing without password inquiry. Therefore, it is often commented out in the `/etc/inetd.conf` file, so that it cannot be accessed from outside.

The Unix login procedure and the access permission scheme protect against unauthorized file access

For TCP/IP-based access on systems where the user is not registered as a trusted user, there is preferably used the `ftp` program. `ftp` includes an ASCII-oriented user interface for the File Transfer Protocol (RFC 765). Nowadays, it is included by default in each Unix-variant.

Currently, there are source codes of some convenient graphical user interfaces available that help the user during `ftp`-based files transfer. They are intended to be used above the X Window System. There are for example the OpenLook-compliant `ftptool` application and the product `moxftp`. They can be created either with the widget sets Xaw or Xaw3d (`xftp`), XView (`oftp`) or Motif (`mftp`). `ftptool` integrates a database where the user can enter "templates" for connections often used. `ftptool` and `moxftp` are not included by default in the Linux distributions. They can be obtained via anonymous `ftp` from various archive servers.

ftptool and moxftp provide graphical user interfaces to ftp

10.5.1 `ftp`

The command

`ftp [option]... [host]`

ftp

establishes an `ftp` connection to a remote system `host` given by host name or domain name or as an IP address. If `ftp` is called up without the `host` argument, the program displays its `ftp` prompt

251

and waits for **ftp** commands to be entered. In this case, one enters the **open host** command to establishing a **ftp** connection.

After the **ftp** connection has been established, the remote **ftp** daemon asks for a user identification and password to be entered. The user can automate this process by setting up the **.netrc** file in his home directory and entering line by line the **ftp** commands **machine**, **login**, and **password** there, each of them followed by the appropriate login parameters. The **$HOME/.netrc** file must have the access permission **400**, **600**, or **700**.

When ~/.netrc is suitably configured, one need not login on the target system

After successfully logging in, the user can look at the directory contents of the remote host with **dir** or **ls** or change to the (remote) working directory with **cd**. The **lcd** command changes the local working directory. If **ls** or **dir** is followed by a directory name, the commands display the contents of the path addressed. A second optional argument (a file name) makes it possible to save the table of contents in a local file. The commands **bye**, **quit**, and **C-d** are killing **ftp**. The **help** command provides a survey of the **ftp** commands available.

cd changes the remote, lcd the local working directory

For the actual file transfer, **ftp** provides the commands **put** (send) and **get** (receive), each of which copies an individual stated file. If **put** or **get** are called up with two arguments, the file stated first gets a new name on the target system.

get file – copies the file content to the standard output

mput and **mget** can copy several files. File names given as argument to these commands can also be wildcards. By default, **ftp** asks the user of the commands **mput** and **mget** to confirm each copy process (interactive transfer). **prompt** switches this inquiry on or off.

prompt switches on or off the interactive transfer mode

ftp always stores copied files in the current (local or remote) working directory, provided the user has write permission on that directory. **mput *** and **mget *** also consider possibly existing subdirectories. Nevertheless, they do not set subdirectories needed for setting files. The user can create them on the remote system with the **ftp** command **mkdir**.

mput and mget also copy directory hierarchies, but do not set any subdirectories

Local subdirectories must be set with the Unix-command **mkdir**. For this purpose, an interactive sub-shell can be started from **ftp** with an exclamation mark **!**. If the latter is followed by a command call, the sub-shell terminates immediately after executing the command stated.

Note, too, that `ftp` differentiates between binary and ASCII mode. In the ASCII mode, the sender converts the data to the standard NVT-ASCII presentation (Network Virtual Terminal), and the recipient changes the data into an internal format. This usually causes no problems when transferring data from one Unix system to another by `ftp`. In the image mode, the data will be transported without converting. Especially binary and compressed files should always be copied by the `ftp` user in the image mode. Under Linux `ftp`, the image mode is set by default.

Binary and compressed files are to be copied in the image mode

10.5.2 Anonymous `ftp`

A great number of the systems accessible via the Internet offer public access to freely available programs, data, documents, publications, pictures, and so on. Any user can access these archive servers via anonymous `ftp` by logging in via `ftp` as user `anonymous` or `ftp` and stating their email address as password.

For anonymous ftp access the individual email address is the password

Anonymous `ftp` contributed considerably to the fact that Linux could be used worldwide within a short period of time. The first Linux archive server was the `nic.funet.fi` node in Finland. Shortly afterward, directories were set on the U.S. American systems `sunsite.unc.edu` and `tsx-11.mit.edu` including exclusively Linux-specific software and the corresponding documentation.

nic.funet.fi was the first Linux archive server

Of course, the GNU products are freely available, too. None of the Linux distributions available today can do it without them. The latter are centrally archived on `prep.ai.mit.edu`. The X Window System, finally, is always provided in its current version on `ftp.x.org`.

prep.ai.mit.edu archives GNU products

Due to the great interest in anonymous `ftp`, some archive servers serve as "mirrors". They mirror the software offered by the official archive servers. For example, the `/pub/OS/Linux` directory of `nic.funet.fi` is mirrored in the U.S.A. on `tsx-11.mit.edu` in the `/pub/linux` directory. The official German Linux mirror is the node `ftp.dfv.rwth-aachen.de` in the Aachen technical university, Rhineland-Westphalia.

Mirror servers mirror the software offered by the official archive servers

*Nearby mirror
servers often offer
the best data
transfer rates*

Every well established archive server includes in each main directory of every product hierarchy a **README** file containing a list of mirror servers. It is always recommended to load this file first (with **get**) and then to contact the mirror server that is nearest geographically. The nearest system can usually be reached with a minimum number of gateways, and for this reason alone it often offers the best data transfer rates.

Furthermore, in the main directory and in each important subdirectory, archive servers normally include an **INDEX** file or a compressed version **INDEX.Z** or **INDEX.gz** containing a list of all files included there. On some archive servers, this file is called **ls-1R** (result of the call **ls -1R**) or **ls-1Rt** (sorted by the modification time). If a user is looking for a certain component, this file can help accordingly. In practice, though, one would rather use the search program **archie** for this purpose.

*In the incoming
directory an
anonymous user
has write
permission*

*LSM-files are
explaining Linux
products*

If a user wants to offer his or her own products to the public, he or she should copy them to a main server. Usually, the main directory of each product hierarchy includes a subdirectory **incoming** where a user has write permission. It is recommended to combine all components in a (compressed) **tar** file in advance, and to create an "LSM file" (Linux Software Map). A total of more than 1000 non-commercial products are now available. With an HTML browser, a user can get a list of additional program packets (under **http://www.boutell.com/lsm**).

*The ftp daemon
enters each copy
process in
/var/log/xferlog*

Finally, we briefly point out that system administrators can also configure their local systems for anonymous **ftp**. The majority of the Linux distributions available today have already been prepared accordingly. Additional information is included in the **Anon-FTP-Setup** document located in the **/usr/doc/HOWTO/mini** directory. By the way, the **ftp** daemon archives all the **ftp** copy processes in the **/var/log/xferlog** file. So, it is always possible to check which file has been loaded where and by whom.

10.6 Electronic Mail

Electronic mail (e-mail) is a service that makes it possible to exchange electronic messages within a network in the form of letters. Essentially, the user works with a mail program (Mail User Agent MUA) to create a message. The MUA is also used for looking at or processing received e-mail.

The MUA realizes the user interface, the MTA sends

E-mail is sent by a Mail Transport Agent MTA that pipes messages to be sent to the target system via a TCP/IP or UUCP connection. So, successfully using e-mail under Linux (and Unix), involves two different programs implementing a transport interface one the one hand and an application interface on the other. Communication between the systems involved is controlled by a number of mail protocols:

10.6.1 Mail Protocols

The oldest protocol for transporting e-mail is the Simple Mail Transfer Protocol SMTP (RFC 821). SMTP describes the encoding of e-mails in two parts. An initial header (mail header) includes the sender and recipient identifications. The following data block contains the actual message. Only the first 7 bits of the data transferred are significant (the 8th bit is set to 0). To send binary data successfully with SMTP, the relevant data has to be converted to a portable ASCII-format before using `uuencode` (with this method, three 8-bit characters are changed to four 6-bit characters). `uudecode` changes the encoded data back to the original format.

SMTP defines the structure of a 7-bit message

uuencode changes binary data to 7-bit ASCII data

This supposed restriction is remedied by the SMTP Service Extensions ESMTP (RFC 1651). ESMTP is "8-bit clean"; each character of the data block is transferred without loss of information. The majority of the Mail Transport Agents used today can handle e-mails encoded with ESMTP.

ESMTP can handle 8-bit messages

In addition, with the Multipurpose Internet Mail Extensions MIME (RFC 1521, RFC 1522), the Network Working Group has created a framework defining further structure within data blocks. A data block conforming to MIME can include several

MIME describes the structure of multimedia e-mail

independent parts, for example representing formatted text or audio or video data. For a complete description of the structure of a MIME data block see the RFC documents.

Systems that are not running continuously define a mail relay host

System that are not running continuously (e.g., private PCs) often use SMTP or ESMTP for sending messages and additionally define a mail relay host backing up incoming e-mails. If a user wants to access received e-mail, the mail user agent establishes a connection to the mail relay host and copies the messages provided there to the local system.

POP and IMAP control the access on a mail relay host

For this purpose, two further protocols have been developed, the Post Office Protocol POP (RFC 1225) and the Interactive Mail Access Protocol IMAP (RFC 1176). POP merely allows e-mails to be loaded. IMAP offers a means for conveniently "manipulating" messages located on the mail relay host. POP and IMAP are mainly used by MS-DOS MUAs.

10.6.2 Linux MTAs

sendmail and smail send email via TCP/IP or UUCP

Linux system administrators can choose between two different mail transport agents. Most widespread is the product `smail`, which was originally developed for mail transport via UUCP, but which can also send TCP/IP-oriented messages.

As standard MTA, some newer Linux distributions offer `sendmail`, popular since 4.2 BSD Unix. In its current version 8.x, the product is also suitably for use under Linux. `sendmail` can also operate UUCP and TCP/IP connections.

~/.forward enables incoming e-mail to be forwarded

As special feature, the mailer daemons `smail` and `sendmail` can forward incoming e-mail to another system. This is especially useful if a user has access permission to several systems and wants to ensure that all e-mail will be centrally stored in a certain system. For this purpose, one must create a `$HOME/.forward` file including one or more e-mail addresses. Then, incoming e-mails are forwarded by the MTA to the users stated there.

The vacation program can automatically answer on incoming e-mail

Furthermore, it is possible to answer incoming e-mails automatically. This option is provided by the `vacation` program, which creates a `.vacation.msg` file in the user's home directory and also creates a new `.forward` file. The `vacation` program answers incoming e-mail by sending the contents of `$HOME/.vacation.msg` to the sender of the received e-mail. `vacation` is not included in every Linux distribution.

The newest `sendmail` and `smail` versions encode the messages to be sent with either SMTP or ESMTP. The Linux Network Administrators Guide, written by Olaf Kirch, describes comprehensively the necessary steps for configuring `smail` and `sendmail`.

The Linux network package additionally includes daemons allowing any Linux system to be use as a mail relay host. The Post Office Protocol is implemented by the `ipopd` daemon. `imapd` supports IMAP access to e-mails held locally. Conversely, the `popclient` program gives Linux users POP access to a remote system.

imapd and ipopd support the use of Linux systems as mail relay hosts

10.6.3 Linux MUAs

By default, Linux distributions include the line-oriented mail user agent `mail` as well as the screen-oriented products `elm` and `pine`, which are operated via an ASCII-oriented menu interface. Linux distributions additionally include the `mailto` program, which can only be used for sending e-mail. Each of the four programs contains online help. Although `mail` offers less convenience, it is guaranteed to be included in every version of Unix.

elm and pine include an ASCII menu interface

Whereas `pine` supports the processing of MIME e-mail, `mail` does not. `mailto` is especially designed for creating MIME e-mail line by line. `elm` can analyze MIME-encoded messages only when a corresponding option has been set when translating the program. To convert a MIME data block, `elm` needs the `metamail` program.

metamail decodes MIME data blocks

Further differences between the programs stated concern the method of creating new messages. For this purpose, `pine` uses the `pico` editor whereas `elm` allows any editor to be used. `mail` and `mailto` take the information to be sent from the standard input, but can also start an external editor with the command `~!command`. The `~r file` command allows insertion of a file.

splitmail splits a comprehensive message into smaller MIME multipart blocks

The `splitmail` program can split comprehensive messages into a MIME multipart e-mail.

mail

mail user creates
and sends an
e-mail to the
address User

Immediately after the program start, `mail` first of all reads the system-scope initialization file `/etc/mail.rc` and then the user file `$HOME/.mailrc`. Normally, in each line the latter includes a `mail` command either assigning a value to a `mail` variable or defining a mail alias (a short name for a mail address). If the user uses a mail alias as recipient address, `mail` automatically replaces the mail alias by the address connected to it.

When the user has
defined the
variable record,
mail saves each
outgoing message

If a user wants to make an automatic backup of the mails created with `mail`, he or she assigns the name of the file for storing outgoing e-mail to the `record` variable in `$/HOME/.mailrc`, for example with

```
set record=~/outbox
```

Furthermore, `mail` automatically copies received and read e-mail to a `$HOME/mbox` file or to the file that has been assigned as value to the mail variable `MBOX`.

elm

elm recognizes
MIME mails and
automatically calls
up metamail

The mail user agent `elm` is somewhat old-fashioned, but still widespread. An `elm` version suitable for MIME additionally requires the `metamail` program to be able to handle received MIME e-mail. `elm` can also send encoded messages on demand.

configoptions
includes a list of
letters

The program takes its configuration files from the directory `$HOME/.elm`. The `elmrc` file combines the variables controlling the behavior of `elm`. Some of these can be set interactively in the program. The `configoptions` variable determines which parameters can be configured. A special menu item stores the currently set parameters in `elmrc`.

If the user has set the **signature** variable, **elm** automatically copies the contents of the file stated there to the end of a newly created message. For this purpose, the user usually creates a **$HOME/.signature** file including his or her personal information (surname, first name, address, telephone number, fax etc.), and assigns the name of this file to **signature**.

/usr/lib/elmrc-info explains each elm variable

Furthermore, **elm** includes an alias editor for simplifying the setting of mail alias entries. The alias editor is opened with the **a** command. In this mode, after **n** is entered, **elm** asks for alias name, surname, first name, comment, and the complete e-mail address later to be replaced by the program when using the alias name. Finally, the **r** command stores the alias names entered in four **aliases** files.

elm includes an internal alias editor

Comprehensive documentation is available on the program, combined in the **elm** documentation package. It includes a Users Guide, Reference Guide, Alias Systems Users Guide, Filter Guide, Forms Mode Guide, and Configuration Guide. An HTML version of these documents can be found, e.g., under **http://www-rohan.sdsu.edu/elmindex.html**.

The elm documentation package is also available in T_EX format

pine

The MUA **pine** has been developed at the University of Washington. Originally, the **elm** program code formed the basis for the system. In the course of time, **pine** was completely reworked, and the current version no longer includes any **elm** code. In operation **pine** is quite similar to **elm**. In contrast to its "predecessor" **elm**, **pine** integrates access to remote mailboxes via IMAP.

pine can access local and remote mail folders

pine takes its configuration parameters from the system-scope **pine.conf** file, for which it usually searches in the **/usr/local/lib** directory. Furthermore, **pine** consults the **$HOME/.pinerc** file (containing user-specific parameters). If the user has set the environment variables **PINECONF** or **PINERC**, **pine** takes its configuration from the files stated there.

An essential extension of **pine** relative to **elm** is that it can run multiple mail folders, which furthermore can be located on

pine accesses remote mail folders using IMAP

remote systems. The latter are set in the folder menu with the **A** command. If a folder name starts with a host name put in braces, `pine` links this folder to a remote mailbox. Messages located there are accessed by `pine` with IMAP.

pine includes an NNTP client

Furthermore, `pine` includes an NNTP client, so it allows users to access the Usenet. This requires, that users have access permission on a news server. Additionally, a user must set a list of the newsgroups to which he or she wants to subscribe. `pine` expects the user to know the titles of the newsgroups wanted.

Complete documentation on pine is available via anonymous ftp

Additional documentation on `pine` which is not covered by the online help can be found with an HTML browser under `http://www.cac.washington.edu/pine`. Furthermore, in the `/pine` directory, the node `ftp.cac.washington.edu` includes complete documentation on `pine`. It is available via anonymous `ftp`.

10.6.4 Graphic Linux MUAs

xmailtool and xmail include an X11 front-end to mail

As Linux accessories, some graphical oriented Linux MUAs are freely available that are designed for use over the X Window System. These include, for example, `xmail` and `xmailtool`. These programs mainly offer an Xaw or Xaw3d based user interface for the standard MUA `mail`.

The command metamail buffer decodes a MIME e-mail

In Sect. 7.3.17, the `rmail` package allowing use of GNU Emacs as a mail user agent was mentioned. Furthermore, in Sect. 7.3.19, the Emacs variant `xemacs` was said to provide an appealing graphic tool for this service. The ELisp library `metamail`, included by default in the product, additionally supports the processing of MIME e-mail.

mumail uses FWF widgets

The X client `mumail`, which can handle MIME e-mail, is an independent mail user agent. `mumail` converts received MIME messages by forwarding the respective data to `metamail`. Creating one's own MIME e-mail is relatively inconvenient. `mumail` is not public domain, but is freely available.

Today, the most sophisticated realization of a graphic MIME compatible, and also freely available mail user agent is Netscape Mail. It is an integral part of the HTML browser `netscape`. Figure 10.2 shows a screenshot of Netscape Mail.

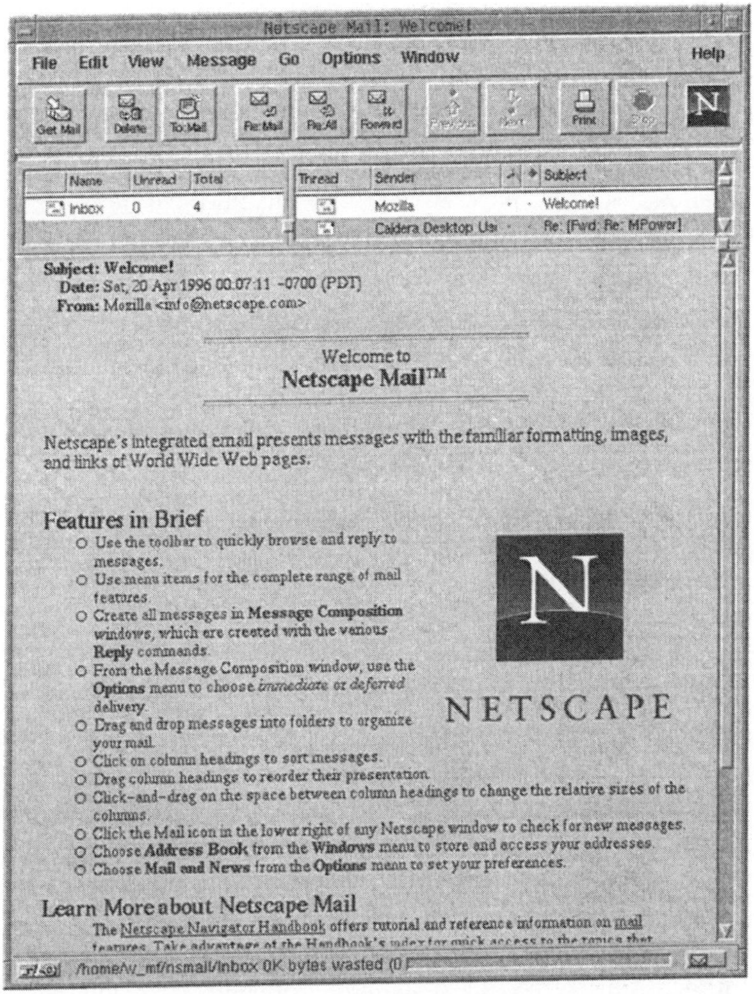

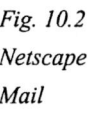

Netscape Mail: Welcome!

File	Edit	View	Message	Go	Options	Window				Help

| Get Mail | Delete | To:Mail | Re:Mail | Re:All | Forward | Previous | Next | Print | Stop | N |

Name	Unread	Total		Thread	Sender		Subject	
Inbox	0	4			Mozilla	- -	Welcome!	
					Caldera Desktop Use -	Re: [Fwd: Re: MPower]	

Subject: Welcome!
Date: Sat, 20 Apr 1996 00:07:11 -0700 (PDT)
From: Mozilla <info@netscape.com>

Welcome to
Netscape Mail™

Netscape's integrated email presents messages with the familiar formatting, images, and links of World Wide Web pages.

Features in Brief
- Use the toolbar to quickly browse and reply to messages.
- Use menu items for the complete range of mail features.
- Create all messages in **Message Composition** windows, which are created with the various **Reply** commands.
- From the Message Composition window, use the **Options** menu to choose *immediate* or *deferred* delivery.
- Drag and drop messages into folders to organize your mail.
- Click on column headings to sort messages.
- Drag column headings to reorder their presentation.
- Click-and-drag on the space between column headings to change the relative sizes of the columns.
- Click the Mail icon in the lower right of any Netscape window to check for new messages.
- Choose **Address Book** from the **Windows** menu to store and access your addresses.
- Choose **Mail and News** from the **Options** menu to set your preferences.

Learn More about Netscape Mail
The Netscape Navigator Handbook offers tutorial and reference information on mail features. Take advantage of the Handbook's index for quick access to the topics that

N E T S C A P E

/home/w_mf/nsmail/inbox OK bytes wasted (0

Fig. 10.2
Netscape
Mail

Graphics (MIME data types `image/jpeg` and `image/gif`) included in a MIME e-mail can be displayed directly by Netscape Mail. Furthermore, the product interprets HTML documents.

Netscape Mail can also follow HTML links

Using Netscape Mail makes sense only in a system with at least 16 MB of main memory. The program `netscape` requires about 3.5 MB of main memory.

10.6.5 Mailbox Systems

A mailbox is a privately or professionally used information database

A mailbox or bulletin board system (BBS) is a database allowing the user to send and collect messages via modem. Each registered mailbox user has his or her own mailbox where other users can leave messages. Conversely, each user can deposit messages for other users of the system. Mailbox users who are not registered usually have limited access to chosen system services under the identification `guest`. Furthermore, modern mailbox systems support bidirectional data transfer (upload/download) and contain a component allowing real-time dialog with other system users.

bbs.list contains a list of mailboxes specializing in Linux

For Linux users without Internet access, a mailbox often provides the only way to contact other Linux users via e-mail. Meanwhile, mailbox systems specializing in Linux are run worldwide. A survey on such systems, together with the telephone numbers under which they may be accessed, is included in the `bbs.list` file in the `/pub/linux/docs` directory of the archive server `tsx-11.mit.edu`. Of course, this file can also be obtained from a mirror server. This file should also be on CD-ROMs including a "`tsx-11` mirror".

Various software packages make it possible to create one's own Linux mailbox

Recently, various software packages have been ported to Linux that make it possible to create one's own mailbox. We mention here the products `ebbs`, `doorway`, `drealmbbs`, and `rocat`. These mailbox systems provide the user with an ASCII menu interface, which means they are largely self-explanatory.

Although installing BBS is not complicated, it requires intensive study of the documentation supplied. If remote access is to be carried out via modem, the superuser must configure the `/etc/inittab` file according to Sect. 9.7.1, so that the operating system kernel can initiate a serial login connection.

10.7 News

News used to be spread via UUCP. Today, News is a TCP/IP service

News is a network service allowing access to the Usenet. The latter is an international discussion forum consisting of nearly 18 000 interest groups (newsgroups). Each user accessing the Usenet can look at information deposited by other users or can leave messages. Usenet should be compared not with a network but rather with a global mailbox.

A user gains access to the Usenet with a special program (news reader) and asking for a system's NNTP service (news server) providing newsgroups. The majority of the globally distributed news servers allow access by their licensees only.

Almost every university runs a news server

The titles of individual newsgroups consist of several components. Beginning at the left, they state the topics discussed in that newsgroup, with the individual topics separated by dots. For example, the newsgroup `comp.os.linux.apps` collects postings on computer topics (`comp`) referring to the operating system kernel (`os`) Linux (`linux`) and focusing on application programs (`apps`). Some of the main topics that occur most often are:

A news group's name indicates the topic discussed there

alt	alternative topics,
comp	computer topics, hardware and software,
de	contributions in German,
news	topics concerning the Usenet,
rec	leisure-time activities, hobbies,
sci	scientific topics,
soc	religion, politics, culture.

One should distinguish between general newsgroups, where anybody can contribute any message at all, and moderated newsgroups, where a moderator decides whether or not a message will be presented to that forum. Moderated newsgroups have the advantage that the articles they include there have little redundancy, if any. Non-moderated newsgroups collect every kind of message, especially inquiries and answers to them.

comp.os.linux. announce is a moderated newsgroup

In some newsgroups, an article is published at regular intervals summarizing frequently asked questions together with the corresponding answers. These "frequently asked questions" (FAQs) normally include comprehensive information on the topic discussed by that newsgroup. For example, these include general background information, a list of relevant literature, software products on the topic, contacts, and so on. The current FAQ versions are located on the archive server `rtfm.mit.edu`.

FAQs include answers to frequently asked questions

Every day, new message's are received amounting to more than 10 MB

There is a considerable flow of information within the Usenet. Therefore, news servers from time to time delete older messages, so that the existing hard disk capacity will be enough to provide the current messages. Depending on the news server configuration, a message will be stored 1-4 weeks, sometimes longer.

10.7.1 Linux News Clients

Netscape and Emacs also contain a news client

Depending on the Linux distribution used, the Linux network package supplied includes at least one of the ASCII-oriented news clients **rtin**, **slrn** or **trn**. If they are not part of the installed Linux distribution, the X11 news readers **xrn** and **xvnews** are additionally available as accessories. **xrn** can be created with the Xaw, Xaw3d, or Motif widgets, whereas **xvnews** requires the XView toolkit.

These programs usually take the news server to be contacted from the environment variable **NNTPSERVER**. However, **rtin** does not need this environment variable if the file **/etc/nntpserver** includes a news server name. **slrn** users can also specify the news server to be contacted in the command line (option **-h**).

~/.newsrc stores the list of news groups subscribed

The news readers take the news groups subscribed from the **$HOME/.newsrc** file. The latter is automatically set by the programs if the user calls them up with the option **-c** (**rtin**) or **-create** (**slrn**). With **trn** the user can create a **$HOME/.newsrc** file, if it does not exist already.

Setting **$HOME/.newsrc** can last a few minutes. For the occasional or daily usage of News, it is advisable to subscribe to a few newsgroups only. During a session, the user can cancel a news group subscription by moving the cursor onto that newsgroup and entering the **u** command (unsubscribe). Nevertheless, it is easier to load the **$HOME/.newsrc** file in an editor and to put an exclamation mark after the names of the newsgroups that should not be subscribed.

Handling a news reader is relatively easy. After a newsgroup is chosen (by moving the cursor to the group name and pressing return), the news reader displays a list of message subjects included in the news server on the topic chosen. To read a certain message, one just moves the cursor to its line in the list and enters return. Then, the news reader asks the news server to send the message.

The user can print a message, store it on the hard disk, answer it via email, or make a statement on it within the newsgroup. Furthermore, one can search for keywords or delete messages (so that in a later session, the news reader will not display it again). A survey of the available commands and their functions can be accessed via the help facility in each news reader.

News readers contain functions for storing and answering messages

10.7.2 Off-line News

Reading news is like reading newspapers. It is time-consuming and linked to considerable costs, especially when using a modem connection. Sometimes, it is more economical to use a news reader off-line. This section introduces a method doing for doing so.

Accessing news via modem can cause considerable telephone expenses

The news reader `rtin` provides a batch mode that automatically copyies new messages from the remote news server to the local hard disk. For example,

```
rtin -S -c -f ~/.newsrc.load \
     -s /usr/spool/news
```

loads every new message from the news groups that have been entered by the user in `~/.newsrc.load` to the local hard disk. The files are saved in the `/usr/spool/news` directory.

A user who does not want to load certain messages must enter line by line the relevant news group names and message numbers into the `~/.newsrc.load` file:

```
comp.os.linux.announce: 1-5230
comp.os.linux.development.apps: 1-24729
comp.os.linux.development.system: 1-36287
```

Several areas or numbers have to be stated separated by commas

The `/usr/spool/news` directory normally has the access permission `755`, so that only its owner and the superuser can successfully execute the command stated. Furthermore, if the `-v` option is additionally stated in the command line , `rtin` outputs a list of messages loaded.

The inetd
automatically
starts the NNTP
daemon if the
service in
/etc/inetd.conf is
activated

If the superuser has activated the service NNTP on the local system, the user can access the local NNTP service using any news reader at all. As an alternative, the `tin` program allows direct access to the local News.

`tin` requires a `/usr/lib/news/active` file containing lines that each give a news group name, the number of the newest and oldest files and one of the letters **m** (moderated), **n**, **j**, **x**, or **y**:

```
comp.os.linux.announce 5289 5231 m
comp.os.linux.development.apps 24995 24730 y
comp.os.linux.development.system 36740 36288 y
```

Thus, all the preconditions are met for reading the local news with the `tin` program from then on.

10.8   Dialog Programs

Dialog programs
communicate in
real time

Dialog programs allow a user to enjoy a real-time dialog with one or more other users active in the LAN or WAN. Here one must distinguish between (text) communication with particular persons and discussions with other participants in a public forum.

10.8.1   `talk` and `ytalk`

Dialog with particular participants is based on a talk service. Within the framework of TCP/IP services, this is implemented by the `talkd` daemon and the talk applications `talk` and `ytalk`. By calling

As argument, talk
requires a user's
e-mail address

```
talk user@host
```

the user addresses the talk daemon of the **host** system. If the user **user** is active there, the talk daemon sends a message to the user's login terminal including the e-mail address of the calling user. After the addressee has established a talk connection to the recipient, the terminal screen splits to show two windows.

Each message entered is transferred directly to the other party by `talk`.

The `ytalk` program works similarly, but allows contact with several users, meaning it establishes a kind of conference circuit. Called up over the X Window System, `ytalk` creates a window for each user taking part in the conference.

ytalk supports conference circuits

Unfortunately, talk connections are not always possible, as there exist two incompatible protocol versions. The talk protocol specified within the framework of 4.2 BSD has been changed in 4.3 BSD.

10.8.2   Internet Relay Chat

Internet Relay Chat, IRC, was developed by Jarkko Oikarinen, Finland, in 1988 (RFC 1459). Extending the talk service common then and so to speak providing a kind of real-time e-mail, IRC is a multiuser communication system. An IRC participant uses an IRC client to get in contact with an IRC server, then logs in on a "channel" to communicate in real time with other users of this channel. IRC thus provides a dialog version of the Usenet.

IRC participants communicate via IRC streams

In contrast to the Usenet, IRC does not determine a specific group. Each IRC participant can open his or her own channel. A channel "dies" when it is no longer used. A user who creates a channel will automatically be the channel operator. He or she can to log out other channel participants without warning, set conditions for accessing the channel, and pass on the operator status to another participant.

Linux distributions by default include the ASCII-oriented IRC client `irc`. The X application `zircon` is available as an accessory, providing an appealing graphical interface by means of the Tcl/tk toolkit.

`irc` provides more than 100 commands, each of which starts with a slash `/`. For example, `/help` activates the internal help function, `/server` establishes a connection to an IRC server, `/list` displays each active channel on an already addressed IRC server, `/who` shows a list of participants, and `/quit` kills the IRC client.

IRC commands start with a slash /

IRC channel names
start with #

With `/join #channel` the user establishes a connection to a communication forum. He or she can ask questions there and answer questions from other participants. Experience shows that communication on some channels is very lively but on others rather sluggish.

For further details on Internet Relay Chat, it is strongly recommended to have a look at thedocument IRCprimer, written by Nicolas Pioch, France. It is available for example via anonymous `ftp` from `nic.funet.fi`. The IRCprimer is located in the directory `/pub/unix/irc/docs`.

10.9 Information Systems

Archive servers
linked with each
other in the
Internet store
programs and
documents

The Internet hosts a practically inexhaustible variety of data and files. Newer archive servers do not just limit their information service to provide programs within the Internet, the user can also access general and specialized documents, like current news from all areas of culture, product information, and technical specifications. Users can even access complete technical articles, dissertations, and theses.

Information systems help the user on the one hand to target and access a certain source. On the other hand, tools are available today that search through the entire Internet for a given keyword.

archie searches for
programs, gopher
searches for
documents

Certain programs or files can be found with `archie`, which asks an addressed Archie server to create a list of archive servers including the element searched. The Gopher service, on the other hand, is designed for accessing text information. Especially its addition Veronica provides a powerful mechanism for searching throughout the Internet for documents including a keyword in their title. Finally, the newest and undoubtly the most powerful information system is the World Wide Web.

10.9.1 FTP Search Help

In Sect. 10.5.2, some archive servers were mentioned that provide complete software packages for public access. Also mentioned was the worldwide infrastructure of mirror servers that mirror the contents of an archive server to reduce the server net-load as well as the user's transport costs. User now face the problem of finding an archive or mirror server that stocks a certain software.

Mirror servers take some of the load off an archive server

The answer to this problem is provided by the ASCII-oriented **archie** program as well as by its graphical variant **xarchie**, both of which access an archive database by using a keyword. The program then provides a list of archive servers and file names including the keyword.

archie displays mirror servers storing a file

Today, more than 25 Archie servers are in active service. Archie server mainly searches through the tables of contents of ftp servers for the keyword stated. Depending on the search criteria set, the Archie server searches for parts of character strings (upper and lowercase either distinguish or not), precise words, or regular expressions. After a certain number of "hits", the search will be aborted (default setting is 99) and the result transferred to the Archie client. Archie servers usually provide the tables of contents of 800 or more ftp servers and update them at regular intervals.

Processing time is determined by the search criteria chosen

If neither the **archie** program nor **xarchie** is on the local system, the user can also establish a Telnet connection to an Archie server and log in as user **archie** there. Although the Telnet-based search is comparatively inconvenient, in any case it provides a way to search for an Archie client after successfully logging in with **find archie**.

Some servers provide the Archie service via telnet

If it is not possible to establish a Telnet connection, as no direct Internet access is provided, it is still possible to question an Archie server via e-mail. For this purpose, one just has to send an Archie command as single part of an e-mail to the user **archie** of an Archie server. Operating instructions can be obtained by entering a **help** command. Figure 10.3 shows a list of selected Archie servers.

Archie inquiries are also possible via email

Newer versions of the **xarchie** program include an integrated ftp client. After an appropriate menu item is chosen, **xarchie**

*xarchie includes
an ftp lient*

establishes an ftp connection to the archive or mirror server previously chosen and copies the desired file to the local hard disk. The other variants just display a list of nodes where the searched software is to be found. In this case, the software itself has to be copied individually with `ftp`.

*Fig. 10.3
Selected Archie
servers and their
locations*

Domain name	IP-Address	Nation
archie.au	139.130.23.2	Australia
archie.th-darmstadt.de	130.83.22.1	Germany
archie.funet.fi	128.214.248.46	Finland
archie.univ-rennes1.fr	129.20.254.2	France
archie.doc.ic.ac.uk	193.63.255.1	UK
archie.unipi.it	131.114.1.3	Italy
archie.wide.ad.jp	133.4.3.6	Japan
archie.uqam.ca	192.77.55.2	Canada
archie.switch.ch	130.59.1.40	Switzerland
archie.uni-linz.ac.at	192.77.55.2	Austria
archie.ncu.edu.tw	192.83.166.12	Taiwan
archie.sura.net	192.239.16.130	USA/MD
archie.unl.edu	129.93.1.14	USA/NE
archie.rutgers.edu	128.6.21.13	USA/NJ
archie.ans.net	147.225.1.10	USA/NY

10.9.2 Gopher

*Gopher describes
how to deal with a
distributed
document database*

Gopher is a distributed information service on the Internet that supports the user in searching for certain information. At the beginning of 1991, scientists at the University of Minnesota had the idea of establishing a distributed information system capable of providing news, announcements, and other information in simple text form. Each department should administer its data in a decentralized database. The information should be available everywhere within the computer network. The gopher, by the way, is the mascot of the U.S. Federal State of Minnesota.

*Gopher can be
accessed with a
Gopher client or
with Telnet*

Today, there are more than 400 Gopher servers world wide providing the user with a single, central menu system. A Linux user can establish a connection to a Gopher server either with the ASCII-oriented Gopher client `gopher` or with the X application `xgopher`. Some systems also offer the option of using the

Gopher service via a Telnet connection. For example, a Telnet-based Gopher session with `consultant.micro.umn.edu` can be opened by using the login name `gopher`.

After a connection is established, the Gopher client displays simple menu items. Choosing a menu item results either in a document being loaded, then immediately displayed by the Gopher client, or in branching to a deeper menu layer, or in establishing a Telnet connection. However, targeted searching with Gopher is not possible without more ado. Normally, the user has to know exactly where to find a certain piece of information. *Gopher-documents are accessed via menu items*

A vital improvement is provided by the Gopher addition Veronica, which can analyze search terms. Veronica does not require any additional software. Some Gopher servers provide it as a menu item. After a keyword is entered, Veronica questions other Gopher servers and as result provides a list of each menu item including the keyword. Afterwards, the Gopher client displays this list as a normal Gopher menu. The user may select a certain menu item to either load the corresponding file, branch to a deeper menu, or reestablish a Telnet connection. *Veronica carries out a world-wide search for titles including a keyword*

10.9.3 World Wide Web

The World Wide Web (WWW or W3) was initiated with the purpose of gaining access to documents of every kind distributed world-wide. There, the documents are not restricted to mere text files; the processing of static and moving images (video files) as well as acoustic information (audio files) is supported, too. The first Web implementations were developed at the Conseil Européen pour la Recherche Nucléaire CERN, a physics research center based in Switzerland. *The World Wide Web was initiated by Tim Berners-Lee*

The net structure of the World Wide Web consists of documents linked with each other by hyperlinks. Each document can refer to further documents that are available either locally or remotely. The information transfer is controlled by the HyperText Transmission Protocol HTTP, and the information itself is usually structured according to the HyperText Markup Language HTML. The latter allows the definition of text structures (headline, *HTTP controls the information transport, HTML defines document structures*

271

paragraph, list, table), fonts (normal, italic, bold), font size, and graphical elements, and can link all the representation objects with hyperlinks.

The World Wide Web is a user service within the Internet. It can be accessed from any computer by running a WWW client (Web or HTML browser). The Web provides hypertext-based or hypermedia based access to information offered by anonymous `ftp`, Archie, Gopher, Veronica, or WAIS (Wide-Area Information System).

The Web links together the Archie, Gopher, and FTP services via hyperlinks

The WWW client's task is to provide a user interface that offers access to the Web, prepares and presents the information loaded, and follows hyperlinks in response to user actions, hence loads new or additional information.

The first product for this purpose was developed at the National Center for Supercomputing NCSA, under the working name "Mosaic". Later, Web browsers were developed such as the ASCII-oriented `lynx` and the X applications `arena`, `chimera`, `jigsaw`, `netscape`, and `tkWWW` that can handle graphics. Although HTML will be extended continuously, not all Web browsers always support the newest HTML specification. Figure 10.4 shows a screenshot of the NCSA Mosaic Web browser.

The first WWW client available was NCSA Mosaic

Each of a Web document's hyperlinks are indicated by a Uniform Resource Locator URL, consisting of a protocol key, a host, and an optional file name. For example, the URL

If there is no file name, the HTTP daemon addressed sends its "home page"

```
http://www.w3.org/pub/WWW/TheProject.html
```

describes the `TheProject.html` document that can be found on the HTTP server `www.w3.org` in the `/pub/WWW` directory. If the user wants to use another service, the URL has to be initiated with a protocol key designed for that service:

```
file://localhost/sound.au
```
loads and interprets an audio file,

```
file://localhost/picture.gif
```
loads and interprets a graphics file,

```
file://localhost/directory/
```
displays directory contents,

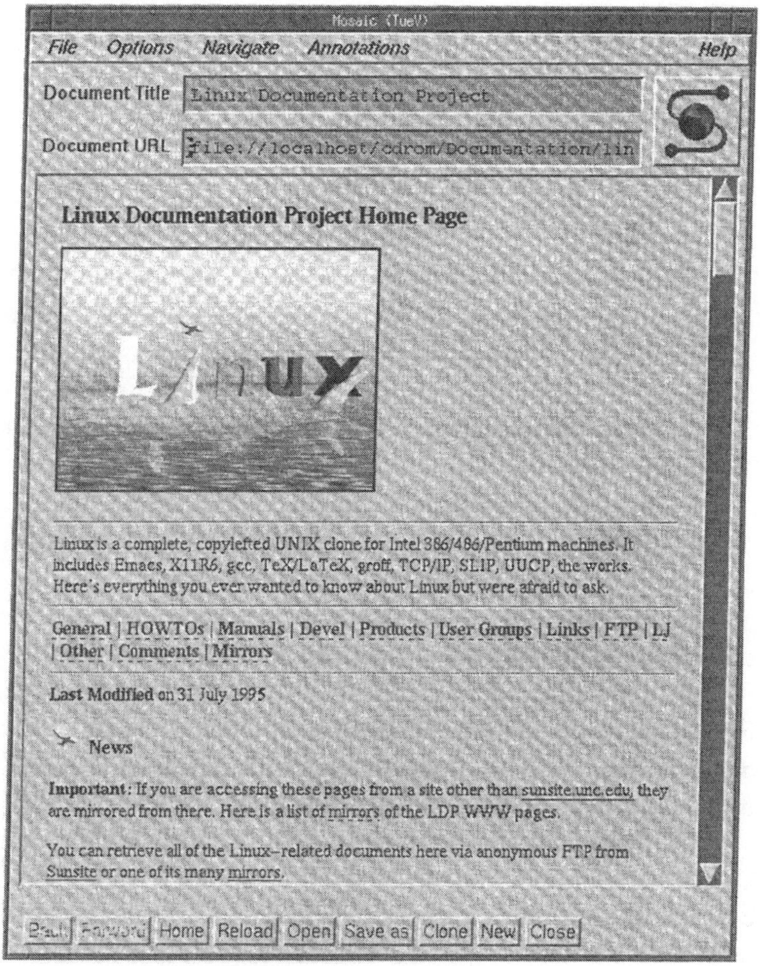

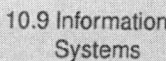

Fig. 10.4
The NCSA Mosaic
Web browser

```
ftp://localhost/pub/text.ps
```
opens an ftp connection to the `localhost` system and
copies the PostScript file **/pub/text.ps** to a directory to
be stated,

```
http://localhost/text.html
```
establishes a connection to the system's HTTP daemon
`localhost` and loads an HTML document,

```
news:comp.os.linux.apps
```
contacts the NNTP server specified in the environment
variable **NNTPSERVER** and loads the headlines of the news
group `comp.os.linux.apps`,

```
telnet://localhost:4711
```
opens a Telnet connection to the `localhost` system (port `4711`).

The majority of the Web browsers on the market today allow the user to input a URL by hand either before or while the browser is running.

Without a doubt, the World Wide Web has contributed greatly to the popularity of the Internet; indeed, it is often mistakenly considered equivalent to the Internet. Practically every well-known organization with an Internet connection now has a home page presenting its public image on the World Wide Web. Meanwhile, the range of information is not just limited to academic or cultural information any longer. Commercial enterprises, too, have long used the World Wide Web for presenting their product range in catalog form or for offering jobs.

A Web server's domain name often starts with "www"

The domain name of a publicly accessible WWW server often follows a standard scheme consisting of a leading character string **www** followed by an organization name and a contraction indicating the geographic location of the server. For example, the domain name **www.springer.de** is the WWW server identification of the Springer publishing company, Germany.

AltaVista, Lycos, and WebCrawler search through URLs for keywords

Some institutions have set up a service providing users with a keyword search within the Web. For example, the system **altavista.digital.com** includes an index capturing 30 million URLs from 275 600 server systems and 4 million articles from 14 000 newsgroups. A keyword search considers not only the headlines but also the document content. Today, the system's operating authority, the U.S. producer Digital Equipment, registers more than 18 million inquiries each day of the week. A similar service is provided by the WWW servers **lycos.cs.cmu.edu**, **www.webcrawler.com**, and various other nodes not stated here.

Many Linux documents are available in HTML format

Furthermore, the universal HTML format structure has set off a wave of conversions of existing documents. A large part of the documentation on Linux and on products included in a Linux distribution is today available in HTML format. This includes the Install Guide, the Kernel Hackers Guide, and the Network

Administrators Guide, each an official part of the Linux Documentation Project LDP.

Of course, it is also possible to extend a Linux system into a World Wide Web server. Some Linux distributions are already suitably prepared by including the HTTP daemon `httpd` by default. If `httpd` is not included in the local Linux distribution, it is recommended to obtain the product from a Linux mirror, or to be more precise, not only the executable program but also the corresponding source code. The latter includes, among other things, comprehensive documentation on the HTTP daemon configuration.

The HTTP daemon httpd makes it possible to structure a Linux Web server

X Window System

An ergonomic alternative for operating Linux via a (virtual) console is offered by the window system X11, where the user can access the system by a graphical interface. Over X11, single applications are displayed in windows and are operated (depending on the application type) via keyboard and/or mouse commands.

X applications are operated with the keyboard or the mouse

The X11 working mode follows a client/server architecture in that the X server controls the local in/output components and thereby runs an in/output interface for one or more X applications (X clients). The information exchange between the components involved is carried out via data packets formatted according to the X protocol. Unix sockets serve as local transport medium. Network-wide data transfer is carried out via TCP/IP.

X applications communicate with the X server via Unix sockets or TCP/IP

11.1 Window Systems

The first significant step towards windows was Smalltalk. It was developed in California at Xerox PARC in the early 1970s and may be said to be the common ancestor of all window systems. Smalltalk was a complete environment with an integrated window system consisting of four functional layers: graphics library, base window system, window manager, and user interface toolkit.

Smalltalk is the common ancestor of all window systems

In 1977, the product Display Lisp was developed at PARC in response to the need to use the graphics-capable Altos 8-bit systems that were in the company laboratories as graphics terminal for a DEC PDP-10. The main feature of Display Lisp was a graphics server running on the application server and controlling Altos systems coupled by Ethernet.

University milestones include NU, presented by the MIT in 1981, which allowed windows to be overlapped, and the window system W developed in 1982 for the experimental operating system V by Paul Asente and Brian Reid at Stanford University. One year later, James Gosling and David Rosenthal at Carnegie Mellon University published the Andrew system. In Andrew, the window system formed an independent process that could operate under Unix without changing the operating system kernel. Andrew applications communicate with the window server via Unix sockets.

Paul Asente and Brian Reid programmed W

About this time, within the framework of the Athena project, the MIT and Digital Equipment developed a first version of the window system X. As development platform, they used a VAX 11/750 and VAXstations 1 and 2 with Ultrix as operating system, connected to monochrome, graphics-capable DEC VS100 terminals.

The source code of W formed the basis for X

The versions 1–6 that resulted were monochrome and available on VAX systems only. Color displays were supported for the first time in X8, and X10 was the first version that could run on different operation systems. Finally, the X10R4, released in 1986, was extolled as a path-finding window system by many enterprises and institutions.

X8 was the first version that could address color displays

In January 1987, leading workstation producers agreed to use X as basis for future working interfaces. Since the foundation of the X Consortium in 1988, with members like Apple, AT&T, DEC, HP, and Sun, X has been officially called X11.

Since 1988, the product has been officially called X11

By that time, several commercial window systems had already been established on the market. At the beginning of 1984, first versions were supplied by Apple's Macintosh, Microsoft Windows, and the Graphical Environment Manager GEM from Digital Research. SunView (Sun) was the first commercial window system for Unix platforms.

Commercial window systems: Macintosh, GEM, MS Windows, and SunView

A common feature of these products was, and still is, that they can run local applications only. Macintosh and MS Windows have maintain their hold on the market to date, whereas GEM and SunView have been more or less ousted.

278

In comparison to its commercial competitors, X11 integrated more powerful concepts from the beginning on. The appearance of individual applications, however, was rather rudimentary. Then, two mergers between producers led to products that defined object representation in window systems as well as a corresponding programming interface.

In cooperation with AT&T and later on with Xerox too, the Openlook specification was created by Sun in 1987. Since 1988, Sun has supplied its operation system software together with Open Windows. It is a software package consisting of an X server, OpenLook-compliant window manager `olwm`, various X clients, and the XView toolkit as development system for proprietary applications.

Since 1988, OpenLook has been part of SunOS

Based on the proposals by Microsoft, HP, and DEC, in 1988 the Open Software Foundation decided to create a graphical user interface with the working title Motif and declare it a standard. The outer appearance of any X client is marked by the Motif window manager `mwm`, whereas the look of the graphical components of a Motif application is controlled by the Motif development system.

Motif is a commercial Open Software Foundation product

The window system X11, or more precisely the porting XFree86 for 80x86 processors, is included by default in every Linux distribution. Above X11, the user can employ the product Smalltalk/X. The latter is contained for example on the second CD of the LST distribution in the `mirror/sunsite/devel/smalltalkx` directory. Additionally, the second CD of the LST distribution includes the window system MGR (in the `mirror/sunsite/apps/MGR` directory), which uses an integrated window manager and is similar to SunView. Although its performance features do not come up to those of X11, MGR is much more "compact" compared to X11.

Linux distributions include XFree86

11.2 Architecture of X11

X11 is a network-transparent, bitmap-oriented window system consisting of an X server, X applications, and the X protocol. The latter forms the basis for (network-wide) data transfer from the X server to the X clients and vice versa.

The X server software consists of hardware dependent (device dependent X ddx) and independent modules (device independent X dix), whereby the hardware dependent part serves the local graphics hardware and takes input from the keyboard and the mouse. The remaining module controls access to font files and the communication interface (sockets, network). In addition, dix processes incoming X protocols and sends X protocols initiated by user action. Figure 11.1 presents the X server and X client components. The arrows show cooperation between hardware and software.

*Fig. 11.1
Communication
between X server
and X client*

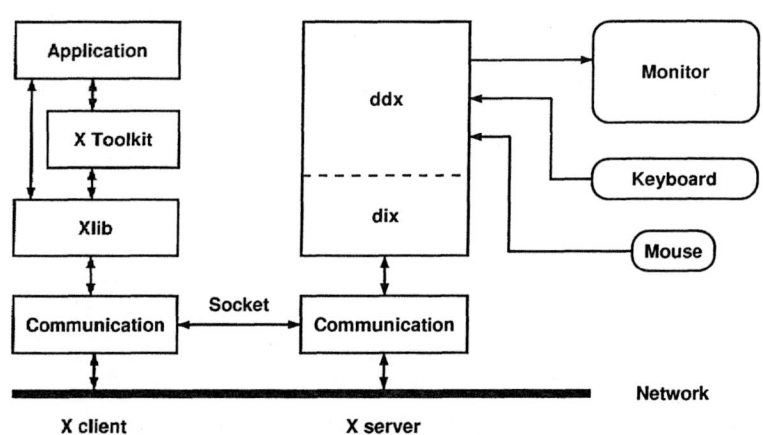

*Xlib functions
establish the
connection to
the X server*

X clients consist of the actual application and a number of functions determining graphical application objects and establishing the connection to the X server. Routines needed for this purpose are combined in the Xlib library, which in a sense is the assembler for the X11 window system.

*X Toolkits make it
easier to program
X clients*

Higher functions based on the Xlib are included in the X Toolkit Intrinsics Library libXt, supplied by default with X11 distributions. This provides useful graphical widgets, like menus, scrollbars, dialog boxes, and so on, and a call-back mechanism for efficient input administration. Furthermore, libXt includes complex application routines that cut the effort needed to develop an X client to a minimum.

The X window manager plays a special role among X applications, as it has special rights. The X window manager controls dimensions and position as well as the appearance of all main windows.

11.3 Widgets

Widgets are abstractions of user interface elements. Each widget corresponds to its own X window where it presents itself. Also, widgets are coupled with actions, which they execute in response to user inputs.

In the course of time, various widget libraries have been developed with different numbers of basic elements. Common to these widget sets is a class hierarchy: each widget represents an object belonging to a class, each widget stems from a common root class. X11 distributions include by default the X Athena widgets Xaw. Figure 11.2 shows the Athena widget class hierarchy.

Widget libraries contain dialog elements

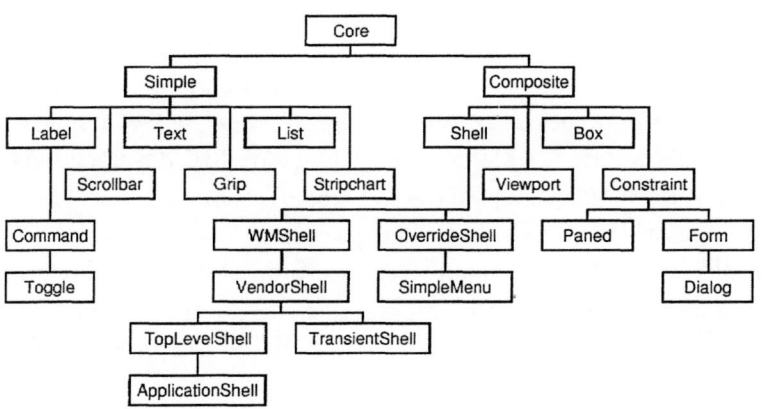

Fig. 11.2
Athena widget class hierarchy

On top of the Athena widget class hierarchy is the class "core". It contains such structures as name, size, position, background, margins, and so on, common to all widgets, as well as functions defining their treatment. The direct subclass "composite"

Athena widgets pass on their attributes to sub-widgets

forms the basis for composed widgets. It controls the addition or removal of sub-widgets. Furthermore, "composite" administers agreements on size and relative position to the next higher widget.

The class "constraint" allows following widgets to be coupled with special demands, like minimum and maximum size. Parallel to this, the class "shell" communicates with the window manager and controls the structure of popup menus.

Xaw3d is Xaw compatible

X applications included within the framework of X11 distributions of the X Consortium use the Athena widgets. As an alternative, the Xaw3d widgets from Kaleb Keithley, USA, are binary compatible with Xaw. In comparison to Xaw, the Xaw3d widgets look three-dimensional, due to shading.

The XView toolkit is freely available

For an appearance compliant with OpenLook, the XView toolkit widgets of the development library also have a 3D look and feel. Although OpenLook has been declared part of System V Release 4 and the XView toolkit is freely available, it has been ousted recently by Motif.

For Motif one needs to pay a license fee

Motif is not freely available. Nevertheless, the product could gain higher acceptance than OpenLook. This could happen because, on the one hand, Motif is similar to the popular MS Windows and, on the other hand, OSF members supply the product by default with their systems.

The FWF Toolkit bundles about 40 free widgets

A comprehensive collection of further widgets is included in the FWF toolkit of the Free Widget Foundation, coordinated by Bert Bos (The Netherlands). With a view to the output of multimedia data, Markku Savela (Finland) has developed the Xew widgets (text, graphics, audio, video).

On the face of it, widget sets are not uniform

Meanwhile, about 40 free and 10 commercial widget sets are available. On the one hand, the variety of available widgets is advantageous for the X11 programmer as he or she can draw on widgets already prepared, when faced with a problem. On the other hand, the variety of widget libraries, which additionally differ from each other in appearance and operation, makes it difficult to write portable program code.

Linux distributions include Xaw, Xaw3d, and the XView toolkit

Linux distributions include by default the Xaw widgets, the XView toolkit, and the Xaw3d widgets. Motif is offered as a licensed product by various distributors. The FWF toolkit with about 40 widgets of different complexity is freely available in the source code via **anonymous ftp**. The newest version can be found on the Dutch FWF server **ftp.let.rug.nl** and on the German FWF mirror **ftp.informatik.tu-muenchen.de**.

11.4 Working with X11

The X11 window system can be accessed in three different ways. Two of them succeed more or less immediately, the third requires preconfiguration. Whereas in the first two access methods the user mainly operates locally running clients, the third method allows the local system to be used the as a terminal for remote computers. X11 makes this possible by coupling X servers with an unambiguous X server address.

X11 runs local and remote applications

After successfully loading the X server, the Linux user is provided with a wide range of X clients. Beside the basic applications that are part of the X11 basic equipment, Linux distributions include various application packages designed for use over X11. The latter are left unconsidered in this section.

The basic equipment includes the MIT X clients only

The aim of this section is to explain access to X11, the structure and content of the X11 start-up files and the X11 addressing scheme. Finally, a short presentation of selected MIT X clients examines the basic applications' range.

11.4.1 Starting and Killing the X Server

The easiest way to access the X11 window system is to call up the initialization program **xinit** from the console. Then, **xinit** analyzes the contents of **$HOME/.xinitrc** and starts the commands entered there in sequence, analogously to shell script processing.

.xinitrc controls the initial X11 desktop

If the **$HOME/.xinitrc** configuration file does not exist, **xinit** opens a command interpreter, started with

```
xterm -geometry +1+1 -n login -display :0
```

283

-display also addresses remote X servers

Here, the $-$geometry $+1+1$ option has the effect that the left corner of the **xterm** window on the upper picture margin is positioned one pixel down and to the right, $-$**n login** assigns the name **login** to the window, and $-$**display :0** causes **xinit** to present the window on the local X server.

The common syntax for specifying the positions at which an X application should appear allows the user in addition to state the window's height and width:

Size and position of X clients are set by -geometry

```
-geometry WxH+-X+-Y
```

positions the X client with width **W** and height **H** at the place (**X,Y**) relative to the left (+) or right (−) or upper (+) or lower (−) screen margin. Note that text-oriented applications use **W** and **H** as row and column number, whereas graphics applications interpret them as pixels.

The user's startup file **$HOME/.xinitrc** usually contains at least one **xterm** application and an X window manager. As an example, Fig. 11.3 shows a mini-.xinitrc. The entries respectively start a clock **xclock**, the **emacs** editor, a mailbox **xbiff**, a command interpreter **xterm**, and the F(?) virtual window manager **fvwm**.

*Fig. 11.3
.xinitrc-file
example*

```
xclock -geometry 60x60+1076+6 &
emacs &
xterm -geometry 92x58+6+108 &
xbiff -geometry 60x60+1000+6 &
fvwm
```

startx and openwin are shell scripts

The second access method is to call up a shell script either **startx** or **openwin**. First, **startx** checks whether or not there is a **.xinitrc** file in the user's home directory. If not, **startx** will ask the **xinit** program to use the start-up file **/usr/X11R6/lib/xinit/xinitrc** instead, and the desktop appears according to the entries located there. However, **openwin** structures the desktop according to the contents of the start-up file **$HOME/.openwin-init**.

Accessing X11 via the X Display Manager **xdm**, originally developed for controlling X terminals, is nowadays the preferred method. Preconditions for this are configuration of the **xdm** control files **Xaccess** and **Xservers** from the directory **/usr/X11R6/lib/X11/xdm** and activation of the X Display Manager. The latter is often automatically started up from one of the shell scripts **rc.6** or **rc.local** located in **/etc/rc.d**.

The xdm is configured by Xaccess and Xservers

The X Display Manager administers several X servers, so it can not only control local but also remote X servers. If the **xdm** is running locally and its **Xaccess** configuration file includes an entry instructing it to control the local system, then **xdm** implicitly starts the local X server **/usr/X11R6/bin/X**.

Otherwise, the user can call up the **X** program with an option contacting a remote **xdm** (the basis for the communication between the X server and the **xdm** is the X Display Manager Control Protocol XDMCP). Following options establish the connection to a X Display Manager:

XDMCP controls the communication between X and xdm

-broadcast sends a **BroadcastQuery** protocol packet to the network broadcast address. The **xdm** of the host answering first takes control of the X server,

-indirect host sends an **IndirectQuery** packet to **host**,

-query host sends a **Query** package to **host**.

When using **xdm** based X11, the login is carried out via a **login** window where the user identification and password must be entered. If the local X server is controlled by several X Display Managers, then the user must first choose from the **chooser** menu which host he or she wishes to access.

The chooser displays a list of the xdm-hosts

After validating the access code, **xdm** analyzes the content of **$HOME/.xsession** and starts the commands stated there. If this file does not exist, then **xdm** activates the window manager **twm**, as background process, and a terminal program **xterm**, running in the foreground.

xdm analyzes .xsession

Both **$HOME/.xinitrc** and **$HOME/.xsession** are used by **xinit** or **xdm** as shell script, whereby, for the **xdm** startup file **$HOME/.xsession**, the execution permission must be set. For both files it is essential that each command line, except the last one, ends with a **&**, which means the respective programs will run as background processes.

.xsession has to be executable

If the last command starts a window manager, the X11 session can be finished by terminating it. In general, an X11 session will be terminated by aborting the last application that was started from `.xinitrc` or `.xsession` and was running in the foreground. Therefore, it is necessary that at least one program started there is running in the foreground, as otherwise the shell script will more or less be considered as processed.

11.4.2 X Server Addresses and Access Permissions

X server addresses consist of host name, display, and screen number

Each X server name consists of the host name, a display, and a screen number. The local X server can be addressed via `:0` or `:0.0`, remote systems via

> `host:0` or `host:0.0`

Here, `host` has to be given either in IP or by domain addressing (see Sect. 9.5).

Normally, the X server controls exactly one display with a single screen. For systems including more than one graphics card or addressing several monitors with a single graphics card, values other than `0` may be necessary for the display and the screen. X applications derive the X server to be addressed from the value of the environment variable `DISPLAY` or from the value stated after entering the `-display` option.

Remote systems can be used by trusted hosts only

For security reasons, the user can access a certain X server as "trusted host" only. X11 controls access permission with an authentication mechanism that initially allows only local clients to communicate with the local X server.

If the user wishes to depict on the local X server an X client processed by a remote host, he or she should first give access permission to the remote system with

> `xhost host`

Unlimited access on the local X server is given by `xhost +` (each host can access the local display).

Additionally, the user should warn X clients started from remote to divert their in/output to the local display. For example, if the local system is called **jeannie** and the remote system **fawn**, the call

```
rsh fawn xterm -display jeannie:0.0
```

will start a command interpreter **xterm**, diverting its in/output to **jeannie:0.0**, on the system **fawn**. Necessary conditions are that **fawn** forms a trusted host for the display **jeannie:0.0** and that the user has provided a suitable **.rhosts** entry on **fawn** allowing the user to initiate applications there from **jeannie**.

*If DISPLAY
contains the target
system's address,
one can forget the
option -display*

11.4.3 MIT X Clients

X11 distributions are supplied with a variety of system and application programs making it possible to interact with the operation system and the window system. This section briefly discusses the most important MIT X clients.

Each MIT X client provides an integrated short help. If an X application is called up with the **-help** option, the corresponding program prints an annotated list of permitted program parameters. Comprehensive descriptions of the individual MIT X clients and each permitted command line option are included in the online manual under **/usr/X11R6/man**.

*xterm -help
provides a
description of the
xterm options*

Already mentioned are the **xterm** program opening a virtual terminal above the window system, **xclock** for displaying an ongoing clock, and **xbiff** informing the user of new e-mail. **xclock** and **xbiff** are X11 desktop tools. Other members of this group are the programs **xcalc**, **xload**, **xedit**, and **xman**.

*xman provides
a graphical online
manual*

xcalc provides a kind of calculator operated by keyboard or mouse. The performance meter **xload** displays the current average system load in the form of a histogram. The full screen editor **xedit** enables elementary word processing. Finally, **xman** provides an elegant way of accessing the **man** command, whereby the user can select individual pages from an alphabetically sorted table of contents. Figure 11.4 presents the desktop tools of the MIT X11 distribution.

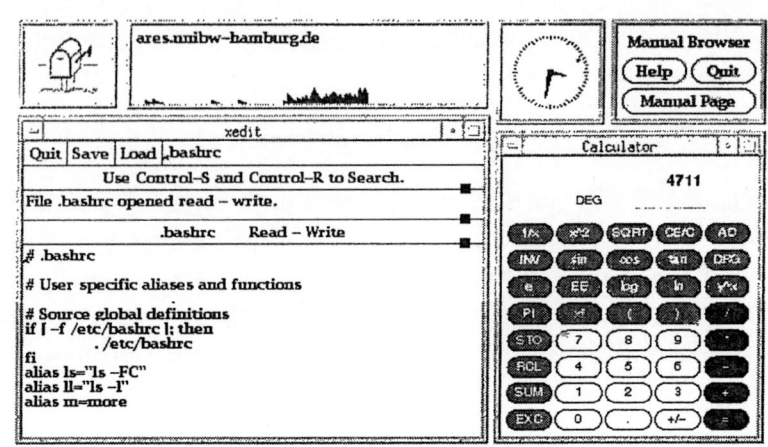

Fig. 11.4

The desktop tools

of the MIT X11

distribution

The MIT X clients **xhost**, **xlsclients**, **xkill**, **xprop**, **xwininfo**, **xset**, **xmag**, **xrefresh**, **xwd**, and **xwud** form the class of session-supporting X applications. **xhost** has already been mentioned in Sect. 11.4.2. Its task is to control the access permissions on an X server.

After xset -s 300 is
called, the screen-
saver will be
activated after 300
seconds idle time

xset makes it possible to set internal server parameters, such as search paths for fonts, mouse parameters, keyboard autorepeat, and screen-savers. A list of X applications running on a certain X server is displayed by the **xlsclients** program. Comprehensive information on a certain X application is provided by **xwininfo**, whereas **xprop** outputs special X client features. Finally, **xkill** tells the X server to sever a connection to an X client.

xwd creates
screen dumps

The other four programs support access to screen contents. **xmag** displays an enlarged screen section in its own window, **xrefresh** refreshes the whole screen content, and **xwd** (X window dump) copies a screen section to a file. Screen sections saved with **xwd** can then be displayed by **xwud** in an individual window.

Information on general X server features are output by **xdpyinfo**. Amongst other things, this includes the server's version number and server extensions installed (extensions). **xrdb** provides access to the X resources database. The **xlsfonts** program creates a list of available fonts, and **showrgb** displays the names of the colors that can be used for specifying hues. Details on the topics X resources, X fonts, and X colors may be found in Sects. 11.5–11.7.

Finally, we mention the X client **twm**. As the standard X11 window manager, it is responsible for the appearance of X clients. Furthermore, it allows the user to interactively enlarge and move individual windows and provides menus allowing access to basic window system functions. More detailed information on window managers can be found in Chap. 12, where also some alternative window managers are mentioned that provide in part essential extensions in comparison to the MIT X window manager **twm**.

The window manager controls X clients' appearance

11.5 X Resources

Each object or graphical element of an X application is linked to attributes determining the position, size, shape, color, font used, and so on. The concept of X resources allows the user to modify some or all attributes without changing the program sources.

X resources control attributes like shape, color, character sets, and so on

For this purpose, the X server runs an internal resources database accessible to the user. With the X client **xrdb**, the user can list the X resources stored there (option **-query**), add new resources (**-merge**), replace existing ones (**-override**), or delete (**-remove**) or redefine (**-load**) all the data.

The X resources processed by a certain X application **client** are output by the call **listres client**. With

        appres client

one can see which X resources are "seen" by **client**. Furthermore, the **editres** program makes it possible to interactively modify individual attributes. Unfortunately, not all X applications are **editres** compatible.

Indicators for X resources are character strings consisting of concatenated class names ending with a colon. At the beginning of the character string stands the application class (usually the program name), followed by a separator (asterisk or dot). Then, individual application components (sub-widgets) follow, and finally the attribute's name. For example, the following X resources control the appearance of the X client **xterm**:

Indicators for X resources consist of class names

```
XTerm*background: navy
XTerm*foreground: yellow
XTerm*cursorColor: yellow
XTerm*pointerColor: red
XTerm*pointerShape: left_ptr
```

These set hues for the attributes `background`, `foreground`, `cursorColor`, and `pointerColor`. Here, `background` belongs to the `Background` class and the other three to the `Foreground` class, and permitted values for these X resources consist of color information (see Sect. 11.7).

mouse pointer belongs to the Cursor class

`pointerShape` belongs to the `Cursor` class. As argument, X resources of the `Cursor` class need the name of a file located in `/usr/X11R6/include/X11/bitmaps`. There, only those files including the definitions `*_x_hot` and `*_y_hot` define a cursor.

The example shows "detailed" X resources specifications in the sense that they are only valid for the X client `xterm` and set special arguments only. With less detailed information, each attribute belonging to a certain class can be set or the attribute's appearance can be determined for each application supporting certain resource classes. The stipulations

```
*foreground: yellow
*pointerColor: red
```

determine that each X client supporting the X resources from the `foreground` class must use the foreground color "yellow" for each element of this class. In contrast, `pointerColor`, also belonging to the `foreground` class, must appear in the color "red".

Usually, the user combines all the X resources determining the general appearance of their desktop in `$HOME/.Xdefaults` and loads them from `$HOME/.xinitrc` or `$HOME/.xsession` using

$HOME/.Xdefaults bundles user-defined X resources

```
xrdb -load $HOME/.Xdefaults
```

For example, if he or she wishes to set the background color for each later `xterm` application to "green", the command sequence

```
echo "XTerm*background: green" | xrdb -merge -
```

suitably modifies the resources database.

Additionally, each X client analyzes the environment variable **XENVIRONMENT** that points to a file including user and host-specific resources. If an X client does not find this variable in its process context, the program searches for **$HOME/.Xdefaults-host** (**host** is the name of the system executing the application).

By default, X clients additionally process the **-xrm** option which allows deliberate allocation of X resources. Several X resources can be set by consecutively entering individual **-xrm** options. For example,

MIT X clients are processing the -xrm option

```
xterm -xrm "XTerm*foreground: red"\
     -xrm "XTerm*background: white"
```

creates an **xterm** terminal emulator with red letters on a white background. However, this method is not very convenient and cannot always be used, as Unix command lines cannot be arbitrarily long.

The common default setting of application specific X resources can be seen by X clients from an application default file. By default, X applications search through the **/usr/lib/X11/app-defaults** directory for a file having the same name as the class name of the X application. For example, **xterm** loads the content of **XTerm**, **xclock** takes the application specific resources from **XClock**, and so on.

Application defaults files contain X resources with are system-wide scope

Note that the files **/usr/lib/X11/app-defaults/*** belong to the superuser and cannot be modified by the user. In addition, each X11 user is free to keep his or her own application defaults files and can cause the system to take the application-specific resource files from alternative search paths. Directories searched for resource files by Xt based X clients are controlled by following environment variables:

Application defaults files belong to the superuser

XAPPLRESDIR allows specification of a search path for X11R3 or earlier versions. From X11R4 onward, the variables ***SEARCHPATH** provide more extensive possibilities. For compatibility reasons, **XAPPLRESDIR** will continue to be supported by "old" X clients.

291

XFILESEARCHPATH can contain a list of search paths, whereby individual entries have to be separated by a colon. Furthermore, certain meta characters can occur in the list.

XUSERFILESEARCHPATH can also consist of a search path list and contain meta characters.

MIT X clients analyze several application defaults files

First, the X client consecutively searches through the XFILE-SEARCHPATH paths until it finds a suitable application defaults file. Then, the X client searches through the XUSERFILE-SEARCHPATH entries and overwrites the resources already set with the contents of the first resource file found. If the X client does not find XFILESEARCHPATH in its process context, it uses

```
/usr/lib/X11/%L/%T/%N%C:\
/usr/lib/X11/%l/%T/%N%C:\
/usr/lib/X11/%T/%N%C:\
/usr/lib/X11/%L/%T/%N:\
/usr/lib/X11/%l/%T/%N:\
/usr/lib/X11/%T/%N
```

The commands and their meaning:

%L language_place.characterset (e.g., en_US.88591)

%l language

%T file type value (here: app-defaults)

%N program or class name

%C resource value *customization

The internal program value of XUSERFILESEARCHPATH is

```
<root>/%L/%N%C:\
<root>/%l/%N%C:\
<root>/%N%C:\
<root>/%L/%N:\
<root>/%l/%N:\
<root>/%N
```

where root is either the value of XAPPLRESDIR or, if this environment variable has not been set, the user's home directory.

11.6 X Fonts

Text representations of all kinds are realized by X clients by using X fonts. It is the server's task to provide the X applications with the X fonts needed. So, in particular, fonts are not part of an X application. Instead, the latter asks the X server to unpack font resources to depict text characters and symbols.

Font resources are resolved by the X server

X Fonts are combined in files that mainly contain pixel information. Each font letter corresponds to a bit-image copied by the X server to the screen memory to depict a character.

Directories through which the X server should search for font files are assigned to the **FontPath** variable in the configuration file **/etc/XF86Config**. Information on the list of paths through which a running X server searches for font files is provided by the **xset -q** command.

FontPath points to directories including X fonts

Furthermore, **xset** allows the value of the internal server **FontPath** variable to be modified. The **fp=path** option calls up the search path **path** for the X server. On the other hand, **xset +fp path[,path]...** adds search paths and **xset -fp path[,path]...** removes one or more search paths.

X fonts included in Linux distributions are usually located under **/usr/X11R6/lib/X11/fonts** in the directories **75dpi**, **100dpi**, **Speedo**, **Type1**, and **misc**. There, **misc** contains only fonts with fixed letter width, whereas the other directories additionally include fonts with proportional spacing.

Each directory has to include the **fonts.dir** file linking font names to file names. Additionally, a **fonts.alias** file is located there, making it possible to access fonts via aliases (font alias). The X server loads these files every time **FontPath** is changed.

fonts.dir links font names to file names

If the system administrator adds new fonts, he or she must then create the **fonts.*** files anew with **mkfontdir** and, if necessary, tell the X server with **xset fp rehash** to load the current files.

The **xlsfonts** command provides a list of font names that can be accessed by the X server. The call **xfd -fn font** structures a window with a table of characters included in **font** and allows the user to look at the appearance of each font letter. After a certain character is selected, **xfd** displays its

xfd shows each X font character

metric values (index, width, etc.). Additionally, **xfontsel** provides a menu-driven font selection.

Font names consist of 14 "values"

In general, an X font name does not correspond to the name of the font file. It consists of a total of 14 "values" which, among other things, encode its origin (Adobe, Bitstream, DEC, Sony, Sun and others), font family (Courier, Helvetica, Times), type line (normal, bold), typeface, font size, and the character encoding included.

This kind of naming has the disadvantage that the complete font name often consists of more than 60 characters. Selecting fonts via their font alias avoids the problem. Furthermore, the system allows the use of wildcards within font resources. Permitted wildcards are the question mark ? for exactly one character and the asterisk * for any number of characters. For example,

```
XTerm*font: *courier-bold-r*
```

causes the X server to use a roman (unslanted) bold font from the Courier family for **xterm** applications. If several fonts match the mask stated, the X server takes the first from the list.

Some X clients process the -fn option

Some X applications process the command line option **-fn font**, to enable the user to set the font resource during the program call. If **font** includes wildcards, the value set has to be protected against interpretation by the shell:

```
xterm -fn "*courier-bold-r*"
```

creates an **xterm** application using the first font matching the mask stated.

11.7   X Colors

Graphics cards encode hues in frames

Today, a principal feature of graphics cards is the administration of screen information in a screen matrix consisting of one or more layers (frames). A one-dimensional screen matrix can simply encode whether a pixel is to be switched on or off. If several layers are available, the screen matrix can administer the hue or brightness of each pixel.

When depicting gray tones, the frames encode a single brightness tone. Color information, on the other hand, requires the frames to be divided into three separate color layers representing brightness tones for the three primary colors red, green, and blue (RGB model).

Furthermore, graphics cards support various operation modes that divide the screen memory into fewer frames for a greater number of pixels (higher resolution). By reducing the resolution it is often possible to increase the number of screen layers.

For example a resolution of 1024x768 pixels, a graphics card with 1 MB RAM can simultaneously display 256 colors (8 frames). If the resolution is reduced to **640x480** pixels, 24 frames will be available if necessary, and the number of colors that can be displayed simultaneously increases to 16 777 216.

The memory space needed is the result of resolution and number of frames

The X11 color model has been designed for presenting X applications on different X servers. Each of them may operate display hardware from a certain performance class (monochrome/ gray scale, small and large range of colors). To achieve an identical appearance as far as possible, the X server enters pixel values in the screen memory and afterwards, with the help of a colormap, codes them as hues. So, the screen does not show the brightness tone (shade of gray) or hue directly corresponding to the pixel tone, but the color value of the corresponding colormap index.

Pixel values refer to a colormap

Depending on the display hardware used, three different methods of indexing should be distinguished. For gray-scale (and monochrome) systems, the color table contains a brightness tone. Systems with a small range of colors derive an intensity value for each of the three colors red, green and blue from the pixel tone. Systems with a large range of colors separately encode the indices for red, green, and blue. Figure 11.5 shows the methods for depicting pixel tones as hues.

Internally, the X server links hues to be used by individual X applications to a "visual", which is a structure controlling the usage of pixel tones. For each of the three performance classes, two visuals are defined, one of which contains predefined hues only while the other administers predefined as well as definable hues. Information on the visuals supported by the local X server is provided by the `xdpyinfo` program.

Use of the pixel tones is controlled by the X application's visual

295

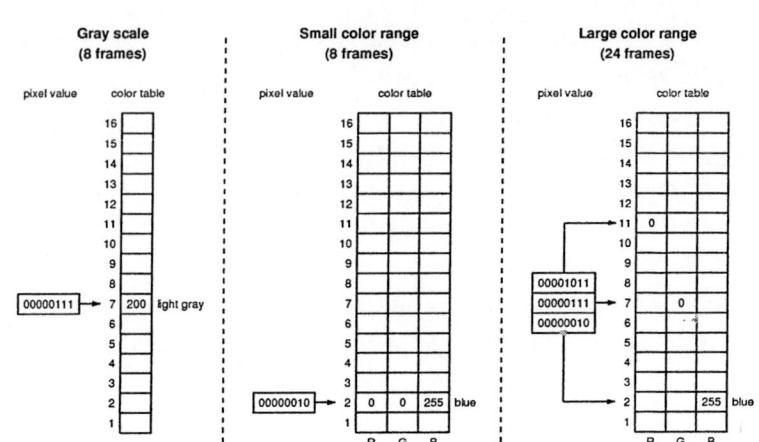

Fig. 11.5

Mapping of

pixel values

onto hues

Visuals with strictly determined color tables are called StaticGray, StaticColor, and TrueColor. They guarantee that the X client's appearance is largely identical on all systems using visuals of the same name.

The colormaps of the visuals GrayScale, PseudoColor, and DirectColor, on the other hand, allow the application to use additional hues that are not contained in the underlying colormap. Thus, for example, it is even possible to get "soft" color borders on an 8-bit display. For this purpose, the user tells the X server to enter additional hues in the colormap used by the X client. The visual PseudoColor uses 216 predefined hues, DirectColor uses 262 144.

rgb.txt X11 provides the user with two ways to select hues and for

links color example to link them to X resources. In the first method, the X

names to server processes color names like **black**, **white**, **purple**, and

RGB tones so on, and derives RGB hues from this. The keys for this mapping are taken from the configuration file **/usr/X11R6/lib/X11/ rgb.txt**. Depending on the platform used, this file can include different values, as some producers adapt individual RGB tones to their hardware.

In the second method, RGB tones are specified with three-digit hexadecimal numbers. Permitted formats are:

#RGB	(4 bits each for red, green, blue)
#RRGGBB	(8 bits each for red, green, blue)
#RRRGGGBBB	(12 bits each for red, green, blue)
#RRRRGGGGBBBB	(16 bits each for red, green, blue)

Since X11R5, it is additionally possible to state hues with reference to alternative color spaces. For this purpose, the hardware producer Tektronix has developed the X color management system Xcms. This allows hues to be encoded in RGB, RGBi, HVC (Hue, Value, Chroma), and various "CIE formats" (CIE is the French Commission Internationale de l'Eclairage, an international standardization commission).

Linux X servers accept color information in RGB, RGBi, HVC, and various CIE formats

HVC and CIE are device-independent color descriptions, each with three components. By contrast, the RGB format is device-dependent. HVC creates colors from values for primary color (hue), intensity (value), and color saturation (chroma). Each hue corresponds to a position on or within a cone. The CIE model, conceived as early as 1931, creates hues by approximating a spectral energy value using three basic functions.

Hues in Xcms-notation consist of a prefix indicating the color space and three " coefficients" separated by a slash /, in general in the format

```
prefix:value1/value2/value3
```

Permitted values for `prefix` are `TekHVC`, `CIEXYZ`, `CIEuvY`, `CIExyY`, `CIELab`, `CIELuv`, `RGB`, and `RGBi`. Figure 11.6 shows the values that can be used by the individual coefficients.

Prefix	value1		value2		value3	
TekHVC	0.0 -	360.0	0.0 -	100.0	0.0 -	100.0
CIEXYZ	0.0 -	1.0	0.0 -	1.0	0.0 -	1.0
CIEuvY	0.0 -	0.6	0.0 -	0.6	0.0 -	1.0
CIExyY	0.0 -	0.75	0.0 -	0.85	0.0 -	1.0
CIELab	0.0 -	100.0	0.0 -	100.0	0.0 -	100.0
CIELuv	0.0 -	100.0	0.0 -	100.0	0.0 -	100.0
RGB	0x0 -	0xffff	0x0 -	0xffff	0x0 -	0xffff
RGBi	0.0 -	1.0	0.0 -	1.0	0.0 -	1.0

*Fig. 11.6
Color spaces
and color values*

A color database with Xcms values can be found in the file `/usr/X11R6/lib/X11/Xcms.txt`. X clients also can process colors given in the Xcms format:

```
xterm -bg CIEXYZ:0.37/0.20/0.06\
      -fg CIEXYZ:0.07/0.03/0.31\
      -cr CIEXYZ:0.32/0.66/0.16
```

creates an **xterm** application with blue letters on a red background and a green cursor. Xcms colors for X resources may be specified analogously, for example with

```
XTerm*background: TekHVC:262.2/16.3/32.8
XTerm*foreground: TekHVC:82.2/95.5/74.9
XTerm*cursorColor: CIEXYZ:0.35/0.55/0.45
```

Color editors: xtici and xcoloredit

Finally, we mention the freely available X clients **xcoloredit** and **xtici**, which support the user during creation of color values (and have a graphical interface). **xcoloredit** generates blended colors based on the RGB or the HSV color model and always displays the corresponding RGB value. **xtici** can additionally create HVC and CIEuvY triples.

X Window Manager

A striking difference between X11 and other window systems is that X11 does not integrate control of X clients in the X server, but rather concentrates it in an independent X application, namely the X window manager. Like window managers of other window systems, it controls the assignment of input devices to an X client and helps the user in modifying various window attributes such as position and size, an X application converting to an icon or vice versa, and positioning a window in the window stack (raising or lowering it).

The X window manager helps the user to modify window attributes

The X window manager is an X client with special rights and abilities. In general, the workplace can be controlled by just one X window manager. One of its special rights is to set a user-defined menu (root-menu) on the X server's root window. After a root menu entry is selected, it can cause the execution of special actions or it can execute them itself, for example starting new X clients or killing existing ones.

The workplace can always be controlled by a single X window manager

Additionally, the X window manager controls the appearance of each window on the desktop. It defines the "window decoration" as well as special functions that can be activated by the user via individual frame components.

It defines the window dressing and the functions of the frame components

The precondition for this is the ability to communicate with the X server as well as with X applications. The X protocol can only partly be used for this task as it only defines the message transfer from the X server to the X client and vice versa. Therefore, in addition, the X Consortium elaborated the Inter-Client Communication Conventions ICCC, which, since X11R4, control information transfer from one X client to another.

*About 30 X window
managers have
been developed
so far*

Within X11, neither the appearance of individual X clients nor the way how to operate them are determined. Several authors therefore felt obliged to translate their own ideas into action. Hence, the user is now presented with a choice of about 30 X window managers offering different desktop appearances and different levels of comfort.

*Tom LaStrange
developed the tab
window manager
twm*

The first version released to the public, X10R3, was supplied with a rather rudimentary universal window manager uwm. With release X11R4, the uwm was replaced by the tab window manager twm. The latter was originally developed by Tom LaStrange, Solbourne Computer. Today, in a completely reworked version, it is the only X11 window manager running under the overall control of the X Consortium.

*olwm and fvwm are
freeware, mwm is a
commercial
product*

In the course of time and influenced by producers' interests, besides twm, the OpenLook window manager olwm (Sun) and the Motif window manager mwm (OSF) became popular, as well as the fvwm developed by Evans & Sutherland since 1988 on the basis of the twm and greatly expanded by Robert Nation, USA, since 1993.

*The expandable
generic window
manager gwm
includes a Lisp
interpreter*

Furthermore, within the framework of the Koala project (Bull), Colas Nahaboo, in France, created as freeware the expandable generic window manager gwm. Like emacs, the gwm includes a Lisp interpreter creating the window manager's functionality and the desktop's appearance by analyzing special WOOL scripts (Window Object Oriented Language). Depending on the configuration, the gwm can emulate either the twm or the mwm. Nevertheless, the gwm has not gained the acceptance claimed by its author, namely to play a similar role among X window managers as the GNU Emacs among universal text editors.

*In the LST
distribution the
fvwm is part of the
default setting*

The LST distribution includes by default the twm, the Open-Look-compliant window manager olwm (Sun) and its "virtual" variant olvwm, and the F(?) virtual window manager fvwm. The motif window manager mwm is part of the Motif toolkit which needs a license.

12.1 Tab Window Manager twm and ctwm

Like all other MIT X clients, the twm uses the libXt functions. Its graphical components are constructed from Athena widgets, it has a two-dimensional appearance, and it only supports two-color bitmap icons. However, a comprehensive supply of window operations, a simple configuration, and the integration of an "icon manager" set new standards then. Furthermore, the twm formed the basis for developing various X window manager programmed afterwards.

The twm's graphical components are constructed from the Athena widget set

Claude Lecommandeur, Switzerland, has developed the ctwm, which can link icons to pixmaps (multicolor icons). Following the vuewm, by the hardware producer Hewlett-Packard, Claude Lecommandeur has extended the ctwm with "virtual screens". These allow application-oriented desktops to be built up, between which the user can switch via the menu.

The ctwm supports virtual screens and multicolor pixmap icons

12.1.1 twm Decorations and Functions

The tab window manager twm provides each window on the desktop with a title bar. It consists of four areas, namely (starting from the left-hand side) the iconify button, application title, focus indicator, and resize button. Figure 12.1 shows the appearance and components of the twm title bar.

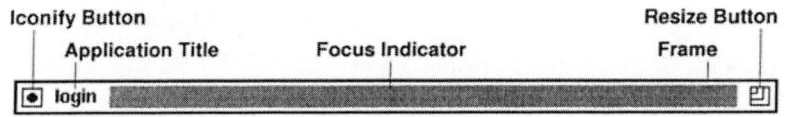

Iconify Button   Resize Button
    Application Title   Focus Indicator   Frame

Fig. 12.1
The twm title bar

The focus indicator shows whether or not a window is active by changing color. Normally, the window in which the cursor is located is active.

After the iconify button is clicked, the twm changes the window into an icon. It can be restored by moving the cursor to the icon and pressing the left or middle mouse button.

The resize button changes a window's size use the. Hold it with any mouse button, and the window will be overlapped by a rectangle indicating the new window size when the mouse is

301

moved (hold the button). When the mouse button is released, the X client will appear in the size indicated by the rectangle.

The area between the iconify and the resize buttons is linked to several actions. Clicking the title bar with the right mouse button brings the X client to the foreground. By holding the mouse button, the user can additionally move the window. This can also be achieved by pressing the left or right mouse button together with the keyboard's meta-key, provided the cursor is located anywhere in the window. Pressing the middle mouse button moves the window either forward or backward within the window stack.

When enlarging or moving a window, the new coordinates are indicated by a rectangle

Clicking the left mouse button on the root window opens the root menu. By default, the root menu provides the user with the operations iconify/restore, resize, move, raise, lower, and delete/kill. Additionally, the root menu makes it possible to focus a certain application, to make it active regardless of where the mouse is positioned, even if the window is completely covered. The unfocus function switches back to the common operation mode. Altogether, the twm provides more than 50 window operations.

By default, the twm root menu provides access on the twm functions resize, move, raise, lower, and delete

A further twm feature, in comparison to its predecessor uwm, is the icon manager which indicates a list of all the clients linked to the X server in its own window. It can be activated and deactivated via the twm root menu. One of its features is to store iconified X applications centrally.

The twm icon manager shows a list of all active and iconified X clients

12.1.2 twm Configuration

The desktop's appearance and the way user actions function is controlled by the `$HOME/.twmrc` file or, if it does not exist, by the system file `/usr/X11R6/lib/X11/twm/system.twmrc`. The twm configuration file consists of three sections:

The start-up file of the tab window manager consists of three sections

variable section: defines fonts and colors for title bars, menu entries, and icons;

binding section: assigns mouse and keyboard events to basic window functions;

menu section: sets the menu contents as well as actions activating individual menu entries.

12.1.3 Variable Section

The variable section includes value assignments to **twm** variables. The whole **twm** is controlled by more than 80 variables. One has to differentiate between logical (their presence changes default values), numeric, and string variables (e.g., font and color names). Some variables, e.g., **color**, **cursors** and **icons**, require as argument a list put in braces with entries of any type permitted. Figure 12.2 illustrates the structure of the variable section of **$HOME/.twmrc**.

The whole twm desktop appearance is controlled by logical, numeric, and string variables

```
DecorateTransients
IconBorderWidth 5
TitleFont "-adobe*bold*"
Color {
    BorderColor       "Slategray"
    DefaultBackground "maroon"
    DefaultForeground "gray85"
    ...
}
```

Fig. 12.2
Part of the variable section of ~/.twmrc

12.1.4 Binding Section

In the binding section are firstly some user-defined functions binding a list of basic operations to a new function name. These followed by an assignment of mouse and keyboard events to function names. Each line consists of an initial key name, an optional abbreviation for a "modifier" (shift, control, meta etc.), the context (window, title, icon, root, frame, iconmgr, all), and the function name. The fields are separated by colons.

If an entry is to be valid for several contexts, the context names are written one after the other, separated by a pipe character. This is also valid if several modifiers are to activate the same function. The functions **f.menu** and **f.function** additionally have to be told the names of actions, in the individual case the name of a menu or a user-defined function. Figure 12.3 shows a part of the binding section.

The f.exec function starts Unix commands

303

Fig. 12.3

Part of the binding

section of ~/.twmrc

```
button1 = : root : f.menu "defops"
button2 = m : window|icon : f.iconify
button1 = : title : f.function "move-or-raise"
button2 = : title : f.raiselower
button1 = : icon : f.function "move-or-iconify"
button3 = : icon : f.menu "window-ops"
button1 = : frame : f.resize
button2 = : frame : f.move
"F1" = window|title|icon : f.iconify
```

12.1.5 Menu Section

A twm menu entry

consists of a menu

label and an action

The menu section of the `twm` configuration file defines the contents of the `twm` menus. A preceding character string `menu` is followed by the menu name and a list of menu entries consisting of the name of the entry and an action. The latter can represent window operations or program calls, where program calls have to be initiated with an exclamation mark and the command itself has to be put in double quotation marks. If there is an action called `f.menu`, in this line the name of a submenu must additionally be entered. Figure 12.4 shows the definition of a `twm` menu.

Fig. 12.4

twm menu

definition

```
menu "Utilities" {
    "Editor"          !"/usr/X11R6/bin/xedit &"
    "Clock"           !"/usr/X11R6/bin/clock &"
    "Calculator"      !"/usr/X11R6/bin/xcalc &"
    "Preferences..." f.menu "Preferences"
}
```

12.2 OpenLook WMs `olwm` and `olvwm`

The olwm is

based on the

XView toolkit

The `olwm` is the standard X window manager of Sun's Open Windows, realizing parts of the OpenLook specification. Based on the XView toolkit, it gives the desktop a 3D Look and Feel. The window operations are also accessible to the `olwm` user via function keys, so in the individual case the window system can also be operated without a mouse.

A precondition for using olwm is the availability of the OpenLook Glyph and Cursor fonts. The corresponding props program allows to set olwm resources interactively. Furthermore, xtoolplaces makes it possible to store the desktop in the start-up file $HOME/.openwin-init.

Its virtual variant olvwm opens a virtual desktop manager, VDM, on the desktop. In its own window, the VDM indicates the content of both the physical and additional virtual screens. Furthermore, the VDM allows windows to be focused and moved via mouse actions on the VDM window. Further additions in comparison to the olwm are menus consisting of several columns and menu entries with two-color bitmaps or multicolor pixmaps.

The olvwm supports virtual screens and menu entries including bitmaps or pixmaps

12.2.1 olwm Decorations and Functions

Like the twm, the OpenLook window manager olwm provides each window on the desktop with a title bar. On the left-hand side there is a menu key (window button) providing access to basic window operations.

The application's name is put in the middle of the remaining title bar space. The latter simultaneously serves as focus indicator, which means active windows on a monochrome display get a title bar with inverse color. On colored displays, the title bar of the active window gets a 3D animated line above and below. Resize operations can be accessed by the olwm user via the window edges. Figure 12.5 shows the olwm title bar structure.

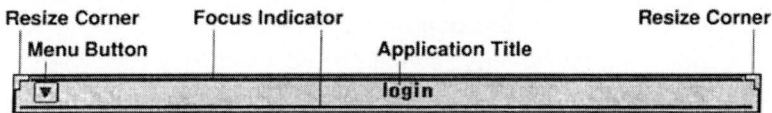

Fig. 12.5 The olwm title bar

Starting from the left, OpenLook assigns the functions select, adjust, and menu to the mouse buttons. If there are only two mouse buttons, the system emulates the middle mouse button when the left and the right mouse button are pressed together. In the case of just one mouse key, OpenLook expects the adjust function to be the mouse shift and menu the mouse control.

OpenLook links the mouse buttons to the functions select, adjust and menu

*The menu key of the
title bar provides
access to the
functions close, full
size, move, back,
refresh, and quit*

Clicking with the right mouse button on the menu key opens a menu providing the user with access to the window operations close, full size (the X application gets the height of the screen), move, resize, back, refresh, and quit.

When the menu key is clicked with the left mouse button, `olwm` carries out the standard action (close), given the appropriate configuration. The menu can also be opened by clicking with the right mouse button on the title bar. Clicking with the left mouse button on the title bar allows the window to be shifted. Double clicking the left mouse button results in maximum or normal window height.

*olwm can
combine several
X applications
in a group*

With Select or Adjust on the root window, several windows and icons can be combined in a group. For this purpose, click and hold the appropriate mouse button and mark an area by indicating a rectangle. Shifting a group's window then causes each client of this group to be moved.

Another difference in the `olwm` in comparison to the `twm` is the "input focus policy". Depending on the value of the `olwm` variable `SetInput`, a window will always be active when the cursor is put there (focus follows mouse) or just when the user clicks the window (click to focus).

*The push-pin locks
a menu on the
desktop*

Pressing the right mouse button opens the root menu (workspace menu) in the root window. A push-pin locks the root menu or a submenu beneath it on the screen. The user is thus permanently provided with a menu from which to start applications entered.

Keyboard-based access to the window operations is controlled by the `olwm` resource `KeyboardCommands`. If its value is `Full`, `olwm` allows access to each window operation via keyboard sequences, otherwise only few can be accessed like this. Figure 12.6 presents the most important keyboard sequences and the window operations linked to them.

Keyboard-based moving the window or changing its size is executed with cursor keys. Each step is either one pixel or, in conjunction with the control key, 10.

Alt-n	next applications
Alt-Shift-n	previous application
Alt-w	next window
Alt-Shift-w	previous window
Alt-m	window menu
Alt-Shift-w	root menu
Alt-t	change the input focus

Fig. 12.6
olwm keyboard
sequences and
window operations

12.2.2 olwm Configuration

The olwm does not use a central configuration file. The
desktop appearance is configured by entries of the application
defaults file Olwm and the internal server resource database. The *olwm consults*
menu entries are determined by a user-specific menu configura- *several startup files*
tion file, defined in the environment variable OLWMMENU. If this
environment variable has not been set, then olwm loads either the
$HOME/.openwin-menu file or the system-scope values from
openwin-menu, located in /usr/openwin/lib.

During a session with olwm, the **props** program allows
interactive modification of the olwm specific resources. Via
various menus the user can set hues for the root window and *props allows the*
window frames, determine the location of each icon (to the left *user to modify*
or right, at the top or bottom) and set the action of Select on *olwm resources via*
the menu key (execute the standard action or display the menu). *menus*
Furthermore, the user can configure the position of the scrollbars
(to the left or right), national settings (language, date format),
mouse features (speed, meaning of the buttons, etc.) and the
input focus policy (click to focus or focus follows mouse). When
the Apply key is pressed, **props** stores the set values of the olwm
resources in $HOME/.Xdefaults.

There is no similar tool for configuring menus. Instead, one *olwm menus are*
must create menus with an editor in the syntax of the olwm menu *programmed in*
language. This is based on each line being divided into three *the olwm menu*
fields. The first field defines the name of the menu entry. This *language*
entry is marked as the standard action by following it with the
optional keyword DEFAULT. olwm interprets the remaining text
on the line as the command normally forwarded to a shell.

307

olwm creates submenus when the keyword **MENU** stands in place of a command. If a file name follows it directly, olwm takes the submenu's definition from there. Otherwise, olwm interprets the following lines as a submenu specification. Its end is indicated by the keyword **END**. If a submenu is to be lockable on the root window, one must additionally use the keyword **PIN**. Figure 12.7 illustrates the syntax of the olwm menu language.

Fig. 12.7
olwm menu
examples

```
Programs MENU
     "Command Tool" DEFAULT cmdtool
     "Text Editor"   emacs
     Others MENU
         Others TITLE
         "Shell Tool"      shelltool
         "Bitmap Editor"   iconedit
         "Clock"           clock
         "Online-Manual"   DEFAULT xman
     Others END
Programs END PIN
```

12.3   F(?) Virtual Window Manager fvwm

The fvwm is based on an early twm version. The question mark in the name is because the author Robert Nation cannot remember the word he abbreviated with the letter "F".

The main features of the fvwm are the 3D-animated appearance of the window display on the desktop as well as support for pixmap icons and virtual screens. Furthermore, the fvwm can start additional modules communicating with the window manager via bidirectional pipelines. Some of the fvwm modules are **FvwmAudio** (outputs acoustic signals), **Fvwm-Banner** (presents a logo), **FvwmIconBox** (an icon manager), **FvwmPager** (virtual desktop manager), and **GoodStuff** (a kind of function menu).

The modular fvwm architecture minimizes its memory need

Based on a fvwm2.x beta version, the Belgian Hector Peraza and the Swiss David Barth made a fvwm2-95 version providing the Unix desktop with an appearance similar to that of the recent and rather well known Windows product by Microsoft.

12.3.1 fvwm Decorations and Functions

The **fvwm** provides each window on the desktop with a configurable decoration, consisting of four bar components along the top, bottom, left-hand, and right-hand sides, L-shaped corners called frames, and a title bar. The title bar serves the purpose of presenting the application name.

To each X application displayed, the fvwm assigns an individual decorations table

Additionally, the title bar can house five buttons on each side, i.e., on the left-hand and right-hand sides. When a title bar button is clicked, the **fvwm** carries out an operation, like iconifying the application or displaying a menu. Fig. 12.8 presents the components of the **fvwm** decorations.

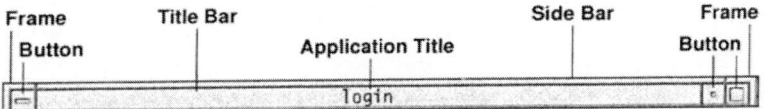

Frame	Title Bar		Side Bar	Frame
Button		Application Title		Button

login

Figure 12.8
Components of the fvwm decorations

The **fvwm** moves a window when the left mouse button is clicked on the title bar or on a side bar element and afterwards the mouse is moved (click and hold the mouse button). The window size can be changed by clicking the frame with the right mouse button. The window gets a new size when the mouse button is released. Clicking on the title bar, frame, or side bar elements with the right mouse button moves the window.

If one of these components is clicked with the middle mouse button, the **fvwm** displays the window operations menu. The latter is displayed by the **fvwm** also when the user clicks on the left corner button with any mouse button. The leftmost of the buttons on the right serves to close the window. The other button increases the window to its full size or restores the normal size.

Clicking the root window with the middle mouse button also opens the menu "window operations"

Additionally, the user can access window operations with cursor and function keys. Used together with the control and the shift key, the cursor keys move the mouse pointer up, down, to the right, or to the left, one pixel for each press of the key. The **fvwm** moves the mouse pointer quickly (10 pixels for each press of the key) when a cursor key is pressed together with Alt-shift. When the control key (Alt key) is used, the window manager scrolls the virtual screen in steps of 10 (100) pixels.

The mouse pointer and the virtual screen can be moved with the cursor keys

The function keys `Alt-F1` to `Alt-F8` are also linked by default to window operations. Figure 12.9 shows the accessible window operations.

Fig. 12.9

Default fvwm

keyboard bindings

Key	Function
`Alt-F1`	utilities menu
`Alt-F2`	window operations menu
`Alt-F3`	display the window list
`Alt-F4`	finish an X application
`Alt-F5`	move an X window
`Alt-F6`	change the window's size
`Alt-F7`	to the next window
`Alt-F8`	to the previous window

Like the `olwm`, the `fvwm` uses a focus policy for controlling whether a window will be activated when the mouse pointer is put on the window or on the window decoration or whether the window will only be activated when clicked on with the mouse.

If the `fvwm` variable `ClickToFocus` is set, the focus policy will be click to focus, otherwise focus follows mouse".

In addition, the `SloppyFocus` variable controls the focus policy in that a window will be inactive only when the mouse points to another window. If the mouse pointer is on the root window, the last window operated remains active.

fvwm automatically brings an activated window to the fore when the auto- raise variable has a positive value

Furthermore, the `AutoRaise` variable controls whether an activated window should be completely to the fore or can be partly covered by another window. A positive value `delay` of `AutoRaise` has the result that a window is brought to the fore after a while `delay` (in milliseconds), if focus-follows-mouse has been set. If the focus policy is set to click-to-focus, an activated window will be brought to the fore immediately, unless the value of `AutoRaise` is negative (no emphasis).

Pressing any mouse button on the root window opens one of three menus. The left mouse button opens the applications menu, the middle mouse button opens the window operations menu, and the right mouse button shows a list of the X clients currently addressed to the X server.

In the **fvwm** version 1.x, all menus are of the **Popup** type. They are only displayed until the user releases the mouse button. Version 2 additionally provides menus of the **Menu** type. The latter are removed by the **fvwm2** when a mouse button is clicked, either on the menu (activating the menu function) or elsewhere (removing the menu). Nevertheless, self-defined functions can realize for **fvwm** 1.x, too, that **Popup** menus "stick" on the desktop.

fvwm2 supports two different types of menus

12.3.2 fvwm Configuration

The **fvwm** configuration is controlled either by the system-scope start-up file **system.fvwmrc**, located in one of the directories **/usr/X11R6/lib/X11/fvwm** or **/etc/X11/fvwm**, or (alternatively) the user-specific **$HOME/.fvwmrc** file. The **fvwm** version 2 searches for files ***fvwm2rc**, and **fvwm2-95** takes its configuration from ***fvwm2-95**.

Each fvwm variant uses an individual startup file

Each of the **fvwm** configuration files stated consists of several logical blocks which together often need over a thousand lines. Figure 12.10 summarizes the individual blocks of a **fvwm** configuration file. Note especially, that individual configurations are entered in the order stated (for blocks 5–7 the order is determined by the references used).

1. color information
2. general parameters
3. path names
4. style options
5. start-up and restart function
6. function definitions
7. menu definitions
8. keyboard and mouse bindings
9. module options

Fig. 12.10
The blocks of the fvwm startup file

12.3.3 Color Information

*fvwm accepts color
information when
given as color
names or as
RGB value*

Color information in the first block controls the decoration of active and inactive windows, and their respective foreground and background colors (**HiForeColor**, **HiBackColor**, **StdFore-Color**, **StdBackColor**). Furthermore, in this block are defined the hues for menus and sticky windows (sticky windows are displayed on each virtual screen). As variable value, either a RGB value or a color name must be entered, according to the **/usr/X11R6/lib/X11/rgb.txt** entries (see Sect. 11.7).

12.3.4 General Parameters

The MWM
*variables give
the desktop
an appearance
similar to mwm*

Some of the general parameters to be entered in the second block are font specifications, namely **Font** for menu entries, **Window-Font** for application titles, **IconFont** for icon labels, and optionally **PagerFont**, if the **FvwmPager** is to display the names of the applications mentioned. Also in this block, one states the focus policy wanted and specifies the variables determining the window and icon positions, the size of the virtual desktop, and other parameters.

*The full size of
the button field
follows the height
of the title bar*

Additionally, in this block the user can select the buttons to be put on the title bar. After the keyword **ButtonStyle**, the user states first the button number and then the relative button size (referring to the full button field size) in the **WxH** format. The buttons on the left-hand side are numbered 1, 3, 5, 7, 9, starting from the left. The numbering of the buttons on the right-hand side is (starting from the right) 2, 4, 6, 8, 0.

Furthermore, the user can define his or her own buttons too. Then, instead of the relative size, one defines coordinates initiated by a number equal to the number of following coordinate points. For example, the sequence

*Each coordinate is
a percentage
number*

```
ButtonStyle 2 4 50x25@1 75x75@0 25x75@0 50x25@1
```

gives the button to be set in the rightmost position the shape of a triangle pointing upward. "Hues" (**@0** and **@1**) added to the individual coordinates cause the **fvwm** to draw the line to the next coordinate in a darker or a brighter color.

Since version 2.0.42, the **fvwm** has included a new button interface that can link buttons to pixmaps, too. For this purpose, instead of the field size, one of the keywords **Pixmap** or **Full-Pixmap** must be entered, followed by the name of a pixmap file. If a second file name is added, **fvwm2** uses the first pixmap for the normal state. When the button is pressed, **fvwm2** masks the button field with the second pixmap.

fvwm2 can link buttons to pixmaps

12.3.5 Path Names

In this section, path names that are to be chosen, determine directories that are to be searched through by the **fvwm** for monochrome bitmap icons (**IconPath**), multicolor pixmap icons (**PixmapPath**), and **fvwm** modules (**ModulePath**). Each path variable can take a list of path names in which individual entries are separated by a colon.

X fonts are provided by the X server

12.3.6 Style Options

The style options enable special **fvwm** decoration parameters to be assigned to individual applications. Each entry includes a line beginning with the keyword **style** followed by a window name and an options list.

Usually, the window has the name of the application or of a widget class for which the options to follow must be set, put in double quotation marks. Wildcards (**?** and *****) may be included and are interpreted by the **fvwm** in the usual Unix way. The interpretation of application-specific options is influenced by the entries' order. The window name **"*"** (all windows), in particular, must always be put at the beginning of the list. The style options specified then can provide individual applications with attributes that redefine the default settings.

Style "*term*" sets attributes for xterm, kterm, and color_xterm

*NoTitle deletes
the title bar,
NoHandles
displays a window
frame without
handles*

The options list contains one or more **fvwm** variables separated by commas. Logical variables set or delete options. A numeric variable must be followed by a number; for example, the option **BorderWidth 5** sets the border width to 5 pixels. Variables that determine hues require as argument either a color name according to an entry in **/usr/X11R6/lib/X11/rgb.txt** or an RGB value (see Sect.11.7). Figure 12.11 summarizes the keywords that can be in the options list.

*Fig. 12.11
fvwm option list
variables*

BackColor	Icon	StartNormal
BorderWidth	IconTitle	StartsAnyWhere
Button	NoButton	StartsOnDesk
CirculateHit	NoHandles	StaysOnTop
CirculateSkip	NoIcon	StaysPut
Color	NoIconTitle	Sticky
ForeColor	NoTitle	Title
HandleWidth	Slippery	WindowListHit
Handles	StartIconic	WindowListSkip

fvwm2 integrates further options controlling graphical attributes of special applications. One of these is the **TitleStyle** option which determines the location of the application title (**Centered, RightJustified, LeftJustified**) and controls its appearance (**Raised, Sunk, Flat**). **fvwm2-95** analyzes the **TitleIcon** option that enables the user to define a pixmap to be set on the title bar's left-hand side.

12.3.7 Function Definitions

*InitFunction is a
user defined
function executed
by fvwm when
being initialized*

In both of the two function definition blocks, the user can determine an **InitFunction** (to be executed at the initialization) and a **RestartFunction** usually having the same content. There, too, the user can define complex functions that call up **fvwm** internal functions.

Function definitions must be preceded by **function**, followed by a function name set in double quotation marks. The end of a function definition is indicated by the keyword **EndFunction**. Function calls entered between these consist of the respective function name, an event (`Click`, `DoubleClick`, `Immediate`, `Motion`), which is the reason for executing the function, and (optional) arguments to the `fvwm` function.

An example of a function definition, `window_ops_func`, is shown in Fig. 12.12. It opens the menu `window Ops` and displays it until the user has made a choice or the menu has closed.

```
Function "window_ops_func"
    PopUp   "Click"        Window Ops
    PopUp   "Motion"       Window Ops
    Close   "DoubleClick"
EndFunction
```

Fig. 12.12
fvwm function definition

The interface to the function definition has been changed in `fvwm2`. First, the keyword `AddToFunc` must be stated followed by the function name, a "trigger indicator" (`I` immediately, `M` motion, `C` click, `D` double-click) and an internal `fvwm2` function. Any following lines must be indicated by a plus sign. `fvwm2` recognizes the end of the definition by a blank line.

12.3.8 Menu Definitions

All the menus and submenus to be run on the desktop by the `fvwm` should be entered in the seventh start-up file block. There, the definitions' order is very important, as `fvwm` does not resolve any forward references. This means the user should define the sub-menus first and then the main menus that will open individual submenus.

The menu entries should be formulated line by line between `Popup` and `EndPopup`. Each entry includes a `fvwm` function, the entry name, and possibly an argument to the `fvwm` function. If the entry name contains an `&` character, `fvwm` presents the next letter of the name with underlining (the `&` character will be removed from the name) and defines this letter as a hot key: entering the underlined letter on the keyboard when the menu is open causes `fvwm` to execute the respective function. Figure 12.13 shows the menu definition `Window Ops`.

If the menu label includes an &-character, fvwm installs the following letter as hot key

Fig. 12.13

The fvwm menu

"Window Ops"

```
Popup "Window Ops"
    Title       "Window Ops"
    Move        "&Move"
    Resize      "&Size"
    Raise       "&Raise"
    Lower       "&Lower"
    Iconify     "(De)&Iconify"
    Nop         ""
    Destroy     "&Destroy"
    Exec        "Hardcopy"       exec xdpr &
EndPopup
```

*Applications must
be started from
fvwm with exec*

Menu entries that directly activate an application use the **fvwm** internal **Exec** function. Normally, a command line is entered that serves as argument to this function. The command call must be preceded by the Unix command **exec**.

To define a **fvwm2** menu, another syntax is used. There, the menu definitions are preceded by **AddToMenu**, followed by the menu name. Each entry includes a menu label and then a **fvwm2** internal function. The following lines are indicated by a plus sign at the beginning of the line. The end of the menu definition is marked in **fvwm2** by a blank line. The argument to the **fvwm2** function **Exec** does not need a preceding Unix **exec** before the actual program call.

*fvwm menu
definitions are not
fvwm2 compatible*

As already mentioned at the end of Sect. 12.3.1, an additional menu type **Menu** is provided in **fvwm2**. So, the "trick" presented in Fig. 12.12 for creating a "locked" menu is not needed in **fvwm2**.

A further addition to **fvwm2**, in contrast to the 1.x versions, allows a pixmap to be integrated into the menu label. One simply enters the name of a pixmap file in the menu label and sets a percentage character to the left and right sides. Figure 12.14 presents a **fvwm2** menu decorated corresponding.

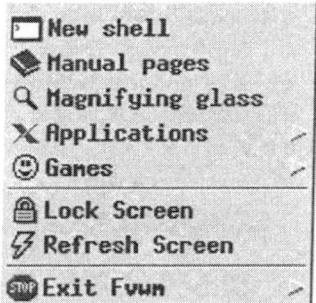

Fig. 12.14
fvwm2 menu
with pixmaps

12.3.9 Keyboard and Mouse Bindings

Having defined the desired functions and menus, the user can allocate them in the eighth block to individual function and mouse buttons. Each line defines a binding. The keyword **Mouse** at the beginning of a line starts a mouse binding, and **Key** activates a keyboard binding.

In the binding section, the user allocates fvwm functions to mouse and function keys

   For mouse definitions, the second entry just describes the number of the mouse button for which a binding should be set. If a 0 stands there, the binding is valid for all mouse keys. When keyboard definitions are being defining, a key name must be entered. Information on permitted key names can be found in the `/usr/include/X11/keysymdef.h` file.

   Next, one must state a "context" and a "modifier" to determine when the **fvwm** function last stated is to be executed. Permitted context values are the letters **R** (root window), **W** (X application), **F** (frame), **S** (sidebar), **T** (title bar), and **I** (icon). A number 0...9 indicates a button. Letters and/or numbers written as a string without spaces define the function on several contexts.

Context and modifier determine when to execute a fvwm function

   In the "Modifier" field, **S** stands for the shift, **C** for control, and **M** for meta. **N** indicates that the function will be executed solely on the basis of the key stated first. In this field too, several modifiers may be combined. For example, if **CS** is stated, the function will be executed by simultaneously pressing the shift and the control keys and the key stated initially. Figure 12.15 shows some **fvwm** bindings as examples.

Fig. 12.15
Keyboard and
mouse bindings in
~/.fvwmrc

```
Mouse 1     R  A  PopUp   "Workplace"
Mouse 2     R  A  PopUp   "Window Ops"
Mouse 3     R  A  PopUp   "WindowList"
Key Left    A  C  Scroll  -100 +0
Key Right   A  C  Scroll  +100 +0
Key Left    A  M  Scroll  -10 +0
Key Right   A  M  Scroll  +10 +0
Key F1      A  M  Popup   "Workplace"
Key F2      A  M  Popup   "Window Ops"
Key F3      A  M  Module  "WindowList" FvwmWinList
Key F4      A  M  Iconify
Key F5      A  M  Move
Key F6      A  M  Resize
Key F7      A  M  CirculateUp
Key F8      A  M  CirculateDown
Key F9      A  M  Delete
Key F10     A  M  Close
```

12.3.10 Module Options

The fvwm modules
take their configu-
ration parameters
from the fvwm
start-up file

Options to be entered in the last block of the **fvwm** start-up
file configure the modules communicating with the **fvwm** via
pipelines. Each module called up by the **fvwm** analyzes the user-
specific start-up file, if it exists, or, if not, the system-scope **fvwm**
start-up file, and takes the configuration parameters determined
for it. For detailed information on module-specific options see
the respective manual pages; these also present comprehensive
example configurations.

Bibliography

Andleigh, Prabhat
Unix System Architecture. Prentice Hall [1990]

Bourne, Steve
The Unix V Environment. Bell Telephone Laboratories, Inc.
[1987]

Goldt, Sven; van der Meer, Sven; Burkett, Scott; Welsh, Matt
The Linux Programmers' Guide 0.4. LDP [1995]

Greenfield, Larry
The Linux Users' Guide 0.4. LDP [1994]

Johnson, Michael
The Linux Kernel Hackers' Guide 0.6. LDP [1995]

Kirch, Olaf
The Linux Network Administrators' Guide 1.0. LDP [1994]

Probst, Stefan; Flaxa, Ralf
Power Linux International Edition. Springer-Verlag [1997]

Tanenbaum, Andrew
Operating Systems: Design and Implementation.
Prentice-Hall [1987]

Welsh, Matt
Linux Installation and Getting Started 2.2.2. LDP [1995]

Wirzenius, Lars
Linux System Administrator's Guide 0.3. LDP [1995]

Index